unlocking the

value of your

business

How to increase it, measure it & negotiate an
actual sale price - in understandable, step-by-step terms

By Tom Horn, author of the
Business Valuation Manual

UNLOCKING THE VALUE OF YOUR BUSINESS:
How to measure it, increase it & negotiate a sale price
in understandable, step-by-step terms

Library of Congress Cataloging in Publication Data:

Horn, Thomas W.
Unlocking the Value of Your Business:
How to measure it, increase it & negotiate a sale price - in understandable, step-by-step terms
Includes Index.
1. Business Enterprises--Management
2. Corporations--Valuation   3. Corporations--Merger
4. Corporations-Finance   I. Title.
HD1393.25.H66 2008 658.1'522 97-094445
ISBN 0-87521-016-3

Third Printing.
Published in 2002, 2008 by:

Charter Oak Press
6 Brook Circle
Ephrata, PA 17522

Printed in the United States of America

Read This First

This book does not have to be read cover-to-cover.

But if your goal is to increase the value of your business, then you will benefit the most by starting from the beginning and going through the entire text.

- If you are in a hurry, you can get some concentrated information from the Intro chapter plus Chapters 1, 19, and 22.

- If you are negotiating the purchase price of a company, then just refer to the Table of Contents and consult the appropriate sections - especially Chapter 20.

- Chapters 13, 14, and 18 are vital if you are borrowing money to buy a business.

If you are conducting a business valuation:

- Start with Chapter 1. That will brief you on some important background concepts and explain the basic procedure.

- Next refer to Chapters 2 and 3 for instructions on how to gather and prepare the information you will need.

- Chapter 4 tells you which valuation methods to use in your case - of those, only use the chapters you need.

- Consult Chapters 15, 16, and 17 to see if special methods apply to your particular type of business.

- Finally, Chapter 19 will tell you what to do with your results.

- Refer to Chapter 21 if your are dealing with a part-interest.

- Chapter 5 is about setting a capitalization rate, which is a measure of business risk. Even if you aren't concerned with capitalization of income, reading that chapter will teach you a lot about risk vs. reward for your particular company.

If you are confused by certain terms referred to in this book, see the Glossary for an explanation. Almost everything is defined there.

Concepts defined in the glossary are often marked in the text with an asterisk (*).

You may find the text repetitive if read through completely, but that's so you won't miss something important if you don't read every chapter.

Acknowledgments

Very special thanks to Mike Wolfe, CPA; Jay Siegrist, CPA; Pete Hicks of Irvin K. Hicks Associates; Kathleen Leidheiser, CPA; Dale Weaver, CPA; Bradley Clark; Leslie Charpentier; Jack Ross, CPA - and all my clients, who have taught me so much about this subject.

Contents

Read This First

Intro: How To Increase the Value of Your Business   1

GETTING STARTED

1. How To Use This Handbook   3
   - You don't have to be a financial genius to get great results from this book!
   - Rule #1: There is no precise value for any business.
   - Valuation methods always assume that the business is being sold.
   - Price and Value are not the same.
   - Is the business really saleable?
   - Valuations can be made misleading.
   - Reshape your firm into something more valuable.
   - The Basic Valuation Procedure
   - 11 Good reasons to do a valuation.
   - How to use your valuation as a negotiating tool.
   - The effect of contract terms on price.
   - How to use the valuation to predict whether an acquisition is feasible.
   - Using a valuation to help borrow money for your company.
   - Letting go.

2. Getting Ready   15
   - How to learn as much as you can about the company.
   - An information checklist to use.
   - Talking to managers and owners for further information.
   - Some confusing financial terminology

3. How to "Adjust" a Financial Statement   25
   - Why financial statements are adjusted
   - Cash vs. accrual accounting
   - What to adjust and how to adjust it.
     - Income statements
     - Adjusting interest expense
     - Partnerships, Sole Proprietorships, and Sub-S Corporations
     - How to adjust balance sheets
     - Dealing with potential hidden liabilities

4. Which Methods To Use In Your Case   37
   (A timesaving chapter that will direct you to the information
   you need. Includes a brief description of each of the classic valuation
   methods.)

5. How to assess the financial risk
   associated with any particular business   41
   - Business risk can be translated into a "Capitalization Rate".
   - An explanation of Capitalization and Discount Rates.
   - Present Value: How to discount the value of something
     to be received in the future.
   - Factors to consider in evaluating business risk.
   - What rate of return should this investment produce? (3 Methods)

THE VALUATION METHODS
6. Economic Value Of Assets Method   59
   - When to use this method
   - Which measure of value to use:
     - Liquidation Value
     - Market Value
     - Book Value
   - Intangible assets
     - The economic life of an intangible asset
     - Methods used to value intangible assets:
       1. Pricing Advantage (or Profit Contribution)
       2. Royalty or Licensing Agreements
       3. Profit contribution by cost savings
       4. Cost to create the intangible asset
       5. Cost to purchase the intangible asset
       6. Contracts that provide income (Sales Contracts)
       7. Employment Contracts

7.   The Net Worth (Book Value) Approach   69

- The concept of "Net Worth" and its role in valuation
- When the Net Worth approach is used
- Why book value departs from economic value

8. **Capitalization Of Income Stream Method** 73
   - The theory behind this method.
   - When to use this method
   - Brief Description
   - Relationship to Rule-Of-Thumb Methods
   - Steps
   - Summary

9. **The Small Business Method** 77

10. **Discounted Cash Flow Method** 81
    - When To Use This Method
    - The theory behind the method
    - Brief description
    - Steps
    - Variation: The Discounted Future Earnings Method
    - Summary

11. **Excess Earnings Method** 99
    - When to use this method
    - Brief Description
    - Steps
    - Asset Appraisals
    - Summary
    - Alternative Approach

12. **The Internal Revenue Service Approach to Valuation** 105
    - When to use this method
    - Brief description
    - Steps (Summarized) to the IRS Income Approach
    - Special considerations for estate tax valuations
    - Note: The actual Internal Revenue Service Rules are reproduced in the appendix, and you should *always* research more recent rulings.

13. **The "Ability To Pay" Method** 109
    - When to use this method
    - Limitation to this method
    - Brief description of the method
    - Steps
    - Summary

14.   Can the acquisition pay for itself?   117
      (Pro Forma Cash Flow Analysis)
  •   Tips on predicting future performance

15.   Popular methods to Avoid   121
  •   Replacement Cost Method
  •   Comparable Sales Method
  •   Price/Earnings Ratio Method ("Multiple Of Earnings Method")
  •   Rule-Of-Thumb Methods for small businesses

16.   Tips on valuing Specific Types of Businesses   133
  •   Retail stores
  •   Medical practices
  •   Other health-care businesses
  •   Accounting firms
  •   Manufacturing company
  •   Golf courses
  •   Wholesale and distribution companies
  •   Restaurants

17.   Special Considerations for the Service Business   155

18.   Secured Loan Value   159
  •   An Explanation of "Secured Loan Value", and why
      it affects market value of any company
  •   How To Determine It
  •   Using Accounts Receivable As Loan Security (Collateral)
  •   Using Inventory As Loan Security
  •   Using Machinery and Equipment As Security
  •   Using Real Estate As Security
  •   Important Limit on Secured Loan Value

19.   Putting it all together   165
  •   The range-of-value concept
  •   Try to be realistic and objective
  •   Negotiation will affect final price
  •   Income taxes don't count
  •   Value the company as it stands now
  •   Divorce situations
  •   When most of the company's assets are inventory
  •   Having an accountant check your work before you rely upon it
  •   Deduct any liabilities to be assumed by the buyer
  •   Can the business pay for itself at this price?
  •   When the buyer pays with its own stock

- Squaring the results from different methods
- No single number will be absolutely ever correct
- Important factors that will affect purchase price
- Devil's advocate: A Pragmatist's Point of View

20. Negotiating tips for buyers and sellers of businesses 185
- Are you a negotiator?
- The basics of negotiation
- Real world negotiation
- Identifying the other side's motives
- Trying to see the real issue
- Identify the other side's negotiating style
- Promising to keep employees
- Should you allow time-extensions?
- Advice for sellers of a company
- Making contract terms specific from the start
- Timing the sale of your company
- General tips for buyers of a business
- Dealing with the seller's emotional needs
- Checking out the details
- Avoiding unrealistic buyers and sellers
- How and when to raise the issue of price
- Hardball tactics
- Tips for both sides
- Targeting companies for acquisition
- How to approach a target company
- Spotting a sick company
- Sellers: Do you really have something to sell yet?
- Option-to-buy vs. preemptive bid
- Due diligence study
- Should decision-makers be at the bargaining table?
- Psychological ploys
- Attorneys and accountants
- Keeping it confidential
- Deadlocks
- Seller warranties
- Letters of intent
- Getting it in writing
- For sellers anxious about letting go
- Negotiating the form of payment
- When should a seller accepting stock as payment?
- Net sale proceeds after-tax
- Bargaining over the accounting method to use
- Earnouts (contingent payments)
- Adjustments to the price at settlement

21.	Valuing a part-interest in a company (Minority interests)	209
22.	Ways to increase the value of a business quickly	215
23.	How new developments in the tax law can affect your deal	221
24.	Glossary of financial terms	225
25.	Illustrative Valuation Example	243
	Appendix - The Internal Revenue Service Rules reproduced	259
	Appendix - Present Value/Future Value Tables	271
	Index	273

Disclaimer

This book is not a substitute for legal, accounting, or other professional advice. By providing the information contained herein, the author and publisher do not purport to render the same. The use of any part of this book is expressly conditioned upon the user's acknowledgment of his or her responsibility for seeking competent professional advice to verify the information contained herein, as well as its application to specific circumstances, particularly before making any decision in reliance upon it.

While effort has been made to make this manual complete and accurate within its intended scope, it is not the purpose of this book to present all relevant information available or necessary to conduct a valuation or arrange an acquisition, and the author and publisher make no representations whatsoever regarding the reliability of the information contained herein. There may be mistakes herein, both typographical and in content, and some information may be out of date, particularly due to frequent changes in the tax law. In addition, this material has limited applicability to the valuation of interests in publicly-held companies. Qualified investment bankers should be consulted with regard to the latter. These caveats and disclaimers supercede any other representations contained herein or in any other materials. The author and the publisher shall have no responsibility or liability to any person or entity with respect to any loss, damage, or claim allegedly caused by, related to, or arising out of, either directly or indirectly, the information contained herein or its use.

How To Increase the Value of Your Business

This book will show you how to determine the value of a business and negotiate a sale price. It will also provide you with an understanding of the factors that contribute to business worth, enabling you to purposely increase the dollar value of your firm over time.

Regardless of whether you created your business from scratch or bought an existing company, you can intentionally cultivate the elements that give a business transferable value, and thereby create a very significant mass of wealth over the course of several years. This is one of the best reasons to own a business, and you should be taking advantage of it.

The way we will accomplish that is by guiding you through a valuation of your firm as it stands now - *using traditional methods explained in very understandable terms. Each one is broken down into easy-to-follow steps.* In the process, you'll learn lots of new things about finance, accounting, business risk, management, and acquisition dealmaking. Most importantly, if you pay attention, you'll learn how to build up the value of any company by operating it in specific ways - ways that increase profitability, reduce risk help limit competition, and increase market share.

You may think you know your business inside-out, but the process of business valuation will teach you even more about its strengths, its weaknesses, and its vulnerabilities. You'll see opportunities you never appreciated. You'll glimpse its future potential, and the things that could cause its demise. You'll gain a better understanding of where you should steer your business, regardless of whether you plan to sell it now or at some point in the future.

Key factors in valuation - There are some basic concepts you should focus on throughout the book:

Business Risk - Think of this as the relationship between your income potential and your vulnerability to disaster. Both tend to increase or decrease together, but not always. Maximum business value is reflected when you have attained the highest level of income combined with the lowest possible level of risk.

Competition - Obviously, this is closely related to risk. No one's market share is secure anymore. These days, anywhere there's an opportunity to make some money, new players flood in. Unless your market is growing, that means someone's got to fall in order for someone else to succeed. Nonetheless, you can position your business in ways that tend to limit the competition.

Profitability - You will become much more conscious of the impact of the bottom-line on your worth. You'll also discover that you have a lot more control over it than you think

Personal Comfort Zone - If you rise to every challenge that really faces your business - if you take it to its maximum potential - will you still be the person you want to be? Or will it ask too much of you - in terms of risk, stress, time, and compromised values? You might thrive on the challenge, or it may simply wear you down and make you miserable. It's important to know your nature, and try to remain congruent with that over the long term. Getting rich in business involves some trade-offs.

How your business is viewed by others: Business value refers to "market value" - what it's worth to those who might buy it. The truth of the matter is, *they* determine its worth. Another way of saying this is that something has value only to the extent that others are willing to buy it - otherwise there's no value. If you're eventually going to sell, you need to start molding your company into a saleable entity that has the features that appeal to those who buy businesses. Valuation isn't concerned with what the business is worth to you. It is *very* important to stand in the shoes of the average buyer, or you won't get anything out of this. You want to start thinking about the attributes that give the business maximum appeal, and the conditions that diminish its appeal in the eyes of others. Some owners will need to confront whether they really have anything at all to sell. At the other extreme are those with profitable, enjoyable businesses having good assets and some insulation from competition.

Timing - The elements that determine the value of your business are in a constant state of flux, so its value can change radically over a short period of time. You need to become aware of those factors and take them into consideration in planning when to sell. I wish I had a dollar for every overly-confident owner who refused to sell when his company was at its best, and ended up carrying a group of shriveling assets to his grave because he could never accept that it was worth less later on. The same thinking applies when you want to buy a business at the lowest price.

"The right time" is usually out of your control, but you should plan ahead and recognize it when it arrives. If your reasons for owning a business have less to do with ultimate wealth than with current income and a certain lifestyle, then maybe you shouldn't worry about this. But more sellers blow it by not selling when their business is at its peak than by selling too early. ("Are you crazy? Why would we want to sell now?") Maybe there's a ton of potential left, but you aren't the one who can capitalize on it. Find that person and and either bring him on-board or sell him the company.

Here's the point: If you want to grow a business of substantial worth, then going through the process of determining its current value will impart you with the very insights you need, and a general mindset toward the creation of value.

For many people, the result will be a full press for maximum financial reward. Others may opt for lower net worth - but a simpler, less-stressful life. Many fall somewhere in between. No matter which path you choose, arming yourself with this background will make you less susceptible to forces that can knock you off course because you'll have taken them into consideration in advance. You're likely formulate concrete financial and career goals, and you'll reinforce a sense of purposefulness in the way you run your business.

"Promises, promises..."

This sounds like a tall order from a book on business valuation, but after many years of guiding owners through this process, I have consistently found this to be the most significant benefit accruing to those who undertake the project in a thoughtful manner. You'll see for yourself.

Chapter 1

How To Use This Handbook

You don't have to be a financial genius to get great results from this book!

The easy-to-follow instructions and practical advice contained here will enable you to appraise a business and negotiate its price even if your financial background is very limited. *This book will guide you through the entire process, step-by-step, in simple terms that anyone can understand.* It's an expanded version of a desk manual that was originally developed by a mergers and acquisitions consultant for his own use in order to make valuation understandable and easy to perform on a regular basis. As a non-accountant, he found other books on the subject too technical and confusing to be consistently helpful. It will enable you to avoid the high cost of professional business appraisals (up to $50,000) - while obtaining the same reliable results.

The author has taken each of the traditional accepted methods used by professional appraisers and broken them down into easy-to-follow steps and plain english, so that even people with little background in accounting or finance can use these time-honored techniques to obtain good, professional results. At the same time, accountants and finance pros will find this the most "user friendly" guide available on the subject - complete in every respect.

Don't read more than you have to!

The methods are explained in unusual detail in order to avoid the need for lots of background reading. At the same time, we avoid burdening the text with long explanations of financial terms that many readers are already familiar with by defining those in the Glossary. If you run into something you aren't familiar with, look it up in the back of the book. Every key financial concept mentioned in this manual is defined there.

Rule Number One: There is no precise value for any business

Even among valuation experts, there is plenty of room for disagreement - as to methods used, how they are applied, and the figures that are plugged into them. As you use this book, you'll quickly begin to understand why there is no single price for a company which is correct under all circumstances. A valuation is nothing more than an opinion of value - an educated guess - and opinions vary widely. That's why no one can guarantee the accuracy their number.

In that regard, these chapters each represent the author's opinion of the best way to implement a particular method. Where variations exist, we try to include those too, but the book does not attempt to cover every subtle nuance of valuation that has ever been discovered. Valuation is such an inexact science that, from a practical standpoint, many of those subtle refinements can be a waste of time. The importance of down-to-the-dollar accuracy can easily get out of hand, and introducing more complexities to the process generally does not change the results enough to justify the additional effort and confusion. In most cases, it is simply not a good expense of your time to be so thoroughly exhaustive. The tools are here if you want to use them, but we try to guide you past much of the nitpicking and still get you good, sensible results.

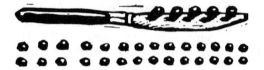

Another reason to avoid overdoing it is because the sale price of any company is the subject of negotiation, so the figure finally agreed upon by everyone will be substantially different from the one you start out with anyway. So don't kill yourself worrying about absolute precision in your results. It's still only a starting point for negotiation.

Nonetheless, if you are going to make an important financial decision based on your results, have a qualified accountant review your work. This is to check for errors in your calculations, verify your methods and assumptions, and give you a second opinion on matters calling for the exercise of personal judgment. If something important has been neglected, you want to make sure it's brought to your attention. Without an up-to-date knowledge of tax and accounting, it is easy to overlook such things.

Valuation is a very subjective process

As you go through each method, you will find that there are many occasions when you are called upon to exercise your own personal judgment. Each time you do, you increase the probability that your figures are going to turn out different from someone else's. Hopefully, you will make informed and intelligent decisions, but there is always room for a difference of opinion. As these judgment-calls accumulate, the odds of variation in results increases exponentially. Subjectivity is also present at the end of the process, when you compare the results obtained by different methods and decide how much weight to give to each one.

This is why two professional appraisers, using the same procedures and the same raw data are going to come up with two different results at the end. There is nothing wrong with this - it's expected. The only assumption is that each will exercise their judgment honestly and intelligently. So use reliable raw data, be scrupulously truthful, document your reasoning so that others can see how you got to your result - and then make your decisions confidently. There is room for reasonable variation in results. Keep in mind that there are also external factors affecting value over which you have no control. These include interest rates, market conditions, supply and demand, tax laws, political conditions, the unforeseeable behavior or perceptions of a particular buyer or seller, and a hundred other things. Many of these become evident during sale price negotiations.

Valuation methods always assume that the business is being sold.

... even if you're doing this for other reasons, such as estate planning. That's because, with few exceptions, the standard basis for value is "market value", no matter what the figure is used for. Market value is defined as that price at which a business is most likely to change hands in an arm's length transaction between buyer and seller, neither being under any particular compulsion to act. The only notable exception to this rule is when someone conducts an appraisal for insurance purposes and the coverage is for "replacement value" of the assets (a topic treated in Chapter 16). So don't get upset when you see us referring to buyers, sellers, acquisitions, sale price, and so on.

Price and value are not the same!

The same company is worth different amounts to different buyers. Market factors, contract terms, egos, negotiation, financing conditions, and even global events can affect the actual price at which a company changes hands. Valuation is supposed to predict that price, but it is always different from the value you calculate. It just depends on the situation.

Important Consideration: Is the business really saleable?

Theory is one thing, and reality is another. Valuation techniques are theory, and they will give you a certain number, but it might have nothing to do with what the business is really worth. Again, we are talking about the difference between calculated value and the price it could actually sell for. Sometimes these valuation techniques fail miserably.

For instance, what if you can't find a willing buyer within a reasonable period of time in that particular market? Then the company is only worth the liquidation (auction) value of its fixed assets. Many entrepreneurs have made lots of money by creating a business that works for them, but wouldn't attract anyone else. The reasons for that can vary. Perhaps there are few people who would want to do what he does for a living. Or maybe its success has resulted

mainly from the unique insights and talents of that particular entrepreneur. Maybe the income requires 80 hour work weeks. Maybe the business is composed of a hodge-podge of jury-rigged assets that are of dubious continuing value. Maybe the only reason the company can produce that income is because it has no debt. (Without a normal measure of debt, the owner is considered to have an artificial situation.)

Maybe the business has high historic income but its heyday has come and gone. Now the owner is treading water amidst greatly increased competition, shifting markets, decreased demand, and other changing factors. Valuation is based on the promise of future income, as indicated by past performance. But if reliable information tells you that the future will be less promising, then you can't base business value on the past record. It might be worth nothing. Sometimes a business will become valueless almost overnight, just from a change in the tax laws or some government regulation.

Pay particular attention to the fact that value is always as-of a specific date.

For instance, Company A may depend, directly or indirectly, on discretionary spending by consumers. If the economy goes into a recession and that market dries up, then it doesn't matter how much income was produced in the past - it might only be worth liquidation value for the foreseeable future. Its eventual recovery along with the economy isn't a certainty. Now, this could represent a opportunity for a patient, cash-endowed buyer. Or, during the interim, entirely new products may hit the market that displace this company permanently. There may be no business to recover. Recessions, by their very nature, are periods of dramatic marketplace transition.

The concept of market value is frequently ignored by those promoting their own agenda. For instance, spouses seeking a divorce settlement from a business owner usually come up with very unrealistic valuations - trying to grab a huge sum of money based on an inflated number. It's easy to find an accountant or appraiser who will use theoretically plausible methodology to place an unrealistic value on  the entrepreneur's business. But what that "expert" is doing is unscrupulous, because he is manipulating his assumptions in a way that produces a very high value while ignoring the fact that, in the real marketplace, no one would ever pay that much for the business. Those who own small professional practices (attorney, doctor, consultant, broker, etc.). are often the victims of this ploy, made worse by the claim that the suing spouse's part-time busy-work at the office was major factor in the other's success.

But market value refers to the price at which the business can be really be sold to someone else. Since that firm's income is almost entirely derived from the services of its current owner, that income will vanish the moment he sells, so the business entity has virtually no value. There's nothing to sell, aside from some fixed assets. In order for a professional service firm to have transferable value, it must be fully-staffed with other equally competent professionals who are employees, bound by contract or otherwise unlikely to leave, all of whom attract and generate business apart from the owner. The latter is saleable - it has market value. The firm might lose some staff and clients when the current owner leaves, but if many are likely to stay, then the firm would have a predictable residual value. Otherwise, it's limited to the liquidation value of its fixed assets.

Accountants and appraisers who don't actually put deals together on a regular basis tend to produce valuations that are too high. They are dealing in theory, with little feedback on whether there really is a market and what it will pay. On the other hand, people who negotiate acquisitions for a living tend take a simpler, but more realistic approach to valuation. Experience has taught them that all the fancy theory in the world is pointless if it leads to a number that no one would actually pay. Their pragmatism can seem insulting at times, and they are often too conservative, but at least they're in the ballpark.

This means that some owners are better off if they don't sell. The company represents a job and an income to them, but nothing to anyone else. Their best bet is to just hang on for as long as they can, then either liquidate or take a chance on owner-financing the sale to an employee or the competition. That can be risky, because the new owner could default on the loan and ruin the business, leaving you with nothing - but it might be the only way.

Sometimes you can simply convert the assets into something that's more saleable. For instance, if a business is situated on commercially-zoned real estate, the owner might gradually cover it with clean multi-use buildings that can be leased. When he's finally ready to get out, he can wind down and convert any remaining space in the same way, giving him a diversified group of rental properties as a nice passive investment. When the general economy is up and the retail markets are strong, they will be very saleable. Throughout the 1980's, retail investment properties regularly sold at cap rates of 8% to 10%, which was a lot more than most businesses sold for. Those rates eventually settled out at between 11% and 14%, but that's still a decent return.

 The Point is, you may be looking at a business that has little or no value as an on-going entity, despite having produced lots of income in the past. In that case, the income-based valuation methods will produce a very misleading result.

The Basic Valuation Procedure:

1. Gather raw data and information needed for your study (See Chapter 2)

2. Adjust the financial statements. (Chapter 3)

3. Consult Chapter 4 to determine which methods to use in your particular case.

4. Use each applicable method according to its instructions

5. Refer to Chapter 19 for instructions on how to wrap up the valuation and "square the results" obtained by each different method.

6. If it's an acquisition that must pay for itself out of the company's own cash flow, refer to Chapter 14.

7. Consult the Glossary (Chapter 24) for an explanation of any terms or concepts you don't understand.

There are usually several different methods that can be used to value any particular company,

...so refer to Chapter 4 for direction on that. While one may seem right on target, you might also find that none are made-to-order for your situation. That's fairly common. But you should use every method that seems the least bit appropriate. Each one will yield a different number, so in the end you will have a range of possible values. At that point you can compare the results and assign more weight to the method that fits your situation the best. That tells you where to focus within the range. The process is often called "correlating the results", and it's explained further in Chapter 19. If one method seems to fit your situation like a glove, you can rely on it principally.

Sometimes you can't use the figures shown on the company's financial statements because they would be misleading. They have to be adjusted to bring them into line with reality. Chapter 3 tells you how to make those adjustments.

11 Good Reasons to Do a Business Valuation:

- To prepare the the sale or purchase of a business.

- To become aware of the factors that account for business worth, so that you can intentionally cultivate company value over time.

- As a management exercise. By viewing your company as a prospective buyer would, you'll gain a better picture of its strengths, its weaknesses, and where improvements can be made.

- To determine the buy-out price for a partner's share. (Agree on the formula ahead of time in order to avoid a big hassle later on.)

- For estate planning. Owners can avoid overpaying gift and estate taxes by having a well-documented valuation study.

- For property settlements following a divorce.

- For an ESOP (Employee Stock Ownership Plan). A valuation must be conducted annually to support the employer's deduction for the ESOP contribution.

- To help obtain a business loan by demonstrating to lenders that the company is worth more than book value shown on its balance sheet.

- When investors in a private firm want to know how they're doing. For companies on the public exchange, you can just check the daily stock prices, but investors in a private company must do a valuation to find this out.

- To assess the income potential and risk in a business you're considering.

- To assess the value of a company's assets prior to dissolution or reorganization.

Since the most common reason for doing a valuation is to prepare for the sale or purchase of the business, this book is oriented toward those transactions. Each chapter includes information on to apply that method to an acquisition, and includes any relevant negotiation tactics.

How to use your valuation as a negotiating tool:

You can't just walk into a negotiating session and say "Here"s my price". At the very least, you'll have to justify that figure on the basis of sound reasoning and accepted financial methods. This isn't a time to look foolish with a lot of wishful thinking or ridiculous demands. Contrary to popular belief, the business world is *not* full of idiots who are willing to let you "make a killing" at their expense.

A well-prepared valuation is your best ammunition for negotiating a fair price for a business. Any time you walk into a negotiating session you can expect that the other side has done some form of valuation as well, and you can also expect that their work has yielded a figure that is vastly different from yours. They're going to argue for the method that gives them the most favorable result. You must be prepared to show why their method is inappropriate to this particular case, or how it is being improperly employed.

Right at the bargaining table, you'll find yourself debating the merits of different valuation methods that might be used in setting the price, but you won't really know what you're talking about unless you know how they apply to the case at hand. If you haven't gone through that exercise, it's going to be very difficult to negotiate effectively on your own behalf. You won't be knowledgeable and you can easily find yourself out-maneuvered by the other party.

Given these facts, it's obvious that *the negotiator should do the valuation*. Don't hire someone else to do it unless they're also negotiating the deal for you.

Price is always a compromise between what the seller wants (sometimes a highly subjective figure) and what the company is actually worth to the buyer. And it's totally legitimate to say that the same company is worth different amounts to different buyers, simply because one might be able to do more with it than another. For instance, a particular buyer might have another business that would integrate well with this company. Combining the two would result in certain mutual advantages (synergies) - so that one-plus-one equals more than two. In addition, certain aspects of the two companies might be duplicated, meaning that you can eliminate some of those departments to produce special efficiencies. Whatever the particular benefits are, the company will be worth more to this buyer than to someone else, so there's a good chance that he'll be willing to pay more for it.

Effect of Contract Terms on Price:

An acquisition agreement contains many provisions in addition to price, and many of those can be translated into a certain monetary value. In order to obtain a certain contract term you often have to trade-off something else, and that sometimes involves an adjustment to the purchase price.

For example, the two most common ways to buy a company are:

1- Purchase its assets (all property used by the company to carry on its business).
Vs.
2- Purchase its stock (the ownership rights to the company, which carries ownership of the assets along with it).

Buyers usually find a purchase of assets to be more advantageous. One reason is because an asset buyer doesn't assume any liabilities (or potential liabilities) of the existing company. In addition, the asset buyer can get stepped-up depreciation on those assets, which increases cash flow and profitability. In that situation, a new corporation is formed to buy the assets and carry on the business.

On the other hand, a sale of stock transfers ownership of the original corporation, and its usually more advantageous to the seller because she gets better tax treatment on the sale proceeds. Either option can be translated into a rough dollar value, and the party who forfeits his advantage usually expects something in return. (Chapter 19 discusses other factors that can increase or decrease sale price in this way.)

In any event, the only thing that brings any buyer and seller to an agreement on price is the strength of their relative desires to buy and sell that company. As mentioned earlier, the figure you arrive at by valuation is only your starting point for negotiation. However,

...by using a number of methods and thereby having a range of values to consider, you'll get a good idea of what should be your bottom line, and what should be the upper limit

Negotiating tips that are applicable to a specific method are usually included in that chapter.

Additional negotiating advice is contained in Chapters 19, 20, and 21, so check those out before you actually try to make a deal.

How to use the valuation to find out whether an acquisition is feasible:

Early in the game, buyers should predict the price they might have to pay in order to gain an idea of whether the deal is even financially feasible. Most buyers borrow the bulk of the purchase price, and the business is then expected to generate enough cash flow to make the loan payments, provide for capital improvements, and give a return to the cash investors. If cash flow isn't adequate to make the payments with a healthy margin left over for safety, then the deal is a waste of time.

Once you forecast cash flow available for loan payments, you can back into a purchase price - and if the seller's expectations are in-line with this, then it's worthwhile to proceed with negotiations.

In this way, a valuation can tell you the limitations of the deal. If the seller expects more, then walk away and find another deal.

The details of cash flow analysis are described in Chapter 14. It's so closely related to some valuation procedures that the two might as well be done together.

Using a valuation to help borrow money:
Buyers will find a valuation helpful when they meet with lenders to borrow money. But for this purpose alone, valuation isn't usually worth the effort because most lenders just want to see whether the cash flow is adequate to support the loan (Chapter 14) and whether the collateral value of the company's assets safely cover the loan amount (Chapter 18).

Valuation brings you down to earth on price. It is important for the seller to be realistic  about price. This is understandably difficult, because of the strong personal attachment most owners have to a business they have nurtured for many years. But those in the buying arena are sophisticated enough to recognize the limitations of a company's worth, and they tend to be very disciplined when it comes to not overpaying for acquisitions. In addition, acquisition lenders are very conservative in this regard, and they try very hard to avoid financing situations where the buyer might be overpaying. Otherwise the deal will be under-secured and the cash flow will be stretched too thin, both of which increase the lender's risk. All-in-all, your chance of actually getting a price in excess of the company's worth is fairly minuscule, so if your expectations are unrealistic the entire process will probably be a huge waste of everyone's time, including your own.

Furthermore, the seller who insists on an unrealistic price will suffer a loss of credibility in the business community. When an owner has been receptive to acquisition offers, even on an informal basis, but his price expectations are unrealistic, word tends to get out very quickly. The company will remain unsold for a long period of time, and thereby gain a shopworn, undesirable appearance in the process. When the owner finally gets serious about selling and comes down to earth on price, he will be at a serious disadvantage by having created a dubious impression of himself and his company in the eyes of buyers and lenders. Still, it is not unusual to encounter a seller who maintains the notion that most acquirers have more money than they know what to do with, or that selling is their way to "make a killing".

There are occasional exceptions, but whenever a company is sold for what seems to be an outrageous price, it was probably worth it. You can also bet that more than one good valuation study bore that out. (Ironically, the caution of both buyers and lenders sometimes goes to the wind when the deal is extremely large, as with some of the more widely publicized mergers.)

Sometimes bidding wars erupt between competing buyers that drive up the price of a promising company. However, these "auctions" are very rare in the case of a smaller company. For one thing, they are very difficult to orchestrate. For another, most buyers consider this a distasteful way of doing business and they flatly refuse to participate. In fact, most serious buyers demand the seller's exclusive attention while they formulate their offer. Then the seller is given a brief period of time to either accept or reject the offer, or to negotiate different terms - and that's it. If they come to agreement, the buyer will demand that the company is taken off of the market immediately, and there will be a written memorandum to that effect. The reason for this procedure is that ...

Buyers don't want their offers "shopped around" to other parties. Using a buyer's offer that way is considered unethical.

Most self-respecting buyers who discover this being done will withdraw from the deal permanently as a matter of principle.

This has been an area of abuse by some outfits. There are firms that charge in excess of $50,000 for valuations that are poorly researched and unrealistic. Some of them ure in the client by tossing around a very high initial estimate. They suggest that they can actually arrange a sale at that price. This entices the owner to sign a contract to have them generate a full blown valuation plus a selling memorandum to distribute to prospective buyers. The would-be seller pays the fee, gets a couple of thick, poorly prepared documents that are mostly fluff pulled out of computer memory, and that's usually as far as it goes. A few inexpensive classified ads in merger and acquisitions publications might be the extent of the marketing. It's often a fluke if they find a buyer at all. But if they do, they get a fat additional commission.

Owners take a real risk when they sign up for services like that. It's just another good reason for doing the valuation yourself. There are too many short-cuts that outside valuators can make - too many ways to screw up the valuation by not being fully informed.

Sometimes an owner will lead buyers to believe that the firm can be purchased, while having no real intention of selling, merely to invite offers that might hint at what the firm is worth. This is usually a mistake. First of all, serious buyers spend lots of time and lots of money evaluating an acquisition prospect, so an owner who engages in this practice is really demonstrating bad faith. Secondly, most interested parties will see through this act before they deliver a real number. Thirdly, any numbers that are discussed in an offer will differ significantly from the fully negotiated price. Lastly, how could that "seller" intelligently discuss a price without first doing a valuation study?

Letting Go

Most owners are accustomed to responsibility and authority, so the act of selling their company can seem quite painful. Many deals fall apart when sellers get cold feet. The excuses vary, but the real reason is always the owner's emotional attachment to the business and his fear of embarking on something new. Sellers should anticipate this hurdle and be mentally prepared.

Often the problem is that the owner just doesn't have a game plan for the rest of his life. It's wise to start the sale process with some serious career planning. Think about your dreams and set some fresh goals. Stretch for something new and different. When you get to the point where you're excited about the next step in your life, then letting go will be much easier. It's important to remember that a full, satisfying life results from a collection of varied experiences, and you'll never achieve that by latching onto the security of sameness. Owning that particular business is just one chapter in your life.

Many sellers rationalize their reluctance to sell by expressing concern about the future welfare of their employees. Selling to someone else usually entails a mixture of pros and cons. In all likelihood, some employees will lose their jobs, but the buyer will also provide new ideas, energy, and resources that improve the lot of those who remain. Most buyers plan to do a lot of things that current ownerss have been unwilling or unable to do.

It's not your responsibility to manage the business forever. Your own financial well-being is just as important. In that regard, settlement can be one of the most exciting days of your life, as you convert a major part of your personal worth into cash and embark on a new future.

If you have a personal computer with  spreadsheet software, we strongly recommend that you use it. If you don't, this would be a great excuse to buy it. In every valuation method, there are many decisions to make and figures to tinker with. Every time you make a change, every other figure will be affected. If you do the job manually, and decide to go back to change something, you'll have re-calculate every other figure. A spreadsheet does this automatically, so it will save you a lot of time and frustration. You're bound to discover little errors made earlier, and you can't just ignore them because they can drastically affect your results. So use a computer, or you'll wish you had.

Chapter 2

Getting Ready

Step One: Learn as much about the company as you reasonably can. This is essential in order to assess its value. You'll need a lot of detailed financial information, plus management input to interpret that data and assess the level of risk associated with an investment in the business. This chapter tells you what questions to ask.

The reason for all this becomes more apparent as you get further into your project. For example, the prior chapter mentioned that there are many points at which you have to exercise your personal judgment to interpret or adjust data. *But* in order to do that, you have to understand the context behind those figures - why they are what they are. Besides, whenever financial data is adjusted, an explanation is mandatory, and you can't offer a plausible reason if you aren't knowledgeable about the company. Remember this: Your goal in adjusting data is only to present a clearer picture of the financial situation, never to misrepresent. You only adjust figures if they are misleading as they currently stand. Chapter 3 of the manual explains how to adjust financial statements.

You'll never get all the information you need in a single meeting, so make sure there's someone in the company you can call whenever you have a question. Then fire away and don't be bashful. Never worry about how numerous or how dumb your questions seem. It's all necessary in order to understand the company's present financial picture and its future potential.

Make sure you take the right approach, otherwise it can become quite an ordeal.

The owners of a private company often perceive these information requests as threatening intrusions into their personal affairs.

That's natural, because up until now all aspects of their business were considered private and personal. But a prospective buyer is entitled to all the facts, and a valuator or intermediary can't do his job without them. So be diplomatic and show some understanding for the owner's sensitivity, but be direct and straight-forward from the start about your need to have all this information. It's best to tell them what you need up front by providing a checklist, and then set a date to meet and go over the answers. It will be frustrating at times, but hang in there. Make sure they understand that you can't proceed until you have all the info.

Keep in mind that it's standard practice to offer the owner complete confidentiality, and make sure you observe your promise. You are now privy to lots of private information, so treat it like you'd expect if it was your business.

Information Checklist

Here is a list you can copy and present to the owner or manager of the business you are evaluating. The items on it are phrased with that in mind. You'll probably add some additional items yourself, depending on the nature of the particular business.

1. Please provide income statements and balance sheets for the past 5 years.

   • The income statements should include a detailed breakdown of the individual expenses, liabilities, and sources of income.

   • Please include the accompanying notes of the accountant.

2. Please provide a comprehensive description of your business activities which includes:

   • Your primary products/services.

   • Any incidental products or services.

   • A breakdown of the sales revenues from each.

- Identify whether any are carried on as separate operations.

- Treat retail, wholesale, distribution, service and consulting activities separately.

- Are there predictable business cycles when revenues are likely to rise and fall? What factors account for this? (condition of the general economy, interest rates, government regulation, inflation, etc.)

3. Please provide a detailed list of the company's individual assets, including the following information:
    - Date acquired
    - Original cost
    - Depreciation taken to date
    - Condition, or whether obsolete
    - Whether "general use" or designed for a specialized process
    - Purchased or leased?
    - Important: Are any of costly assets in need of replacement?

Minor items (such as office supplies, office furniture, etc.) can be grouped together as a category, but try to provide details on any major items that stand out as valuable and individually important (vehicles, expensive computer systems, real estate, etc.)

4. What product development costs or major capital expenditures do you anticipate during the next 5 years in order to remain competitive and keep operating at present levels?

5. Do you anticipate an increase or decrease in certain costs during the next 5 years? Can you predict the change in percent?

6. Please provide your sales projections for the next several years. Remember that a company is valued as it stands now, not based on how it might perform in the future. However, these projections will help us determine the degree of risk associated with the business so that we can determine appropriate capitalization rates.

- Annual Sales - Please give try to predict your total sales revenue for the next three years.

- Does your accountant prepare a cash-flow projection or a pro-forma income statement for you? If so, please provide a copy.

- Do you have a business plan? If so, please provide a copy.

7. Please provide a schedule of inventory, broken down as follows (giving the original cost or book value for each):
   - raw materials
   - work in progress (WIP)
   - finished product
   - obsolete inventory
   Make sure you indicate whether each is at its normal operating level.

8. Please provide copies of any appraisals on the value of your business assets.. (These are often obtained for insurance purposes.)

9. Please provide your best estimate of the following:
   - Total annual sales of your products or service by all companies in your market area.
   - Projected annual growth of your market in the future.
   - What % of the total is sold by your firm? (your current market share)
   - Trends in the market, and new product developments.
   (Some of this information can be obtained from trade associations or from trade magazines.)

10. Amount of accounts receivable*, including agings* as follows:
    - 30 days old - current dollar amount
    - 60 days old -   "
    - 90 days old -   "
    - 120+ days old -   "
    - Number of customers with balances due
    - Credit terms extended to customers
    - Average amount of bad debt each year

11. Amount of accounts payable*, including agings* as follows:

Current amount of payables owed on payment terms of 15 days or less:
- Amount past due:
- Average number of days past due:
- Current amount of payables owed on payment terms of 30 days or less:
- Amount past due:
- Average number of days past due:

Current amount of payables owed on payment terms of 31 days or more:
- Amount past due:
- Average number of days past due:

Who pays you? The recipient, an institution or government, or a third-party (such as insurance company)?

12. Your competition: who are they, what are their products, what are their estimated sales, what geographic areas do they serve?

What distinguishes your company from the competition?

13. Employees:
- Breakdown by category
- Number and average wage/salary level - for past three years
- Average length of employment, or turnover rate
- Benefits and incentives
- Is there an agreement with a union?
- Training costs per employee

14. List your top 10 customers, with annual sales to each, and how long each has been a customer.

15. What do you perceive to be the weak points of your company? How would you remedy them?

16.   Please provide an honest explanation for each major fluctuation in the company's performance over the past 5-10 years. (Remember: all facts are confidential.)

17.   Marketing and sales:

- How do you advertise and market your product?
- How are actual sales conducted?
- Factors emphasized in making sales (service, price, quality, delivery)
- Product areas you avoid and reasons for that
- Products emphasized and the reasons for that
- Promotional techniques employed
- Is there a logical relationship between the location of facilities and the location of your customers or suppliers?

18.   Please provide a description of the management structure, and key individuals involved.

- If the company is sold, will management stay afterwards? Do any have employment contracts?

- Do managers who might leave have non-compete agreements?

19.   Are there any pending or threatened law suits?

20.   Leases and contracts (Provide copies, or at least a summary of their essential terms).

21.   Capitalization (How the company is funded):

- Short term debt:
    - Accounts payable
    - Accrued expenses
    - Income taxes payable
    - Other taxes payable
    - Interest payable
    - Short term loans - balance, payments, interest rate, and terms.

- Long term debt: Balance, monthly payments, interest rate, security (collateral) for loan, lender.
- Stock or Equity: Type of security, number of shares, owners, par value.
- Are there any accounts payable, accrued expenses, income taxes payable, or interest payable on your current balance sheet which warrant an explanation?

22. Please provide a brief company history (date founded and by whom, former shareholders/partners and buy-outs, major expansions, acquisitions, and other milestones in the development of the company.)

23. Pricing: method used and reasoning behind it.
    - Provide product list and price schedule.
    - Effect of cost increases on pricing.
    - Price protection afforded to company by suppliers, and to customers by company.
    - Government regulations restricting prices.
    - How are bids for important contracts solicited? How do you formulate your bid?

24. Facilities - for each property:
    - Is it owned or leased?
    - Size of site and size of building
    - Zoning and types of surrounding properties
    - Age, condition, and type of construction
    - Expansion potential at that site
    - Quality of road access to site
    - Percentage of total production capacity is being used
    - Description of office improvements
    - If leased, what are the basic terms of that lease? (length of term, rent, other expenses paid by tenant, etc.)
    - Did the landlord provide valuable office improvements as part of the lease, or do you have a sizeable company investment in those improvements?

25. The names of each major supplier, including:
    • Date they started doing business with company
    • Annual purchase volume from each
    • Type of products they supply
    • Credit and purchase terms
    • Quality of the company's relationship with them
    • The number of backup suppliers for those items

26. Insurance, fire, and police protection
    • Include premium amount for each insurance

27. Are there any operating restrictions or reporting requirements imposed by the Government?

28. Important: Please take a copy of your most recent annual income statement, and adjust the figures to show what you think it will probably look like next year.

Talk to owners and managers for further information.

Once you've obtained all this input, you should have a fairly good handle on the health of this company, and you should also understand the risks involved in that line of business. The next step is to talk to the people who manage the company and get them to really fill you in on the following topics:

1. **Where can operations be tightened up and how much?** (without detracting from the quality of products and services, or relationships with employees and clients).

2. **Potential sources of sales growth, and what it would cost to develop them,** including:
- New customers in current market area.
- New geographic market areas.
- New products or services that could be offered.
- Possible enlargement of the sales and marketing staff.

3. **Possible acquisitions of other businesses**

4. **Excessive salaries, perquisites, and other generous benefits to managers and owners** which could be scaled down. Also, any personal expenses of the owners being paid for by the company and written off as "business expenses".

5. **Any unusual accounting or bookkeeping methods being used by the company.** Anything out of the ordinary that might cause the income statement or the balance sheet to look different than it otherwise might.

6. **External factors affecting this company,** including:
- The state of the nation's economy, interest rates, and inflation.
- Technological developments in that field.
- Developments in different but related fields that might have an impact.
- Population growth and movement.
- Changes in consumer taste/demands.

You might include these items in the checklist you give to the managers. The information will give you some insight into the company's future potential. If part of your job is to predict the future performance of the company, this input is essential. In that case, you will need to translate the effect of each foreseeable change into a dollar result, and then create a new income statement showing the combined financial effect of all those changes. This is known as a "pro forma*" income statement. It's essential analysis for anyone thinking about buying a business.

Most buyers want to determine that they can do more with the company than those before them. However, considering the inherent uncertainty in the business world, pro forma predictions are nothing to count on. The acquisition has to make sense even if none of the expected growth takes place.

After you have gathered all this information, proceed to Chapter 4 to determine which valuation methods to use in your particular case.

There are a couple of financial expressions that might seem confusing to some readers, because they tend to be used interchangeably. The term "Net Operating Income" (NOI) refers to the *profit* a company makes after deducting all of the normal "costs of doing business" (which are known as "operating expenses"). The confusion arises because many people think of "income" as the money you take in *before* expenses are deducted. But in financial circles, that's referred to as "sales", "gross sales", "revenues", or "gross revenues". Some just call it "the gross". Then you deduct all the normal operating expenses, and the profit that's left over is called "net income", "net operating income", "net profit", or "net operating profit". These terms are used interchangeably, but they all refer to the same thing.

However, net income does not include income from sources that are incidental to the real business of the company, such as interest on loans to employees, interest from bank accounts, investment income, or rent from excess warehouse space. Those things are "non-operating income".

Also, income isn't reduced by the costs of owning the company - such as depreciation and interest. Those are called "non-operating expenses". Those are considered to be financial or investment expenses of the owners.

Lastly, understand that all income figures are before taxes are deducted, unless it specifically says "after-tax".

Got that straight? OK - now on to the methods!

Chapter 3

Next Step: Adjust the Financial Statements

An "adjusted" income statement is one in which certain figures have been changed. The changes are made to compensate for any unusual spending or accounting practices of the current owner.

The goal is to produce an income statement that shows the real present earning power of the company. It reflects your prediction of earnings over the next 12-months.

 We also do this in order to show what the statement would look like if a corporate parent was operating the company as a subsidiary. Balance Sheets are also adjusted in some cases. We often refer to an adjusted statement as an "economic statement" since **the changes are intended to reflect economic reality**, as opposed to the owner's personal accounting practices.

Valuation is based on pre-tax earnings. That's because tax consequences vary so much, depending on choices the owners make with regard to different tax treatments, as well as the type of business entity they select. Most people agree that the value of a business shouldn't be affected by the owner's tax bracket, so methods based on pre-tax earnings give more consistent and fair results. Sub-S corporations are very popular because the earnings are taxed only to the owners at their individual rates, and not to the corporation as well.

Basic form for an Income Statement:

Gross Sales
  (minus) Sales returns, customer
    allowances, and discounts

= Net Sales
  (minus)) Cost of Goods Sold*

= Gross Income (or Gross Profit)
  (minus) Operating Expenses - including:
    Sales and Delivery Expenses
    Administrative & General Expenses
    (including executive salaries)

= Net Operating Income (Net Operating Profit)
  (minus) Interest, Depreciation, and other
    Financial Expenses (Called "non-operating expenses" or "other expenses")

= Net Income Before Tax

*Cost of Goods Sold = the materials and labor used to produce the company's goods.

A publicly-held corporation wants to please its stockholders by showing the largest "bottom-line" profit possible. Conversely, the aim of a private company is to show the smallest bottom-line profit as possible. It isn't that the private company wants to make less money. It wants to make all the money it can, but at the same time it wants to show the smallest possible amount of net income, which is taxable. As you know, the government taxes all income remaining after business expenses are deducted. Therefore, if you can pay an expense through the company, with the money it earns before taxes, and thereby reduce the company's taxable net income, you will be better off than if you paid the expense out of your own pocket with after-tax dollars.

It's common for the owners of a private company to include a business purpose in many personal activities so they can write-off the cost of that event as a business expense.

Most businesspeople do that in an honest and legitimate way, and the IRS accepts the deductions as bona fide business expenses that benefit the company. (Consult your accountant and the tax laws.) However, when you do a valuation, think of your company as a subsidiary of a larger corporation that has no interest in bestowing excess benefits on the local managers. They want the sales manager to meet with prospective customers in the office - not at an expensive country club. So in any valuation it's important to use figures from an income statement that has been "adjusted" to exclude these unusual expenses.

Don't use figures from tax returns, since they don't always reflect generally accepted accounting principles..

The figures on tax returns are designed for one specific purpose - to determine taxable income according to IRS regulations. For example, tax laws may allow cash basis accounting in a case where accepted accounting principles dictate accrual accounting - and the result can be a significant difference in calculated earnings. You don't have to understand all these different accounting concepts - just make sure your valuation is based on financial statements instead of tax returns.

Whenever an income statement has been adjusted, make sure you disclose that fact in your valuation report.

Include the "before" income statement and the "after" income statement, as well as detailed notes on the items that have been adjusted. If you don't, your conclusions could prove misleading to someone else. Most adjustments involve an element of personal judgment that others may disagree with, so they should have the opportunity to replace your revised figures with their own.

This is not a time for wishful thinking. Don't try to disguise real problems in the business. Your statement will be scrutinized carefully if a deal is undertaken, and misleading or unrealistic adjustments will destroy your credibility, if not the transaction itself.

Keep in mind that there are certain disadvantages associated with adjusted statements. First of all, they are always suspect, because they are based on supposition. Buyers and sellers always seem to find ways to argue with each other's replacement figures. Secondly, you might stir up an IRS challenge if they see an adjusted statement showing a larger bottom line than has been reported. For instance, they might claim that excess salaries were actually dividends.

Cash Vs. Accrual Accounting:

Many small businesses use the "cash" basis of accounting, which means that expenses are recorded when actually paid, and income is recorded when actually received. "Accrual accounting", on the other hand, records expenses on the date the business becomes liable for them. It records income as soon as it's owed to the company, whether or not received. Obviously, cash accounting can be misleading in some cases. For instance, the last income statement may show a big surge in earnings if the company holds back on paying some bills. That could manipulate a buyer into paying too much for the firm. Another tricky item is bad debt. Some firms know that certain accounts won't be paid, or they experience a predictable amount of bad debt each year, and yet they don't recognize bad debt until it's formally judged uncollectible. That overstates the income. Keep an eye out for these things, and adjust the statement accordingly.

Income Statements: What to adjust and how to do it

Salaries: Unusually small or unusually generous salaries drawn by the owner/managers.

- We usually assume that the business is incorporated, even if it isn't. In the case of salaries, that means the expenses should include a reasonable salary for the owner. In an unincorporated business, the entire bottom-line income goes to the owners as their "salary". But that amount is likely to be either excessive or inadequate for a hired manager. The salary expense should reflect appropriate compensation for a capable replacement to carry out the owners' duties.

- An incorporated business is taxed differently. Its net income is taxed at a special corporate rate, then the remaining amount is either kept by the company ("retained earnings") or distributed to the owners (stockholders) as their share of the profit from the business ("dividends"). Once dividends are in the hands of the individual owner, that income is taxed again, this time at the owner's personal tax rate, just like any other income they receive. To avoid this double taxation, owners who work in their own incorporated business pay themselves the largest salary possible. (Although the IRS may question the reasonableness of that amount.) When paid as salaries, these sums are deductible business expenses to the company, and therefore they are taxed only at the corporate level, and not at the personal level.

- Sometimes the owner underpays himself to make the company look more profitable, or sometimes the owner just doesn't need the money and would prefer to leave it in retained earnings. In that case, you have to add more salary to the expenses.

...less if your company writes it off as a business expense than if you pay for it out of your own pocket with dollars that have already been taxed twice. So ask yourself if a large corporation would provide an auto-mobile for that employee. Does it have to be a Porsche? Follow the same reasoning used for salaries and adjust the income statement accordingly.

- Don't forget to also exclude any related expenses to the same extent - such as auto insurance, gas, repairs, parking, etc.

Life insurance premiums:

- Small companies often pay the premiums for an owner's life insurance. If the company is the beneficiary of the policy, it's key-man insurance. In other words, that person's talents and abilities are essential to the firm's success, and it would be very expensive to go out and find an equally capable replacement for him if he were to die, but the insurance would pay for this if it happened. In that case, it's a legitimate expense. Otherwise, kick it out.

- If the beneficiary of the policy is another owner, then the reason for the insurance is to allow him to buy out the insured's share of the company upon the latter's death. This keeps the deceased owner's relatives from screwing things up by inheriting the stock and trying to run the company. It's a good idea, but the expense should be taken out.

-If someone else is the beneficiary of the policy, then the insurance is just part of the employee's compensation package. It should be taken out of the statement if it would not be part of the expected compensation of a replacement manager.

Travel and Entertainment Expense ("T&E"):

-Owners often write off country club dues, boats, vacations, resort properties, meals, and other extravagances as business expenses. This may be completely legit for the private owner, but the question to ask is: how much T&E expense would a corporate parent allow this company to spend in promoting its business? It may be less than you think. Large companies like to promote their business in other ways.

- On the other hand, travel expenses not associated with entertainment (for example, a sales trip) usually aren't questioned. However, always be aware of current IRS limitations on T&E deductions.

Relatives employed by the business:

-Sometimes a relative is put on the payroll in order to take more money out of the

business in the form of *deductible* employee wages. That "employee" may be overpaid, or never even show up at work. However, the advantage is that the income is reported on the personal tax return of someone who is in a much lower tax bracket than the owner. If you pay yourself a handsome salary, all of it will be taxed at the highest individual tax rate. If you split that same amount between several family members filing separate returns, it's spread out and taxed at lower bracket rates. That way is a lot more money is left over after taxes, which makes this one of the least expensive ways to take money out of the company. However, when the current tax rates are relatively low, this device is less attractive. To adjust, simply ask whether that employee is necessary, and how much they would normally be paid

.

Cost of Goods Sold:

- In a very profitable year, the company may be more aggressive in writing off inventory because that reduces taxable income. If that's the case, compare it to previous years and adjust Cost of Goods Sold to a more reasonable figure. In addition, the inventory accounting method they use may not fairly reflect the market value of the inventory, so you should also adjust that (on the Balance Sheet).

- For instance, recasting from LIFO to FIFO (see Glossary) might reduce the deduction for Cost of Goods Sold, and increase profit on the bottom line. Most owners anticipating a sale would not elect LIFO if the cost of new inventory is much higher than that of old inventory, because that weakens the bottom line. However, the result might be lots of valuable inventory on the books at the old, lower values.

Leases for equipment or machinery

that could have been purchased outright by the company and financed with debt:

In order to keep the balance sheet liabilities as low as possible, many businesses lease items they might have purchased. This is known as "off the balance sheet financing". It makes the firm look healthier, but it can sometimes be misleading. Go by this rule: If leasing still gives the company most of the risks and benefits of owning that property, then the lease obligation should appear on the balance sheet as a liability. (Sometimes called a "financing lease".) In other words, the lease is just another way to finance the property, and the lease payments are like loan payments, with part of them representing interest and the rest representing repayment of the principal amount financed.

The other type of lease is called an "operating lease" - where you lease and use the item, but most of the risks of ownership and the tax benefits still belong to the firm that leases the property to you.

How do you adjust the statements when an operating lease is really a financing lease? First of all, the income statement should show only the interest portion of the lease payment. Normally it's listed as an operating expense. But if you are using a valuation method that requires you to remove interest payments from the income statement, then you show it as a non-operating expense. Secondly, on the balance sheet, you should list the leased item as a fixed asset (at original cost minus depreciation to date). Then the principal portion of the lease payments should be shown as a liability.

Remove "unrelated" (non-operating) income or expenses from the statement:

- This includes any income or expenses which do not directly result from the primary business operations of the company. On the statement, these are referred to as "other income" or "other expenses".

- Interest is usually an "other expense", so it should be deducted from the statement if it arises from obligations that are not expected to continue in the future, or if it is not directly related to the primary business operations of this company.

- "Other income" might include such things as income from rental properties, investments, or other sources which have little to do with the business operations being evaluated. Allowing these items to remain on the statement would give the misleading impression that the additional income is derived from the production and sale of the products or services which are the normal business of that company.

Depreciation: Look up "Income Statement" in the Glossary to see where depreciation appears on the statement. It's usually shown as some type of "operating expense". For example, it might be listed under "Cost of

Goods Sold", or "Administrative and General Expenses".

But while depreciation may be listed on the income statement as an operating expense, it's not really "a cost of doing business". Some valuation methods are based on operating income before any deduction for financial expenses, so in those cases we move all depreciation down to a different part of the statement (to the section for "financial, non-operating, and other expenses"). In effect, we are adding the depreciation expense back into the net operating income. We do this for the Capitalization of Income method, the Excess Earnings method, and any rule-of-thumb method that uses a multiplier of earnings. For now, just leave it on the statement where it is. The step-by-step instructions for the particular method will tell you whether or not to add it back.

What adjustment should we make at this point? Since the depreciation methods used for accounting and tax purposes do not necessarily reflect the actual annual reduction in the value of those assets, you want to figure out how much their value really declines each year, and substitute that amount for the depreciation expense already shown.

In some cases we adjust the depreciation expense to what it would be *after* the company is acquired. We do this for methods that forecast earnings or cash flow into the future - such as the Discounted Cash Flow method and the Ability to Pay method. These are buyer's methods. They don't measure overall value as much as they predict what the company will be worth to that particular buyer, considering the specific way it will be purchased, financed, and run.

For example, let's say you are relying on income statements from past years to do your valuation, and you are anticipating an acquisition that will take the form of a sale of assets rather than a sale of stock (see Chapter 14), so that after the acquisition, the assets will have a stepped-up "basis" for deprecia-

tion, which will increase that annual write-off. On the other hand, if the company is transferred by means of a purchase of stock, the buyer will inherit the existing depreciation schedule for the assets, wherein most of the depreciation may already be used up. (There is a way around that, using Section 338 of the tax code. See your accountant.) Higher depreciation increases your "cash flow*", and since most buyers of privately-held companies need that boost in cash flow to make the deal financially feasible, the majority of acquisitions involving companies with older (more fully depreciated) assets take the form of a purchase of assets. The prospective seller of such a company should bear this is mind and expect to go this route if they want to make their deal. Anyway, buyers should conduct their valuation and cash flow analysis using the predicted (stepped-up) post-acquisition depreciation expense instead of the old schedule. See Step 3 of Chapter 10 (Discounted Cash Flow Method) for instructions on how to do this.

Asset Values on the Balance Sheet:

Again, the asset values listed on the balance sheet reflect original cost minus depreciation taken to date, so these should be adjusted to show the true economic value of the assets.

Interest Expense:

In some of the methods described in this book, you remove the interest expense from the statement entirely (Capitalization of Income Method, Rule of Thumb Methods that use multipliers, and the Excess Earnings Method). For others, such as the Ability to Pay and Discounted Cash Flow Methods, you leave the interest expense on the income statement, but you adjust it to show what interest costs would be in the future. In other words, you add back any current interest expense that would not exist after the acquisition, and you deduct any new interest expenses that will exist after the acquisition.

From this you can see that it's possible to have two different valuations for the same company, depending on how much interest expense is expected in the future. Methods that leave the interest expense on the statement are usually "buyer's methods" since they are designed to help a buyer figure out what the business is worth to *him*. Those methods usually don't deduct liabilities from the end result. But if the interest expense *is* removed from the income statement, we deduct the liabilities that create it from the end result.

Non-recurring circumstances that have affected earnings positively or negatively in the current year:

These wouldn't occur under normal circumstances, so adjust their effect out of the statement. They could include things like a large legal fee or judgment against the company, a casualty loss, moving expense, or gains and losses from the sale of assets.

Some other things to watch out for:

- Professional fees (legal, accounting, etc) billed to the business as company expenses. These may actually be personal expenses of the owners.

- Interest paid to owners for loans they made to the company. Were the loans necessary? Was the interest higher than market rates?

- Rent paid to owners by the company. If the owners have purchased real estate or equipment and leased it back to the company, ask whether the lease payments are more than they'd be if the company rented from someone else. Otherwise, there's nothing wrong with these arrangements - they make good business sense.

- Under-insurance. A firm may not carry adequate insurance protection, and in that case you should get premium estimates for the proper amount of coverage and add that to the expenses.

- Any dramatic increase or decrease in a particular expense from one year to another. Look into the reason for it - it may reveal something unusual. On the record, make sure you ask about any "imminent changes" that may affect income or costs. Something big may be about to change soon, even though there's no hint of it on the financial statements. Your appraisal should reflect the conditions in effect at the present time, but if you become aware of something that's going to affect value in the future, then you should take note of it, particularly if you or your client is a prospective buyer.

- Research & Development expenses. This label is sometimes used by companies to write off non-deductible gifts and expenditures that benefit particular individuals.

- Skimmed Cash: Sellers sometimes claim to have skimmed amounts from their cash take (implying that the net profits were actually greater to that extent) - but it's best to not rely upon such claims. Only use figures that are verified by income tax returns.

How to Adjust Income:

1. Take out any non-operating income. That means any income that isn't derived from the primary business activity of the company. It could include rent from excess building space or interest from loans to employees.

2. If income has fluctuated over the past several years, then use a weighted average*. If it has increased consistently over the years, then use the latest year. If it has declined fairly consistently over the years, then use the latest year.

3. Take out any non-recurring income - income that results from unusual events, such as collection of a legal judgment, repayment of money owed to the company, or the sale of assets. Also adjust-out any temporary surge in income that is unlikely to continue - for example, an unusual wave of orders from the military due to a war, or an increase in business due to a natural disaster such as a hurricane.

ಬಿಂಬ

Should you use pre-tax or after-tax income?

The methods in this book always refer to before-tax earnings. However, some appraisers argue that valuation methods should compare an investor's *pre*-tax return from investments of equivalent risk to the *after*-tax return of the company being valued. They feel this is appropriate because the after-tax earnings of the company will be taxed again at the personal income tax rates after they pass to the investors - the same as with any investment security. (Corporate earnings are taxed twice - once to the corporation, and then again to the stockholders when they get their share of what is left.) Despite this logic, we suggest that you stick with before-tax earnings because the methods will produce more-consistent results.

ಬಿಂಬ

Note - On Adjusting Statements for Partnerships, Sole Proprietorships, and Sub-Chapter S Corporations:

A sole proprietorship is an unincorporated business with one owner. A partnership is an unincorporated business with more than one owner. A Sub-S Corporation is a type of corporation that's taxed like a partnership.

These types of businesses won't show an owner's salary among the expenses. The owners take their salary as a "draw" - a distribution of the bottom-line earnings. In other words, net profits pile up in a bank account from which the owners can write themselves checks on a regular basis - and the whole amount is taxed on the owner's personal return. Corporations, on the other hand, have their earnings taxed first at the corporate level, and then taxed again at the individual level when the remainder is distributed to the owners as dividends. It's the price you pay for taking advantage of the legal protection of a corporation. But with corporations, the owners' salaries are a deductible business expense, so they show up as an expense on the income statement as well.

In valuation, we usually regard every business as a corporation. Therefore, no matter what form the business really takes, your adjusted statement should show a reasonable salary expense for everyone working in the business. Some methods also ask you to determine the corporate income tax.

How to Adjust Balance Sheets:

Watch for Fluctuating Values - items that seem unusually high or low in a particular year. For example, if accounts receivable are much lower in one year than in most other years, then you need to find out why and adjust for it on the balance sheet.

In most cases, you *compare balance sheet items from year-to-year by calculating them as a percentage of Total Assets* in that year. This means you divide the dollar amount of the item by the dollar amount of Total Assets for that year. This will give you a percentage. Do the same for the other years and then compare them. However, if the item is listed on the Liabilities or Stockholders Equity side of the balance sheet, then compare it to other years as a percentage of Total Liabilities plus Total Stockholder's Equity.

Inventory levels...

should be scrutinized. If a particular adjustment is difficult to estimate, ask the company's controller for help. Necessary inventory levels are usually a percentage of the corresponding amount of annualized gross sales during that period.

Inventory is usually valued according to the LIFO or FIFO* methods. (See Glossary). However, if all inventory is useable, you can adjust its value to current replacement cost. Any obsolete or unusable inventory should be excluded. If the company uses LIFO, you might want to adjust it to FIFO if you feel the latter reflects more realistic conditions. Besides, you want to compare apples to apples when looking at more than one company in the same industry - and if one firm uses FIFO and the other uses LIFO, your conclusions could be off. So adjust all of your comparables to the same basis. Usually the company's accountant can tell you how to translate LIFO to FIFO.

Materials inventory accounted for under the LIFO method may have significant hidden value. This is because some older inventory is still carried on the books at its original cost, yet today's market price for those materials is probably higher. Value those inventories at their current market cost if all of it is useable. Remember that inventory is not depreciated.

Note that Work In Progress and Finished Inventory value should include the cost of the labor and allocated overhead expense incurred thus far in producing it. The value of Finished Goods, however, should not include any of the expected profit, unless it's pre-sold. This is because additional funds and resources must still be expended to sell them, and because there is still uncertainty regarding their sale.

Refer to the section earlier in this chapter regarding "Cost of Goods Sold".

Cash and Equivalents:

No adjustment is normally required. "Equivalents" include any investment that can be quickly and easily converted to cash.

Marketable Securities:

If these are non-operating assets, then remove them from the balance sheet. But if they constitute the company's cash reserve, then leave them on the balance sheet and adjust them to market value.

Accounts Receivable:

Delete any receivables that are unlikely to be collected. In other words, if bills are due in 30 days, but receivables older than 90 days are unlikely to be collected, then remove any receivable older than 90 days from the total. Another approach is to reduce total receivables by the company's historical percentage of bad debt.

Even though the IRS no longer allows companies to deduct an allowance for doubtful accounts, you can still use this approach for your adjusted balance sheet, based on the amount of debt that is usually not collected. For example, a mall jewelry retailer offers financing to a large percentage of its customers and routinely experiences 30% bad debt each year, so you would reduce the current value of his receivables by 30%.

Note that a company using cash-basis accounting does not include receivables on its balance sheet, but those should be included for your purposes here.

Even if the seller plans to retain the pre-existing accounts receivable when the company is sold, the buyer should analyze them in order to gain an understanding of the payment habits of its paying customers because that contributes to the level of risk associated with the business.

Pre-paid Expenses:

Remove these from the balance sheet if they don't really benefit the business in some way, or if they are not transferable to a new owner.

Some pre-paid items are cashed out by the owner when the business is transferred - such as rent or deposits on utilities. Make sure these are excluded from the balance sheet.

Equipment, Furniture, and Fixtures:

Since book value does not usually reflect the real economic value of these assets, this has to be adjusted. The main question is whether to use market value, replacement cost, or liquidation value. In general, use market value if the company is a profitable, viable, going-concern that will probably be transferred as a whole to a new owner. In other cases, use liquidation value.

Market value can be approached in a couple of different ways. The best, but not the cheapest, is to hire an equipment appraiser. If there is a reliable market for the resale of those items, then equipment dealers can help you figure out what the stuff is worth. Otherwise, use "depreciated replacement cost". In other words, find the cost for a new replacement item, then deduct the percentage of that cost that corresponds to how much of its useful life has already been used up. Don't use the useful life listed in the tax laws for this, since it may be shorter or longer than the real useful life of the asset.

If assets are already fully depreciated, no value will show up for them on the current balance sheet, but you should add their real economic value. In addition, due to inflation, equipment that's in excellent condition and not obsolete has probably depreciated very little. In that case, it may be worth more than book value.

Some assets may not contribute to the company's sales and profits. These should be valued at their orderly liquidation value - the price they'd probably bring at auction or in a quick sale.

By the way, this is a good time to find out whether the equipment is up-to-date with the rest of the industry, and whether additional equipment should be purchased to carry out that business effectively and competitively.

Tools & Dies:

Tools, dies, molds, and certain other types of equipment are subject to lots of wear, so they have short useful lives. They also grow obsolete very quickly. Their value is probably less than book value and they may not even be resalable. If they are marketable, don't be afraid to depreciate them heavily. They seldom bring anything near cost or replacement value.

Leasehold Improvements (Money spent out-of-pocket to improve leased property):

These are valued by multiplying their original cost by the percentage of remaining lease term. However, if the real useful life of the improvements is less than the remaining lease term, then base it on the useful life instead. If the lease is not assignable to a new owner, then these should be deleted from the balance sheet.

Real Estate:

Use market value. Real estate and leasehold improvements are often worth more than their book value, for several reasons:

a) Contrary to popular belief, most real estate does not rise in value right along with the rate of inflation. This is especially true in the case of industrial buildings. However, real estate will usually hold its original value if it's well-maintained and doesn't become functionally obsolete. The point is that this runs counter to the practice of *depreciating* real estate on the books over time.

(b) Accelerated methods of depreciation can result in an even lower book value, which would be even more misleading.

(c) Sometimes management will "expense"* the cost of improvements to real estate, rather than adding it to the cost basis of the real estate or its book value on the balance sheet. In that case, the balance sheet would understate the value of the realty to that extent.

Rather than hire real estate appraisers to calculate value, many people just solicit the opinions of several commercial-industrial real estate brokers to get an average estimate of property value, based on their experience in selling similar properties in that market. Just make sure they are specialists in that kind of property, not residential agents who dabble occasionally in commercial property.

If the real estate won't be transferred with the sale of the company, then don't count it among the assets. Instead, knock it off the balance sheet and add fair rent for equivalent space to the expenses on the income statement. With small businesses, the value of any real estate is often a disproportionately large part of the total asset value. In fact, most small businesses do not own their own real estate, so most valuators remove it from the balance sheet and add rent to the expenses.

Intangible Assets:

Refer to the Economic Value of Assets Method for instructions on how to value these. Note that certain methods, such as the Excess Earnings Method, tell you to remove intangibles from the balance sheet, since their value is calculated separately. However, that normally doesn't include those having value apart from the business, such as liquor licenses and transferrable franchise rights.

Loans to Shareholders (Notes)

- These are generally removed from the balance sheet when the company is owned by one person, since the net effect of owing yourself money is a wash. Besides, most sellers don't want the debt to continue after the company is sold.

- In other cases, keep the note on the balance sheet as an asset, but make sure the debtor is paying market rate interest. List its value as the remaining amount of unpaid principal. If it's an interest-free loan to the stockholder, then reduce it to present value* using a discount rate equal to the rate of interest that should be paid on the loan.

Liabilities of the Business:

No adjustment is necessary unless there are special circumstances. Keep in mind that a business using cash-basis accounting may not list certain liabilities on the balance sheet, such as trade payables and payroll, but you should make sure they are included.

Even if you are working on an acquisition where the buyer won't assume liabilities, you  should examine these debts because if the company has been slow in paying its bills, that can result in overstated profits, in which case the buyer might overpay for the company. Watch for a general reduction in operating expenses that started shortly before the company is put on the market.

 *Investigate the possibility of unrecorded or undisclosed liabilities*

- Potential lawsuits or fines

- Regulatory compliance, particularly with regard to environmental contamination

- Warranty work or replacements. If the company has a warranty or replacement policy, there should be a warranty reserve. If not, part of the purchase price should be set aside in an escrow account to cover warranty costs from sales occurring before settlement. When the warranty period expires, the balance can be paid over to the seller.

- Unfunded pension plan obligations. These can result in huge liabilities that carry over to the new owner. The plan may have been set up to cover a number of employees, but since the payout is years away, the company may not have accumulated enough money in the plan to cover the amount owed for service to date.

- Many of these liabilities are contingent, so it's hard to predict what they might amount to. In a real acquisition, the solution will be a combination of guesswork, reserves, insurance, and seller indemnification.

ଞୋଗ

Now you should have the idea.

Just make sure you start with a very detailed breakdown of all business expenses so you'll have the chance to spot these things. If you're dealing with your own company, you should already know what to adjust. If it isn't your own company, don't be afraid to ask. Although this is often a sensitive topic, you should assume that the owners have been acting ethically and therefore won't mind answering honestly, provided you assure them of the confidentiality to which they are entitled. In fact, if the owners want to achieve as high a valuation as possible, then it's in their best interest to reveal these things to the valuator, since most adjustments increase the net income, and therefore increase the apparent value of the company.

Chapter 4

Which Methods to Use in Your Case

This section gives a brief description of each valuation method and explains when it's used. Use every method that seems to apply to your case. When you're done, compare the different results according to the instructions in Chapter 19. That will tell you how to narrow down the range of values and zero in on a specific number.

Economic Value of Assets Method
(Chapter 6)

When To Use:

• Whenever the Excess Earnings Method, or some other method, shows that company's earnings are not significant enough to warrant any "goodwill*" value.

• To value any business with a stagnant, unsteady, or downward trend in sales or earnings.

• Any time a business might bring a higher price if it's broken up and its assets are sold individually.

Brief Description: Determine the market or liquidation value of the individual assets by independent appraisal, and total them up. Do not use "replacement value" appraisals conducted for insurance purposes. Determine the value of any intangible asset* for which there is a resale market, and add those to the total.

Net Worth (Book Value) Approach
(Chapter 7)

When To Use: This is not really a valuation method. It is sometimes used in price negotiations, but only as a supplement to Economic Value of Assets Method. Net Worth, or total Book Value, is often viewed as a target price by buyers in leveraged buyouts* and corporate divestitures.

Brief Description: Total Assets minus Total Liabilities, using the figures given on the balance sheet.

Capitalization of Income Stream Method (Chapter 8)

When To Use: Anytime a business produces sufficient after-tax earnings to result in "goodwill* value" over and above the value of the company's assets.

Brief Description: An "adjusted" income statement is prepared to show how the company is likely to perform over the next 12 months. Take the net operating income before tax from that statement. Then add back all depreciation expenses and interest expenses. Then subtract the real average annual decline in the value of the company's fixed assets. Divide the result by the rate of return an investor would expect from another investment of equivalent risk. The resulting figure is reduced by any liabilities assumed by someone purchasing the company. The result is the value of the company.

The Small Business Method (Chapter 9)

When To Use: For businesses with net operating income of $200,000 or less - before deducting interest, depreciation, and taxes. (The $200,000 should include any manager and owner salaries.) Applies well to small retail and service-type businesses.

Brief Description: Take the Net Operating Income and add back any interest, depreciation, and non-operating expenses. Do this for the last 5 years and calculate the weighted average. Divide the result by an appropriate capitalization rate. Add the real economic value of any non-operating assets and real estate that will be included in the sale. Add the net working capital, if current assets and current liabilities are will be transferred to the new owner. Deduct any other liabilities that go with the business.

Discounted Cash Flow Method
(Chapter 10)

This is primarily a buyer's method.

When To Use:

- When the company will be purchased as an "investment" to be held for a limited number of years (no more than 10).

- When the acquisition will be highly leveraged (financed mostly with borrowed money).

- Any extremely risky situation.

Brief Description: Project the annual cash flow* for each year of the projected holding period of the company. Deduct the taxes, capital expenditures*, and debt service (loan payments) expected in each of those years. Then, for each year, compute the "present value*" of the remaining amount. Add them together. To this, add the present value* of assets expected to remain at the end of the entire period. Subtract liabilities expected to remain at the end of that period.

-

Excess Earnings Method (Chapter 11)

When To Use: To value any profitable company.

Brief Description: This method assumes that a business is worth the market value of its tangible assets, plus a premium for "goodwill*" if earnings are high enough.

Internal Revenue Service Method
(Chapter 12)

When To Use:

- Primarily for estate and gift tax purposes.

- For any situation where tax considerations are involved.

Brief Description: Add the value of the Net Tangible Assets* of the company (Total Assets, minus Intangible Assets*, minus Liabilities) to the capitalized value* of "excess earnings" (earnings in excess of the "normal return" those tangible assets would yield for a typical company).

Ability-To-Pay Method (Chapter 13)

When to use it: This is primarily a buyer's method. While it can give a strong indication of value, its main purpose is to tell the buyer if the company's earnings can support the proposed purchase price. In other words, if you are borrowing the money needed to buy a business, use this method to make sure the company can make the acquisition loan payments out of its own cash flow* ("Pay for itself").

Sellers: Use it to find the *maximum price* your company's cash flow can support, on the assumption that its cash flow must provide all the payments for the buyer's acquisition loan.

Brief Description: Here you are saying that the company will provide cash flow of $X to make debt payments - so, what is the highest loan those loan payments will support? (Ie, you "back into" the loan amount, hence the price as well).

Start by projecting the annual *net* cash flow for 8 to 10 years. Then find the average. Deduct the expected yearly Capital Expenditures*. The result is the Average Annual Cash Flow Available for Debt Service. Deduct a conservative percentage as a safety buffer, and assume that the remainder can be used for loan payments. Figure out how large a loan those payments will support? Assuming that the loan amount is about 80% of the purchase price, determine the purchase price.

Comparable Sales Method (Chapter 16)

When To Use: Only use when valuing a publicly-held company and when detailed data on recent acquisitions of "similar" publicly-held companies is available. The method has serious limitations for privately-held or closely-held companies, but can provide valuable ammunition for price negotiations.

Brief Description: Recent acquisitions of comparable companies are analyzed and the sales price of each is painstakingly adjusted to reflect what it would have been had that company been identical in all significant respects to the subject company. Those sale prices are then translated into a different form - a "multiple" of after-tax earnings. This process is repeated for a large number of transactions, and then you determine the average of the resulting "multiples". The value of the subject company is arrived at by multiplying its own after-tax earnings by this average multiple.

Price/Earnings Ratio Method ("Multiple" of Earnings Method) (Chapter 16)

When To Use: Best suited for valuation of publicly-held companies. Not practical for privately-held situations. However, as with the Comparable Sales Method, the study can sometimes provide useful insights and data to support positions taken during price negotiation.

Brief Description: Find a group of publicly-held, publicly-traded companies that are similar to the one being valued. In each case, find the stock's current market price and divide that by the net after-tax earnings per share of the company, as reported on the same date. Find the average of all these "P/E Ratios". Multiply it by net after-tax earnings of the subject company.

Replacement Cost Approach (Chapter 16)

When To Use: Only used for insurance purposes, and then only when the coverage is for the "replacement cost" of the insured property.

Brief Description: Generally, replacement cost for individual assets is estimated by a qualified independent appraiser. Technically, the replacement cost for an entire business would be the cost of recreating that business, in every respect, from scratch. Obviously, this is an inappropriate measure of value for almost all situations, besides being almost impossible to accurately ascertain.

Rule-of-Thumb Pricing Methods Used For Particular Types Of Businesses
(Chapter 16)

When To Use:

• When there is a well-established, time-honored, specific short-cut formula that is consistently used in the subject industry - and when you will probably be selling to someone who will insist on using that method. Even though the formula may seem like an oversimplification, if the price for businesses sold in that industry are customarily determined by that method, then you may be stuck with it. Whenever possible, always rely more heavily on other methods.

• Useful for rough comparison of different deals.

Brief Description: Multiply Gross Monthly Sales (or some other base figure) by an industry-accepted "multiplier".

Secured Loan Value (Chapter 18)

When To Use: This is only used to determine the amount you can borrow by using the company's assets as collateral ("security") for the loan. Use it whenever you are assuming that an acquisition loan will be needed.

Brief Description: Multiply the lender's "advance rates" by the value of the assets. Different advance rates apply to different kinds of assets. Add up the result for each category of assets to get the total Secured Loan Value.

Service-type Businesses
- Also see Chapter 15.

Manufacturing Businesses
- Also see Chapter 17.

Wholesale or Distribution Businesses
- Also see Chapter 17.

Medical practice or health-care
- Also see Chapter 17

Retail Businesses - Also see Chapter 17.

Golf Course - Also see Chapter 17

Accounting Firm - Also see Chapter 17

Restaurants - Also see Chapter 17

After you have determined which method(s) to use, proceed to the appropriate chapter and follow the step-by-step instructions. When you have completed every applicable method, go to Chapter 19 for instructions on how to complete the study.

Chapter 5

How to Evaluate the Financial Risk Associated with any Business

↓

and How to Translate that into a Capitalization Rate

This chapter is really a short-course on how to assess the risk associated with any particular business. You will probably benefit from reading it, even if you don't need a capitalization rate for the methods you are using.

What is a capitalization rate? What is a discount rate?

"Discount Rate" - The most common use of this term refers to the interest rate charged by the Federal Reserve in loans made to its member banks. This is how banks get most of the money they lend to customers. They borrow it at the government's current "discount rate" and then lend it out at higher rates to make a profit.

In valuation, however, the term refers to the interest rate used to calculate the present value* of a sum of money to be received in the future. The "discount rate" is thus converted into one of two forms, each of which has a different application:

1. Capitalization Rate - This is a single percentage rate used to convert a *series* of payments (or a "stream of earnings") into a

single present value in one step. A discount rate is called a "capitalization rate" when it is used in this way. Accordingly, "capitalization of income" is the process of estimating the economic worth of a company by computing the present value of *average annual* net income it is expected to produce during the future. A "cap rate" is something you will use in almost all of the income-based valuation methods.

2. Present Value Discount Factor - A "discount factor" is a form of discount rate that's used to determine the *present value** of the right to receive a *single* payment at a *specified time* in the future. Present value is determined by simply *multiplying* the amount to be received by the discount factor (not dividing it). In other words, a thousand dollars received a year from now is worth less than a thousand dollars received today. The discount factor tells you *how much less* it's worth.

Capitalization of Income

The best way to explain this concept is by example. Let's say you want to make an investment in something that will earn you a return of $2500 per year indefinitely. You are basically buying a stream of income, at a consistent annual amount. Over the long-haul you want to get more back than the investment cost you to begin with. That additional income is called your "return". You might receive income checks annually and get your initial cash investment back at the end of the holding period, or you might want to get a portion of your initial investment back with each income payment. The latter is called "amortizing", and it's the same as when you make a mortgage payment on a house. The point is, each year you receive a certain amount of income in return for the use of your money, and that return is a percentage of how much you initially invested.

> *The investment world lives by this concept: "Return is commensurate with risk". The greater the risk, the higher the return.*

For relatively "risk-free" investments like insured savings accounts, CD's, and government bonds, you are willing to settle for a fairly low rate of return because you're confident that you won't lose your initial investment. But for high risk investments, like unsecured loans to unproven companies (junk bonds), you want a much higher rate of return in order to compensate you for the risk of losing your investment if the company fails.

Here's how this all relates to capitalization rate: Let's say you're offered a chance to invest in something, but you don't know how much to pay for it. However, you are told that your share will earn you a return of $X per year. Secondly, you are aware of the risk level involved in this investment. You can equate that level of risk to other investments that usually produce annual returns of about Y% per year. If you divide the anticipated $X annual return by the Y%, the result is deemed to be the "value" of that investment. That's about how much you should pay for it in the beginning. What you have done is "capitalize" the annual income stream of $X at a rate of Y%.

So let's say I see a business I want to invest in, and I know my annual return will be $2500. If I feel this investment carries about the same risk level as other investments that I know produce returns averaging 12% per year, then:

$2500 divided by .12 = $20,833

So I know I don't want to pay any more than $20,833 for it. I have "capitalized" the net income, using a "cap rate" of 12%. $20,833 is the "value" (but a shrewd investor will try to pay less).

> *Note that the capitalization rate you use should be the same as the "rate of return" that is currently being paid on other financial investments that have an equivalent amount of risk and an equivalent holding period.*

For example, if a deal was very risky, an investor might demand a return of 30% per year in exchange for the use of his money. For a less risky investment, investors might demand a return of 8%. For a riskier deal, you obviously don't want to leave your money hanging out there for a long period of time.

Don't be confused by other common uses of the term, "capitalization".
The word also refers to how a business is financed - i.e., where the money comes from to create it, how much is there, and what it costs to borrow. When someone asks how a firm is capitalized, they want to know how much cash equity the owners put in, how much came from the sale of corporate stock or bonds, and how much was borrowed from banks. You often hear people say a firm is "undercapitalized", meaning that the owners

haven't put in enough cash to run it properly. This is a common cause of post-acquisition failures.

"Capitalization" also refers to an accounting practice whereby the cost of a capital asset (a fixed asset) is written off over the course of several years instead of deducted all at once in the year purchased. When expenditures are capitalized, that means they are recorded as long-term assets on the balance sheet, which are then depreciated*. The alternative is to record them on the income statement as an "expense", in which case they are written off entirely in one year.

When we refer to capitalization in this book, we will be talking about "capitalization of income" unless we say otherwise.

What is a "multiplier"?

A "multiplier" is just another way of stating the cap rate. The only difference is that you *multiply* net income by the multiplier but you *divide* net income by a cap rate to get value. A multiplier is just a "capitalization rate" which has been mathematically inverted (that is, 1 is divided by the capitalization rate to produce the multiplier).

Example:

Dividing by 12% is the same as multiplying by 8.33, because:

$$\frac{1}{.12} = 8.33$$

Divide 1 by any cap rate and you will get the corresponding "multiplier". So when you hear the phrase "multiple of earnings", that is the same as capitalized earnings. We prefer to stick with the capitalization version because a percentage rate is the form most people relate to as the measure of return from an investment. What we want you to understand here is that this rate is an indicator of the relative risk inherent in the investment.

You usually hear about multipliers in the context of "rule of thumb" valuation methods, which are discussed more thoroughly in Chapter 16.

Since these often represent an over-simplification of otherwise good valuation methods, there are caveats that accompany their use. In practice, those who use rules of thumb rarely go to the trouble of formulating their multiplier accurately, and they rarely take the time to properly refine the figure they to apply it to.

Key Point: When you appraise a business, you either value its income stream (using capitalization) or you add up the market value of its assets, but you don't combine both.

With all income-based methods, the value of the income stream is not separable from the assets that produce it. A business is composed of a group of assets, and when you value the business you don't get to add the capitalized value of the operating income to the value of the assets themselves. You have to pick one or the other. If you capitalize the income produced by those assets, that's just another way of looking at the value of those assets. The alternative is to base your value on the real economic value of those assets. Which one do you go with?: The one that is theoretically correct for the subject company and produces the highest value. When a business is profitable, has manageable risk, and has plenty of future promise, that usually means you should use an income method.

43

Discounting to Present Value:

Present value is the value today of something that will be received in the future. Present value discounting is based on the premise that a dollar received today is worth more than a dollar received tomorrow.

Disregarding the effects of inflation, this is because, until you receive that dollar, you lose out on the investment income you would otherwise earn from it.

"Present value" tells you what to pay today for the right to receive a sum-certain in the future. We use present value to appraise a business because the buyer is, in effect, purchasing a stream of future earnings. Those earnings must be discounted in order to arrive at the present value of the business.

To calculate present value, we use an interest rate that corresponds to the rate of return you would expect from a different investment bearing the same degree of risk. If there is relatively little risk, then you might use the risk-free rate. To the extent that the risk is higher you use a higher interest rate.

In calculating present value, that interest rate is translated into something called a "discount factor". There is a formula to calculate the factor, but you don't really have to use it since there are tables that give you the discount factors corresponding to different interest rates. One is included in the Appendix, but most good financial calculators can perform this function easily.

(For you math geeks out there, it's the reciprocal of one, plus the discount rate, or $(1 + i)^{-n}$. Here, "i" equals the estimated rate of interest you would earn on the money if you had it now, and "n" refers to the number of periods that will pass before you get it. The period is one year if you are working with an annual rate of return, one month if it's a monthly interest rate, etc..)

For example, if the discount rate is 10 percent per year, the discount factor for three periods (years) is $(1.10)^{-3} = 0.75131$. If the amount to be received in three years is $10,000, then the right to receive that amount has a present value today of $10,000 X .75131 = $7,513.10. In this form, the discount rate represents the alternative return the investor has sacrificed by committing his funds to the investment being valued.

When do you use "present value" instead of capitalization?

Capitalization is a short cut to finding the present value of an investment when the same amount of income will be received each year indefinitely into the future. But if you expect to receive different amounts of income each year, you must bring each one back to present value separately (using a present value discount rate) and then add them up. Likewise, if equal payments will be received for only a limited number of years, then you must use present value.

For example, let's say you want to buy a business that produces net operating income of $50,000 per year. You assume the business is worth the capitalized value of its net operating income. You've rated the risk associated with that business, and decided that its about the same as for a 6-month bank CD, which pays 6% at the time. So you pay:

$$\frac{\$50,000}{.06} = \$833,333$$

But later you find out that the risk is much higher. In fact you should have used the current junk bond rate plus 3% - or 19%. In other words, you should have paid:

$$\frac{\$50,000}{.19} = \$263,157$$

So, you would have paid more than 3 times too much for that business because of a mistake in picking the cap rate.

Here's how that applies to "discounting to present value". Let's say you agree to invest some money in a company, based their promise to pay you $30,000 five years from now.

You rashly accept a proposal to pay $22,417 for that right, which corresponds to a 6% discount rate. In other words, if you invest $22,417 with them today at 6%, it will grow to $30,000 in five years. However, you later discover that there's a lot of risk involved with this business. Public companies with equivalent risk are selling bonds that pay 15% interest. You should have used a discount rate of at least 15%, meaning you would have paid no more than $14,915 for the investment. If you had known that you were investing $22,417 in a risk rated at 15%, you would demanded more money back - $45,088. You blew it by not assessing the risk level correctly. You overpaid for your investment.

For example, the interest paid on pass-book savings accounts, bank CD's, and treasury bonds changes constantly. That's because the government, through the Treasury Department, has the power to speed up or slow down the speed at which money flows through the economy by manipulating that rate. They do it by changing the interest rates charged by the Treasury for money loaned to participating banks, and by changing the interest rate it pays to investors on the bonds it sells. For instance, if inflation is running too high and the government wants to slow down the economy, it will offer bonds paying higher interest, thus attracting more private money back into the Treasury's coffers. Simultaneously, it will raise the rate it charges member banks for the money they borrow, so lending will slow down. This tightens up the money supply, but it raises interest rates everywhere else. If a bank borrows money from the government at 6%, it has to charge its own borrowers more interest in order to make a profit - say 9%. So when a company, in turn, tries to borrow money from individual investors by selling bonds, it has to offer an even higher rate of interest (say 12%) in order to attract them, or else they'll just leave their money in safer government securities and bank deposits.

What this means is that the risk associated with that business may remain the same over time, but the interest rate paid by the company to borrow money will change as the cost of money changes. When the government's prime lending rate goes to 8%, the bank's prime lending rate may go to 10%, and a company borrowing directly from individual investors must offer as much as 15% to 16% - even though the risk involved with that business is the same as it was before.

But the risk associated with a given business can also change over time. It might lose a major account. Foreign competition could arise. A big lawsuit might be filed. The economy could go into a tailspin, or that particular industry might grow weak. For lots of reasons, business risk can change over time, and the cap rate associated with that firm will go down or up accordingly. The point is that cap rates are not fixed. Every time you use a cap rate, start from scratch in selecting an appropriate one.

Factors to Consider When Evaluating Business Risk

Cap rates and discount rates are both selected in the same way. The rate of return from an investment is always commensurate with the degree of risk it entails, so your main job is to assess that risk as accurately as possible. A number of different factors should be considered:

"Quality of the earnings":

- How steady have sales and profits been over the years?:

- How profitable is the company?
  - negative to break-even?
  - profitable but below the industry norm?
  - at the industry norm? higher?

- Has the company been profitable for over 7 years, without wide fluctuations in sales or profits?

- Is the firm profitable, but too young (less than 5 years old) to know whether it will be consistent?

- Is the firm is profitable, but with sales that are flat or growing only at the rate of inflation?

- Have sales been growing, but not enough to keep pace with inflation?

Type of business

- How long has the company been in operation?

- Is the cost of entry into this business very high?
  - Does the need for lots of expensive fixed assets limit competition, and yet provide good loan security?

- Or is it a service business with few securable fixed assets?

- Is inventory and equipment a large part of total value?

- Does the business depend on the health of other industries over which it has no control?

Prospects for the future
- What is the outlook for this industry as a whole? Is it growing, declining, or stable?

- Does it deal with mundane products in a field with little growth?

- Or does it deal with products that are faddish and characterized by rapid and constant change.

- Could its products and processes soon be outmoded? Does it possess up-to-date technologies and a well-developed R&D program?

- Is foreign competition emerging?

- If the company's health depends on that of the general economy, what is the outlook for the latter?

Competition
- How competitive is the market for this company's products or services? How does this company stand among its competition?

- Does low cost of entry encourage new competition? Or are there high start-up costs or proprietary products to reduce competitive threats?

For Small Businesses:
- What work skills are required, and how desirable is the work?

- Does it require special skills, education, and licensing?

- Is it low status, rough, or dirty work that is considered less "respectable"?

- Is the work challenging and does it take place in a pleasant environment?

Quality of fixed assets
- Real estate: Assess the location and desirability of facilities, degree of obsolescence, adaptability to other uses, deferred maintenance, environmental cleanup liabilities, underlying land value, and quality of title.

- Machinery and Equipment: Assess the degree of obsolescence, and cost of deferred purchases.

Structure of the transaction
- Will the purchase be highly leveraged (lots of debt)?

- Or will the buyer sink lots of cash equity into the deal? (safer)

- Is the company adequately and safely capitalized? Or have the owners taken a riskier "lean and mean" approach?

- How do this company's financial ratios compare to those of average profitable companies in that same industry?

- If the purchase involves a transfer of stock, will it carry potential liabilities carry with it?

Other risk factors

- Labor union present?
- Depth and quality of management remaining after the sale
- Risk of competition from former owners or employees
- Governmental regulation
- Dependence on constant availability of lending sources
- Health and personalities of key personnel
- Economy health of the local area
- Diversity of customer accounts
- Diversification of products/services
- Susceptibility to weather, international events, or other uncontrollables - and relative likelihood of their occurrence

Also look at the checklist in Chapter 2 - it will suggest some other things to consider, and you'll probably think of more yourself as you dig into your investigation of the company.

The most important of these is always the reliability of the earnings.

Select your Cap Rate on the basis of good research. Avoid rule-of-thumb multipliers if you can.

There are several ways to determine your cap rate. However, try to avoid using an arbitrary "rule-of-thumb" that ignores actual market rates of return and gives no consideration to the risk factors associated with your particular company.

For instance, I've met business brokers who actually employ this rule of thumb to virtually all businesses: "Price equals 8 to 10 times earnings". That's it. It's equivalent to assuming every investment pays a return of 10% to 12%. It totally ignores the real returns being earned in the financial markets and the particular risks associated with the subject company. Haphazard assumptions like this will carry you far afield.

Use average rates of return from a long period of time.

We are trying to predict the rate of return this company will produce in the future, given the degree of risk associated with it. To make that prediction, we look to investment results of the past. Short-term investment returns jump up and down all the time, so they aren't a reliable measure. We encourage you to refer to long-term averages instead.

Look, for example, at the situation in back in late 1992. The United States was still in an economic recession, and we had just elected a democratic president, so business investments were seen as more risky than during the prior 12 years. However, in an effort to control the recession, the government (through the Federal Reserve) brought interest rates down lower than they had been for 25 years. So, while most business should have been viewed as riskier in the short term perspective, and hence worth less, anyone basing a cap rate on those abnormally low interest rates would have totally over-valued their company.

One exception to the use of long-term averages might be where the risk for your company is so low that it equates to investments paying a guaranteed return over a long period of time, such as 30-year Treasury

Bonds. There are always low risk institutional investments with guaranteed returns, but very few private companies offer such low risk.

You want to use the average annual return over many years, from investments of equivalent risk.

For instance, let's say you want to base your cap rate on the average return from publicly-traded stocks during the prior 12 months. If that was a bull year, then you will have a very high cap rate, which will produce a low value. On the other hand, if there was a bear market that year, with low returns, your cap rate will be low, and your value will be unrealistically high. This isn't how valuation is supposed to work. For that reason we encourage you to base your cap rates on the long-term averages that go back to about 1925. You can get that data from investment almanacs, such as the one published annually by Irwin Business One.

Twelve months is too short a period, but so is just a few years. That makes it possible to manipulate the rate. For example, if you cut off the period just before the year in which a dramatic market crash occurred, you will produce an unfairly high cap rate. Again, use the averages that go back to 1925. The whole point is to consider the overall performance of investments at that level of risk - a number that reflects all of their ups and downs over the years. This is the only way to safely and fairly estimate the probable return over an indefinite period of time.

Another unfair way to manipulate the return is to base your average on a small or special group of stocks. For instance, the Dow-Jones Average covers only 30 stocks, so it really doesn't give you a good average return. Instead, choose an average that represents a huge number of stocks. And make sure it represents all industries.

An exception to this is where you can find the average return from a large number of companies in exactly the same business as your subject company. However, you have to be very specific, and you can't include companies whose returns also reflect other types of business activity. For instance, let's say you are valuing a home healthcare nursing firm. Value Line has an industry classification called "medical services", but that category would be much too broad. Likewise, many reference books list companies by SIC (Standard Industrial Classification) category, but those lists always include companies that are not in that business exclusively. There is an SIC category for home healthcare companies, and the companies in that category in Standard & Poors and Dun & Bradstreet all have home healthcare subsidiaries, but in most cases their earnings are derived from many other businesses at the same time, each of which carries a completely different level of risk and produces a different return. Therefore, stay away from specialized averages unless you know the companies included in the sample are only involved in that particular business.

Demanding a very high rate of return is not unreasonable under certain circumstances. Most venture capital firms demand a compounded annual return of 25% to 30%, and many leveraged buyouts have been risky enough to warrant interest rates of 20% to 25% on their secured borrowing. If your research seems to justify a very high cap rate, then don't be afraid to use it.

Method 1
Survey of Alternative Investment Returns

One common method of picking a rate is to take a survey of the rates of return offered by other investments having the same degree of risk as your subject company, then average those rates. You can find most of these rates of return in financial publications, like Money magazine and the Wall Street Journal. Here are some average returns to consider:

Low Risk:
- money market funds with banks
- one-year certificates of deposit at commercial banks
- municipal bonds (insured)
- government securities: treasury bills, bonds and notes
- zero coupon bonds
- mutual funds that invest in government or insured securities
- 10 year industrial bonds, AAA rated
- insured municipal bond trusts
- tax deferred annuities

Medium Risk:
- uninsured municipal bonds or bond unit trusts
- A rated industrial bonds
- mutual funds investing in "income" or "growth" type stocks
- the average total yield on "blue-chip" common stocks
- average return on the 10 or 12 most popular stock options taken by investors in the last full investment cycle
- the dividend yield on utility stocks
- 30 year residential mortgages

High Risk:
- stocks of emerging "growth" companies (particularly over-the-counter issues)
- oil and gas limited partnerships
- index options
- real estate limited partnerships
- managed futures

It may be difficult to find an average return for some of these investments. Financial magazines often publish an annual recap of returns from the previous year, and they usually compare those to the long-term averages. A stock broker or financial planner might also provide you with this information.

We have reservations about this approach, since you are probably generalizing too much if you simply grade your company's risk as high, medium, or low.

You really should be more specific than that, so we are going to explain two methods that are preferred by valuation professionals - the Built-up Rate Method, and the Weighted Cost of Capital Method.

Method 2
The Built-up Rate

In this method, you build-up an appropriate cap rate by starting with the risk-free rate of return, and then add more percentage points to account for the particular risk characteristics of your company.

The "risk-free rate of return" is the interest rate currently offered on investments where there is almost no chance that you will lose your initial capital. CD's and passbook savings accounts at insured banks are very safe, but long-term (30 year) U.S. government bonds usually offer the same low risk with a better rate of return, so they are commonly used as the benchmark for the risk-free rate. Next, you add more percentage points, based on the relative extra amount of risk you perceive in that business.

The problem is that, even if you have a well-thought-out system for estimating the additional risk, it's still one that you or someone else invented, so it's rather subjective. That means there's no such thing as an "accurate" result. Somebody else's system could be just as sensible, but it will lead to a different rate. However, we warned you in the beginning that the entire valuation process is filled with subjective decisions, and each one of those adds to the deviation of your results.

However you establish your cap rate, you should document the reasoning behind it so that it can be examined later by those relying on your work.

The cap rate you select will have a substantial impact on your result, and anyone negotiating the sale price of a company would be foolish to accept those figures without taking a hard look at how you arrived at your rate.

Whatever system you use, it must have a rational basis. Some systems seem more well-reasoned than others, but all are sort-of a stab in the dark. As an example, here is a system used by members of a professional appraisal society:

Risk Premium	Type of Business
6-10%	Large, established business with stable earnings and well-developed management team. Not carrying more debt than industry average. Future outlook is stable to growing.
11-15%	Same, but in a more competitive industry.
16-20%	In a very competitive industry with low capital entry costs. Also, small service businesses that depend on the particular skills of a small number of individuals.
21-25%	A business that is subject to wide fluctuation in sales and earnings due to uncontrollable cycles of demand for products/services.

Some of these rating systems also include a category for 1-2 person service businesses that depend on the unique skills or relationships of those people. However, if their skills or relationships can not be easily duplicated by someone else, then the owner really has nothing to sell except the hard assets of the business.

Here's a better system for building up a cap rate:

Risk-free rate
+ Equity risk premium
+ Small company risk premium
+ Specific industry risk premium
+ Private company/specific company risk premium
- Conservative estimate of average annual growth
= Built-up capitalization rate

(a) For your risk-free rate, use the rate being offered on 30-year U.S. government bonds. You should probably use the average rate offered over the past 30 days. This rate amounts to an assured return for a long number of years.

(b) Next you add a premium to reflect the additional amount of return that investors traditionally demand when holding stock instead of risk-free debt investments.

If you look at the average total return (dividends plus appreciation) from all stocks since 1925, that will give you a pretty good indication. That average is about 12.2% at the time of this writing. So, if your risk-free rate is 6% - then the Equity Risk <u>Premium</u> would be 6.2%.

However, as the risk-free rate rises and falls, the equity risk premium changes slightly as well. So, to further refine these estimates, a firm from Chicago (Ibbotson Associates) has studied the matter extensively and determined that (as of 1993) the Equity Risk Premium for publicly-traded companies is about 7.3%. The annual Ibbotson study is called "Stocks, Bonds, Treasury Bills, Inflation Rate Yearbook". It is updated each year, based on the investment results from all stocks traded on the New York Stock Exchange since 1925 (plus those traded on the American Stock Exchange and over-the-counter since 1982), so the average changes very little from year to year.

The Ibbotson equity premium doesn't reflect the total return - just the premium - so you must add the current risk-free rate. In one recent study, the two totaled 12.2%. This average actually changes very little from year to year, since it is based on such long-term data.

(c) Next you add a premium to reflect the additional risk involved with a small company. A smaller company is seen as carrying more risk. The Ibbotson average is based on smallest 20% of all publicly-traded companies, but a small public company is considerably larger than a small private company. The Ibbotson group has found that investors demand an additional return of about 5.2% in order to justify the added risk of investing in a small private company. Presumably, that figure is updated in each year's study.

(d) Next you must add a premium for any additional risk inherent in the specific industry you are studying. This is a very subjective call. Remember that the average equity return you have been using thus far is based on a huge number of companies representing all industries. That means that, so far, your rate reflects the average risk of all those industries combined. However, some industries are more stable (more consistently profitable) than others. Your job is to assess whether your subject industry is safer than the average one, or whether it is riskier - and then either add or subtract percentage points accordingly.

To assess Specific Industry Risk, you will have to do some research. The trade association for your industry probably publishes some information that will help you. You should also read the advice of stock market analysts specializing in that industry. Look up the Value Line forecasts. Check the latest U.S. Industrial Outlook, available at your library. Look at average data in Robert Morris Associates annual report on key financial ratios. Look at the degree of competition within that industry, its average rate of business failure, its capital intensity, the extent and effect of government regulation, the effect of economic cycles and other uncontrollables such as seasonality, weather dependence, and so on. Look at the checklist earlier in this chapter to stimulate your thinking on this.

It won't take long to get a feel for the relative strength of that industry. The hard part is *quantifying* it. You'll have to use your own judgment, so be conservative and have a rational basis for defending your decisions.

There are investment services that do this for other purposes, and sometimes that can be helpful. For example, Merrill Lynch and Value Line both try to calculate a risk coefficient for *each* publicly-traded company - which they call a "beta". You might try to find the average beta for companies engaged exclusively in that particular industry. If you have a large enough sample (20 or more), the average might be a meaningful indicator of the difference in risk between that business and the all-industry mean. 1.00 is the mean, so anything lower than that is less risky, and anything higher is more risky. Therefore, if companies in a particular industry have an average beta of .89 - you could say that type of business is 11% less risky than the all-industry average.

However, in practice, it seems that most valuators limit the adjustment for specific industry risk to somewhere between 0 and 10%. Again, this factor is very hard to quantify, so be conservative.

(e) Next you add a premium to account for the fact that you are dealing with a privately-held company. Since private owners are less-accountable for their decisions, there will certainly be an added element of risk there. On average, this might add another 5%.

(f) You also must consider the Specific Company risk. At this point, you should know enough about your subject company to realize how it stacks up against the competition. In other words, how does it compare to other small, privately-held companies in the very same market and industry?

For example, let's say your subject company is extremely strong. It has:

- a consistent trend of increasing sales and profits over many years
- dominant market share in its trade area
- a diversified customer base
- excellent receivables management
- good banking credit and payables history
- low employee turnover and no union
- more than adequate working capital
- financial ratios that compare favorably to the averages for its SIC group (published by Robert Morris Associates and others)
- good fixed assets
- a diversified group of products or services
- relative insulation from increased competition
- no unprotected hidden liabilities
- strong management and competent staff
- and all kinds of upside potential

In that case, you wouldn't be adding additional risk - in fact, you might even subtract risk points - perhaps enough to offset the private-company risk well into the negative. But to the extent that the company doesn't display these virtues, you will want to add risk points, which can often increase it by another 10% or more.

(g) Finally, subtract the average annual growth rate you expect this company to experience, based on the way it is currently put together. Don't factor in potential growth from changes that haven't yet been made. You have to base it on the average annual growth this company has experienced in the past. In effect, you are projecting the past returns into the future.

This should be backed-up by industry-wide growth projections from a credible, unbiased source. You should have every indication that your company's local trade area will facilitate equal growth.

So in order to justify a "credit" for annual growth, you need to see:

1. a consistent pattern of growth during each of the past years
2. a strong forecast for overall growth within that industry, and
3. equally strong predictions for growth in its local market.

Since this growth factor is supposed to reflect a fairly long period of time, it should be conservative. For example, you might be dealing with a high-tech company in a volatile product field, with projections of 30% growth per year for the next 5 years. But beyond that, no one can predict a thing. Even the immediate projections have an element of uncertainty. Remember, a cap rate is supposed to reflect results indefinitely into the future. So in this case you wouldn't try to use 30% as your growth rate deduction. You realize that high-tech industries can change overnight. But, if the 10 and 20 year forecasts for that industry were still very strong, you would probably be safe in deducting a few points for average future growth, yet you would be wise to scale it back to less than 10%.

The theoretical justification for factoring-in this growth rate is worth mentioning. Bear in mind that with capitalization of income, you are basing value on the net income from a single year - the year of the valuation. Since you are valuing the company as it stands today, you are assuming that the company will continue to produce this same amount of income every year into the future. But in most cases the operating income will change from year to year.

For instance, the industry as a whole may experience growth (and pull that company's income up along with it), or the company may have steadily increasing income every year. In cases where a certain amount of growth appears to be inevitable, you should reflect that in your results, and you do it by adjusting your cap rate, not by projecting higher income. But be conservative because there's no certainty for

what the future will bring. It 's said that industries reinvent themselves every 3-5 years.

And, once again, don't factor in growth from changes that haven't been implemented yet. Also keep in mind that the long-term, overall rate of growth may differ from the short term rate of growth. For example, your company may have experienced 20% to 30% annual growth over the past 4 years, but that will eventually slow down. Over 40 years, the average annual growth rate might be more like 4%.

Keep in mind that an industry with huge growth potential also has very high risk. Therefore, you probably won't even use a method that capitalizes net income, since you can't make reliable income prediction far into the future. Instead, you would use the discounted cash flow method, and predict sales and income only as far forward as you can with reasonable certainty. Then you would bring the Net Income from each year back to present value using a discount rate, and add them up. The discount rate is selected in the same way as a capitalization rate, except that it doesn't look so far into the future when assessing risk.

Warning:

What many appraisers don't like about the built-up rate method is that, when you add up all the different elements of risk, the total is often much higher than the return any investor would realistically demand from that kind of investment.

For example, venture capital firms often help new companies get off the ground by investing money in exchange for stock. These are very risky, totally unproven situations. They frequently depend on little more than a good idea and some capable people. In addition, these venture capitalists often take a minority interest - which adds even more risk. As a result, venture capitalists are notorious for the very high investment returns they expect, ranging from 25% to 30% per year. Many regard these as the highest rates of return demanded anywhere, from perhaps the riskiest situations around. Yet you might find yourself with a built-up rate that's even higher. So the bottom line is that, whatever rate you work up to, it still has to make sense when compared to the real expectations of investors. You may have to go back and adjust your assumptions in order to scale down the rate to a reasonable level.

- Small firms are less likely to maintain up-to-date capital assets. Larger firms can afford the latest technology, and are less likely to "make do" with old equipment.

- Larger companies tend to have a more diversified customer base, more diversified products, and serve a wider variety of geographic markets.

- Most small businesses require little or no formal training, and it doesn't take a lot of money to get started. That means competition can multiply overnight.

Capitalization Rates for Smaller Businesses

One place very high cap rates are often justified is with regard to smaller businesses - the size normally dealt with by business brokers (retail stores, service establishments, professional practices, and so on). There, prices are based on what has been paid for similar businesses in the past. You can't refer to stock market returns and venture capital rates. The experience of hundreds of business brokers, selling thousands of small establishments per year, seems to indicate that prices for these are based on discount rates ranging from 20% to 100%.

Here are some of the reasons why smaller businesses carry a greater risk:
- Large companies tend to be better capitalized, and they have easier access to funds when they need them. The smaller firm is more likely to get into a financial pinch.

- Large companies have greater depth of management, and decisions are less likely to be made on an emotional basis (due to the likes or dislikes of the owner).

Method 3
Weighted Average Cost of Capital

The "capital" with which most businesses are financed is a combination of debt and equity (borrowed money and cash). Each source of funds is obtained at a different cost. This method determines the average cost of those funds, and then uses that as the cap rate. The amount of debt vs. equity is usually based on the way most firms in that industry are capitalized.

Here is a simple example:

Data from Robert Morris Associates shows that firms in a certain industry have a 25:75 debt to equity ratio. With their average cost of debt at 6% and their average cost of equity at 12%, a cap rate is calculated as follows:

component			cost	weighted average
Debt	25%	X	6%	1.5%
Equity	75%	X	12%	9.0%
			Total	10.5%

So the general formula for this method is:

$$WACC = (Pe \ X \ Ke) + (Pd \ X \ Kd)$$

Where Pe is the percentage of equity
Ke is the cost of equity
Pd is the percentage of debt
Kd is the cost of debt

In other words, the cap rate is equal to:

% of equity to total capital X cost of equity
+ % of debt to total capital X cost of debt

The cost of debt is usually an estimate of the average annual interest rate for borrowed money during the projection period. In other words, what fixed rate of interest would a commercial lender demand from this company on a long-term loan?

This interest rate must then be adjusted to its after-tax cost. That's because business interest is deductible, and we want to focus on its real out of pocket cost. If the average effective tax rate for your subject company is 35%, then multiply your interest rate by 1.00 - .35 = .65 to find the real cost of the loan interest. The formula is usually stated as:

$$Kd = \text{interest rate} \ X \ (1.00 - \text{average tax rate})$$

So, if you predict that the average long-term cost of debt will be 9.25%, then:
$$Kd = 9.25 \ X \ (1.00 - .35) = 6\%$$
(approximately)

The Cost of Equity is a little trickier to calculate. It is usually determined by a method referred to as the Capital Asset Pricing Model. The formula is:

Risk free rate of return (30 yr. Treasury Bonds)

+ Beta X [Average historic stock market total return (-) risk-free rate]

+ Small stock/private company premium

= Cost of Equity

Risk free rate of return described in the earlier section on the Built-Up Rate Method. Most people just use the average rate for 30-year U.S. Treasury Bonds during the past month or so.

Beta is a coefficient that measures the risk or volatility of the subject industry, as compared to the average risk in "all industries". The all-industry average is assumed to be 1.00. A lower beta means that industry carries less risk than the average publicly-listed company.

Analysts at Merrill Lynch and Value Line calculate the beta for many, many stocks. The Value Line service is available at many public libraries. Try to find betas for a large number of companies that are exclusively involved in the same business as your subject company. You will need at least 10 betas in order to have a meaningful sample, and even that's pretty skimpy. You should check out each company before you use its beta, because many of them are involved in several other lines of business at once, which means you can't use that beta.

What if you can't find enough betas to constitute a meaningful sample? Then you have to come up with another plausible way to gauge the relative risk of this type of company versus the "all-industries" average. Where the performance of your subject company has been relatively stable compared to the stock market as a whole, you might base your beta on the difference between its average Net Operating Income Before Tax and the average historic return from the stock market.

The former should be obtained from the company's adjusted financial statements. The latter can be obtained from an investment almanac at your library (such as Irwin Business One). For instance, at the time of this writing, one source says the average total return from all stock since 1925 was 12.2%. (This average doesn't vary much from one year to the next.)

So you might go back and prepare adjusted income statements for the past five years. Then calculate the weighted average* of the Net Operating Income Before Tax from those five years. Then figure out the percentage by which that average differs from the stock market's historic average return. If that's a negative percentage, subtract it from 1.00 and if it's a positive percentage, add it to 1.00.

For example, let's say the adjusted NOIBT for your subject company, over the past five years, has been as follows:

year 1: 15.45%
year 2: 21.43%
year 3: 20.45%
year 4: 15.21%
year 5: 17.43%

The weighted average is 17.85% That's 5.65 percentage points higher than the long-term stock market average return of 12.2%.

5.65 divided by 12.2 = 46% greater return

Here we are assuming that getting a consistently higher return than the market as a whole means less risk than the market as a whole, by the same percentage. Therefore, where average stock market performance is indicated by a coefficient of 1.00 (100%), the beta for this company could be estimated as 1.00 - .46 = .54   But whoa - that's really a wide deviation - one that might be unrealistic. Again, these techniques sound good in theory, but the end result still has to make sense.

Obviously, the more years you include in your weighted average, the more valid these

assumptions seem to be. After all, you are looking back to 1925 for your average market return, but only going back a few years for your company.

Some people say this approach is theoretically more sound than averaging the Value Line betas for companies in that industry, because it places more focus on the performance of the specific subject company. In addition, the analysts who calculate those betas base their risk assessment, to a large extent, on the degree to which the company's stock price jumps up and down compared to the daily market average. However, the daily movements in the prices of publicly-listed stocks reflect investor behavior more than actual changes in the company's financial performance, so a beta based on those movements might be a poor indicator of the risk of owning a privately-held company.

The small stock/private company premium can be obtained from the same sources referred to in part (c) of the section on the Built-Up Rate Method. Many people rely on data from Ibottson Associates. We understand that the premium was estimated at 5.2% before this was written.

Example:

6.75%		Risk free rate.
+	[12.2% - 6.75%]	Average stock market return minus risk-free rate.
X	.54	Beta in example above.
=	2.94%	
+	5.20%	Small stock premium
=	14.89%	Cost of Equity (Ke)

The total Weighted Average Cost of Capital would then be calculated by using the formula provided earlier (page 56). The percentage of equity and percent of debt is usually based on the average Debt-to-equity ratio for companies in the subject industry. Refer to sources such as Robert Morris Associates and Duns Analytical Service for key financial ratios of companies classified under the same SIC number. The problem is that those averages can be very misleading. Those two services seem to use different methods for calculating the same ratio, because they often differ from one another.

That data could be misleading for other reasons too. For instance, the average company in a sleepy industry might be very mature. If there have been relatively few recent acquisitions and recapitalizations in that industry, those averages would show a very low debt-to-equity ratio. Conversely, hot acquisition activity and aggressive recapitalization could result in averages that are unrealistically debt-heavy.

You will probably find that the average private company acquisition is financed with a debt/equity ratio of something like 75/25.

Final considerations for all methods:

• What "form" does this business interest take? If you invest in a business and receive some form of debt instrument - a bond or unsecured note - then your risk is much higher than when you receive equity security like preferred stock. There is a strong argument for applying lower rates to equity interests than to debt interests. Let's say you equate the risk of your business to that of another company that has recently issued corporate bonds at a certain interest rate. However, *your* investment in the subject company is for stock. You might decide to use 3/4 of the bond rate. But then you still have to ask whether the result makes sense when considering the investment yields from other stocks of comparable risk, and if so, why didn't you refer to those to begin with?

• You might also want to adjust your rate according to the percentage of debt in the capitalization. If you are looking at something that can only be acquired by using a lot of borrowed money, that "leverage"increases the risk.

• Method of transfer also affects risk. If the transaction will take the form of a purchase of stock, the buyer loses out on stepped-up depreciation and may inherit hidden liabilities of the former owner. That adds risk. Also consider the additional risk of owning less than a controlling interest in the company (See the chapter on Minority Interests.)

• It also helps to talk with corporate lending officers at commercial banks to get their input on how they would view the investment and what kind of return they would expect in order to justify the loan.

• Your analysis may seem to make sense, but if companies in that industry just don't sell at prices corresponding to the cap rate you've chosen, then there's no point in trying to use it. It always comes down to what the market will really pay.

• In these methods, we are imagining a situation where you invest your money in exchange for an annual return that includes both principal and income. But many acquisition investors think in terms of how many years it will take them to get their money back. Only after that do they consider themselves to be making a profit. For a risky situation, the might want their principal investment back in 3 years.

• If you can, it's always best to use more than one method to calculate the cap rate, and then average the results.

Chapter 6

Economic Value of Assets Method

In many cases, the value of a business can't be based on its income. Instead, we use the value of its assets, minus any liabilities the buyer would assume. It's as if you are selling off the real estate, inventory, machinery, and other property .while ignoring the "ongoing business".

When this method is used:

- *When inflation has made the assets of a company very valuable.* The company doesn't have to be losing money. It might be very profitable and yet still bring a higher price based on the value of its individual assets. For that reason we encourage you to look at total asset value in every case.

  For instance, let's say you have a nice little business that's throwing-off net earnings of $500,000 a year. Let's say the discounted cash flow method tells you this income stream (including the assets that produce it) is worth $5 million. But wait a minute. What if the surrounding community has grown up around the company's property, making that location a very logical site for a regional shopping mall, and developers are willing to pay

$7 million for the ground? In that case, you'd make a big mistake if you assumed that an income-based method would give the highest value.

- *With a service business where sales are derived from the particular talents or contacts of the departing owners.* In that case, it doesn't matter whether the business is profitable or not.

- *When the company has been profitable in the past, but there are reasons to believe its future is endangered.*

For instance, what if you learn that a new technological breakthrough by another company is going to make your product line obsolete in 12 months? It would be inappropriate to base value on the profitable performance of the past.

- *Where sales or earnings (according to an adjusted income statement) have been flat, declining, or sporadic over the years. In these cases, there's no certainty of a profitable future.*

In that case, any cap rate used in an income-based method must be fairly high, which will produce a low calculated value. Asset value may be higher.

When sales and earnings have fluctuated over the years, potential buyers view it as a "turnaround"* situation, and they won't succeed in turning that business around if they buy-in at too high a price. In that case the deal may only be attractive if they can acquire the assets for less than market value. Otherwise they'd be better off just starting up a new company from scratch.

It's important to understand what we mean by "flat" or "stagnant" earnings. Even when sales and earnings have grown, if the rate of growth has been less than the rate of inflation, then the trend is considered to be stagnant, and an income-based method is probably not the best measure of value.

Another way to look at these situations is in terms of "goodwill". Our Glossary defines it as "that portion of the value of a company which is in excess of the value of its assets." A company with goodwill value is usually one that stands out among its competitors and has a trend of increasing profitability. It's a common misconception that every ongoing business is entitled to some premium for "goodwill".

Look at how income-based valuation methods work and you will see that each illustrates the goodwill concept in a slightly different way. For instance, one technique holds that a business is worth the value of its tangible assets, plus a premium for earnings in excess of the "normal return" produced by the average company from such assets. Another method says that a business is worth the value of its assets, plus a premium for earnings in excess of the cost of financing the purchase of those assets. In both cases, this "premium" is goodwill. In both cases you can see that if earnings are down, then the business is only worth the value of the assets.

In this method, we don't always include every asset.

First, go to the Glossary and read the definition of "assets" so you understand the difference between "tangible assets" and "intangible assets". Generally, you want to include any asset for which there is an ascertainable value and a ready market in which to sell it. That's where we usually draw the line.

Intangible assets may be included in the total asset value, but *only...*

(1) if their value is separately ascertainable on some reliable basis,

and

(2a) there is an established secondary market in which to sell them,

or

(2b) if they carry some distinct advantage to the buyer of that business.

The valuation of intangible assets is covered later in this chapter.

Don't assume that the assets will be sold piecemeal. They can still be sold to a single buyer who intends to keep the business together. However, we value them as if they are each being sold separately.

In addition, when we talk about asset value, it's different from when we talk about the *form of the transaction* being a purchase of assets. The latter just means that the buyer is purchasing the assets, as opposed to buying all the stock of the company (in which case ownership of the assets passes automatically). It's a technical distinction that gives certain legal, accounting, and tax advantages to the buyer or seller.

Market Value vs. Liquidation Value:

There are two ways to dispose of the assets:

1. You can sell everything together so that someone else can carry on the business. (This approach generally corresponds to "market value".)

2. Or you can dissolve the operation and sell the assets individually, converting them into cash. This is known as "liquidation", and sellers sometimes get more for the business this way. However, it often produces lower proceeds if it's conducted under an expeditious timeframe. If you have the luxury of more time, you can market the assets carefully and hold out for the best prices. But we usually envision a quick sale or an auction when we think of liquidation.

If you don't know how the assets will be sold, then use both methods and choose the one that produces the highest value. Most people assume that market value will produce the highest price, but that's not always the case. Auctions are generally the route chosen for liquidation, and they can yield high prices if they attract a large group of interested purchasers and create a highly-charged buying atmosphere. This is especially true for real estate and general-use machinery.

Liquidation value is also the best approach for any business that is relatively new or can't show a history of operating success. There is too much uncertainty in those situations to warrant speculation on whether the assets merit value as a going concern.

"Book Value" is never a good measure because it doesn't reflect the true economic value of the property.

Book value is based on original cost of the asset minus depreciation taken to date for tax purposes. That can be a very small number - a fiction that has no relation to the true value of the property. (See the next chapter.)

Rules-of-Thumb for Estimating Liquidation Value:

The following guidelines are sometimes used to estimate liquidation value in the absence of a professional appraisal:

Accounts Receivable	80-90% of Book Value

Inventory:

Raw Materials	50-70% of Cost
Work In Progress	10-25% of Cost
Finished Goods	50% of Market Value at wholesale

Equipment & Machinery	80% of Market Value
Land & Building	65-80% of Market Value

Alternatively, the following relationships are sometimes used as a rough guide:

Replacement Cost	100%
Market Value (used)	60%
Liquidation Value	30-35%
Net Book Value	20-25%

These are completely speculative, and any valuator would be justified in feeling a little nervous about using them. The results they produce could be way off in a particular case. There's no substitute for a professional asset appraisal. It's well worth the cost.

Market Value implies a sale negotiated at arm's length between buyer and seller, each being fully informed of all relevant facts and neither being under any particular compulsion to act. It does not refer to the "best" price that could possibly be obtained. It refers to the most likely price that would be received today in the very same market where the asset is expected to be sold. It is based on data from recent actual sales of similar property. *See Step 2 of Chapter 11 for more* information on determining market value. A professional asset appraisal is the only reliable way to get these figures.

Whichever measure of value is used, the valuator should be careful to exclude the value of any assets that are not necessary or relevant to the operation of that business.

Most buyers refuse to pay extra for assets that they don't want or need, so it's usually a waste of time to try to include them in the total asset value, especially if they have no real value apart from the business.

Can a business be worth less than its asset value? With poor earnings, an income based method can produce smaller number than asset value. A business can always be liquidated, so we usually think of liquidation value as the lowest amount that it would be worth.

Remember to deduct liabilities and sale expenses!

Don't forget to deduct any liabilities that a buyer would assume. Also remember to deduct any predictable expenses that will be incurred in selling the assets or stock, such as appraisal fees, real estate brokerage commissions, auction commissions, legal fees, accounting fees, and sales tax.

Sellers are sometimes very unrealistic about the value of a particular asset. Things like secret processes or customized equipment may perform special functions, but that doesn't mean that anyone wants or needs those functions performed.

Valuing Intangible Assets:

These are assets having no physical nature and no intrinsic value. Their value lies in the advantages they represent to their owners in terms of income, competition, security, control, and so on.

The most obvious intangible asset is goodwill, which is discussed above and in the chapter on the Excess Earnings Method. Goodwill takes in a lot of specific intangibles at once. There may be other intangible assets associated with a business, but that doesn't mean they have an ascertainable value. Valuing intangibles is one of the most difficult aspects of these projects.

The figure produced by any income-based valuation method automatically includes all of the assets, including goodwill and other intangibles. Whether you are dealing with an income-based method or an asset-value method, the situations in which you can add extra value for an intangible are very limited:

1- The intangible must provide a specific and unique advantage of some kind to the new owner. Even so, it's hard to convince a buyer to pay more for these intangibles. In practice, their value is incidental to the whole. It's a lot more convenient and a lot less costly to sell all of the assets to one buyer than it is to dispose of them piecemeal, so most sellers decide that it's worthwhile to forget about trying to demand additional payment for intangibles in that situation.

2- The seller's case for getting paid separately for an intangible is bolstered when there is a recognized, secondary market for its resale apart from the business. An example might be a liquor license.

Although it may be possible to separately define them, remember that most intangibles are really just a component of goodwill or excess earnings, and have no value when separated from the company. Intangibles such as brandnames and customer lists are what make a collection of assets a "business", so the value associated with them is merged with the general "ongoing business value" that is necessarily included with transfer of the company.

Economic life of intangible assets:

This refers to how long the intangible will bring an economic benefit to its owner. Keep in mind, that this can be much shorter than its legal life. A patent, for instance, may be legally valid for a certain number of years, but it will probably only produce a financial advantage for its holder for a few years before it becomes outmoded by other products.

Also keep in mind that the advantage gained from an intangible *gradually* diminishes over time. Your calculations should reflect this gradual reduction.

Ways To Value Intangible Assets:

1. Pricing Advantage (or Profit Contribution)

This boils down to: How much additional net income does the intangible asset bring in? For instance, consider a brand name with high level of recognition among consumers that enables you to charge more per unit for your products than your competitors can.

Here's how to calculate Pricing Advantage:

(a) Determine how much additional price the company can charge for each unit of the product sold, over and above the price charged by competitors for equivalent products. Use wholesale price to distributors, not retail price, unless the manufacturer is also the retailer.

(b) Translate that from gross income per unit to net income per unit. In other words, just because you can charge more per unit more at wholesale doesn't mean you can take that entire amount to your bottom line. There are costs associated with developing it that have to be amortized over its useful life. There are costs to manufacture it, advertise and sell it, maintain the equipment and people who produce it, additional packaging cost and shipping cost, legal fees from enforcing the patent rights, and so on. These all have to be deducted from the gross income you receive.

(c) Multiply that "price advantage" by the number of units sold annually. Use volume sold in the current year.

(d) Determine the number of years this intangible will probably continue to benefit its owner in this way (its "economic life").

(e) For each year of it's remaining economic life, calculate the present value* of the additional net income that will be received because of the intangible. Use a discount rate equal to the annual rate of return an investor would expect on a medium risk investment made for the same number of years.

(f) Add up the present values for all these years. The result is the value of the intangible.

For example, let's say you have a patent for a special feature that lets you charge $13.00 more (wholesale) per unit than your competitors, and that translates into $3.00 per unit in net earnings after deducting all the expenses of developing, producing, selling, and maintaining the intangible. Last year you sold 300,000 units. So your additional income is $900,000 per year. The patent is valid for another five years. So...

- For year one, the total pricing advantage is a straight $900,000. Assume no present value discount for the first year.
- For year 2, assume the income will be received one year from now, so the present value of the $900,000 you'll receive (using an 8% discount rate) is $833,333.
- For year 3, figure you'll get your $900,000 (on average) 2 years from now, so the present value is $771,605.
- For year 4, the present value is $714,449.
- For year 5, the present value is $661,527.

The total pricing advantage is $3,880,914. This assumes that sales remain level during those five years, and that the costs associated with the feature do not increase. If you think they will, you must reflect that in your calculations. Also, don't speculate that you'll sell more units or that you'll get a higher sales price in the future.

This method is best for items which have a determinable life, such as a patent or copyright. Remember that the realistic economic useful life of a patent, copyright, licensing agreement, etc. may be much shorter that its legal life.

Some specific uses for this method:

- Brand names and registered trademarks

- Copyrights

- Patents - Remember that if competitors come out with newer technology, it will diminish the value of your patent well before its legal life expires, so be realistic and study the developing technology before making your decision.

- Unpatented special processes - Use a high-risk capitalization rate to determine present value, and use one-half to one-third of the average economic life of a similar patented process. This is done in order to reflect the higher risk resulting from the lack of patent protection.

- Customer Lists:

    (1) Determine the annual sales contribution made by each individual repeat customer on the list. Add these up. Determine the resulting net profit after tax. (Do that by multiplying their total sales contribution by the percentage of Net Profit After Tax shown on the company's last full income statement.)

    (2) Determine the useful life of the list by dividing 100% by the average % of customers lost each year (attrition) . For example, a 10% annual turnover means the list has a useful life of 10 years.

    (3) Assume that the net profit determined in Step 1 will continue for the number of years determined in Step 2. However, reduce the net profit contribution for each succeeding year by the average annual attrition from Step 2. In other words, if the turnover rate is 10%, then the first year will be 100% of the total profit con-

tribution by customers now on the list, the second year will be 90%, the third year 80%, and so on for 10 years.

    (4) Bring the profit contribution from each year to present value* using a high risk capitalization rate. Add up the present values.

2. Royalty and Licensing Agreements:

(a) Determine the realistic economic life of the agreement.

(b) Project sales of the item for each year of that period.

(c) Apply the royalty rate to the sales figure for each year.

(d) Deduct any special expenses associated with the license or agreement, including special accounting or audit costs.

(e) Bring the result for each year to present value*.

(f) Add up the present values from each year.

This method can also be used to value *un*licensed brand names or trademarks, but it requires a great deal of speculation on the royalty percentage that can be received, on the length of economic life, and on the number of units that might be sold under the license. Even the assumption that it can be successfully licensed may be too speculative. In sum, there are usually too many unpredictable factors to allow you to attribute value to a presently unlicensed intangible.

3. Profit contribution by cost savings

Use this method when the intangible provides the company with a unique cost savings which is not enjoyed by its competition. Here are the steps:

(a) Determine the additional costs per unit experienced by competitors who lack this asset. Multiply that by the number of units sold in the current year, or by a weighted average (if fluctuation has occurred).

(b) Determine the realistic life of this advantage before it expires or before the competition catches up.

(c) Determine the present value* of the cost savings for each year. Use a discount rate equal to an investor's expected rate of return on a medium risk investment of the same duration. (For example, 11% for 6 years.)

(d) Add up the present values for each year.

Some specific uses for this method:

- Contract entitling the company to purchase materials at advantageous prices. Bring each year's cost advantage to present value.

- Covenant Not To Compete (A contractual promise made by competitors, or potential competitors, not to compete with the company in certain areas of business, lasting for a specified period of years.) Specific directions for this:

(1) Compute the amount of sales that would lost be to competitors if the covenant didn't exist. Do this for each year of the economic life of the agreement. Remember that the new owner of a business gradually builds up his own unique clientele, so the value of a covenant not to compete will diminish with time, and the potential lost sales should decline each year.

(2) For each year, translate the potential lost sales into lost Net Income After Tax. In other words, deduct the normal expenses.

(3) Bring the result of the prior step to present value. Use a high risk capitalization rate.

(4) Add the present values together.

- Patented Processes - Use a medium risk capitalization rate in determining present value.

- *Un*patented Special Processes - To reflect the greater risk due to the lack of patent protection, use a high risk capitalization rate, and use only one-half to one-third of the realistic economic life of a similar patented process.

- Tax Loss Carryforwards - (An accumulation of losses experienced by the company, which it could not use on past tax returns because they exceeded taxable income. These can be carried-forward to offset taxable income in future years. Consult your accountant, because there are important restrictions involved.) Bring the resulting tax savings predicted for each year to present value using a high risk capitalization rate. Use a high risk rate because the company has obviously had some difficulty in the past which led to the loss.

4. Cost to create an intangible asset:

Add up the original cost to create the intangible. Be careful, because cost is not usually indicative of true value. It can really overstate it, so you may have to scale back your figure, perhaps significantly. Tremendous costs may have been incurred in the creation of an intangible which actually brings no traceable income advantage to the company. Unfortunately, that happens a lot. Some specific uses:

- Copyrights
- Specialized mailing lists - For useful life, use 100% divided by annual customer turnover rate.
- Patented processes developed through extensive research
- Patents applied for - Research & development work done for a yet-ungranted patent
- Customer lists

5. Cost to purchase an intangible asset:

Used only for intangibles which have an active secondary market for their resale - such as:

- Franchise agreements - Reduce its anticipated value to reflect any restrictions on transferability or buy-back rights in the agreement.

- Transferable licenses - (Liquor license, etc.)

6. Contracts that provide income (Sales Contracts):

Bring the Net Income After Tax expected for each future year of the contract to present value and them add up.

7. Employment Contracts:

Calculate the cost to replace the person covered by the contract. Generally, you include cost of training only to the point where the replacement person will be as proficient as the departing employee in carrying out those duties reserved for the company by the employment contract. Value only the *additional* costs *over and above* those of maintaining the individual covered by the contract.

For example, there is someone under contract who is important to the company because of her marketing ability. If only 50% of her time is spent on marketing and the rest is spent on general management, the company would probably have to hire two people to effectively replace her - a marketing person and a general manager. So...

(1) Add the costs of the two anticipated salaries.

(2) Deduct the amount of salary paid to the covered individual.

(3) Deduct a portion of each replacement salary to the extent that those people would be able to provide additional services to the company, over and above the subject employee.

(4) Assume that this additional cost will be incurred in each remaining year of the contract term. Bring the amount for each year to present value using a medium risk discount rate.

(5) Add up those present values.

(6) Add any other costs that are likely to be incurred in replacing the individual, such as recruiter's fees, training seminars, and so on.

After you subtract the part of the replacement salaries that represents additional contributions to the firm (Step 3), you often find there's no additional cost after all, other than hiring costs.

If only one person is hired to replace the covered individual, then focus on the cost of training and maintaining this person only to the point where he is as effective as the covered person at those duties. For instance, if it would take six months for the replacement to come up to par with the covered employee, then the cost to the company is only the present value of six-month's salary, plus hiring costs and additional training costs, minus the gradually increasing value of the new employee's contribution to the company during that period. If you have to pay the new person a higher salary, then the difference between the two salaries incurred during the *remaining* contract term would also be included.

ഇന്ദ്ര

Remember: Intangible Assets are not valued separately in an income-based valuation. They are only valued separately when you are appraising a business by adding up the values for each asset of the business.

Chapter 7

The Net Worth Approach
(Book Value)

When there aren't enough profits to justify the use of an income-based method, you have to value the company solely on the basis of its assets. In that case, book value is sometimes used as a measure of total asset value, but it shouldn't be.

Book value is easy to determine, and it's useful as a point of reference for comparing different companies. But if a buyer suggests a purchase price at book value, it's often a low-ball offer for something that should be priced at the economic value of those assets.

For more on that, see Chapter 6. Book value also doesn't apply well to service businesses because they have very few assets.

Net worth and *book value* are terms that are often used synonymously, although technically they are different. Again, they don't really constitute a valuation method because they don't accurately reflect the true economic value of the assets being sold.

Net Worth is the difference between Total Assets and Total Liabilities, as shown on the company's balance sheet.

It's also referred to as Owner's Equity, since it represents the worth of the business to its owners in terms of balance sheet values. While the term "Book Value" is often used as slang for Net Worth, it actually refers to the value at which an individual asset is carried on the balance sheet.

Book Value is original cost minus any depreciation taken to date.

On the balance sheet, assets are usually grouped together in categories - machinery & equipment, tools & dies, data processing equipment, and so on. The figure shown on the balance sheet for each category is the total of the book values for all assets in that class. There are ledgers on which the book value for each asset is recalculated each year as additional depreciation is taken. Upon the expiration of it's useful life, the asset has been completely "written off".

Although these terms are used somewhat interchangeably, a purchase price at "Net Worth" would refer to an arrangement where the buyer assumes all of the company's existing liabilities, such as when the transaction is carried out as a purchase of stock. On the other hand, *a purchase price at "Book Value" technically refers to the sum of the book values for every asset of the company, without assuming any liabilities.*

ຂ⊃ଠ୫

When the Net Worth approach is used:

Net Worth should probably never be used as the sole determinant of purchase price, but there are times when it is.

• One is in leveraged buy-outs (LBO's), because the buyer needs to end up with a purchase price that's below market or liquidation value, so that the deal can be financed completely with secured loans. That's what the ideal leveraged buyout is: all of the purchase price is borrowed, and the lenders have recourse only to the assets of the company.

• Bargain-hunters will often make an offer at book value and try to put a rational-sounding spin on it, hoping that the seller can't see through it. Of course, this is a savvy move only if you're sure that value is understated by net worth.

• Even in conventionally-financed deals at a higher price, lenders may attribute book value to the assets as loan security. When they don't include intangible assets, they call this "tangible book value". LBO buyers often do the same thing. They exclude intangibles such as goodwill, capitalized research and development expenditures, patents, processes, and so on.

• Book Value often represents the lowest price at which a subsidiary can be bought from a parent corporation. The parent company wants a price that will at least cover their remaining investment in it (i.e., the undepreciated amount, which is the value at which they carry it on their books.) It's usually a waste of time to offer less than book value, since someone in the parent corporation will look like a schmuck if they sell at a loss, especially the person who insisted on acquiring that business in the first place. Selling at a loss also lowers their reported earnings, and hence the value of their stock, which is the last thing they want to do.

One exception might be where a subsidiary is hemorrhaging badly - causing uncomfortable losses for the parent, who has neither the interest nor the inclination to turn it around. In that case, you could buy it for less than book, but it might not be the bargain it seems. For instance, it could harbor hidden potential legal liabilities. Or it might depend on government spending in areas threatened by budget cuts. Buyers should do their homework to discover the real reason for the low price.

• Another time you might see a sale at book value is when an entrepreneur has pieced-together a very eccentric business, extracting profits from a hodge-podge of jury-rigged assets. It works for him, but it isn't attractive to potential buyers, particularly when a load of debt is added. Book Value of Liquidation value might be the only way he can sell.

• Another appropriate use of book value is when a company hasn't really kept pace with the changes it needs to remain competitive - installing new technologies, making routine maintenance and repairs, snd so on. Either way, the buyer will have to spend a lot more than the purchase price to get that business up to par.

There may be times when book value is greater than the real economic value of the assets. In that case, book value obviously overstates the worth of the business.

For instance, very specialized machinery may be installed at great expense, and even though it can't be resold six months later for a fraction of that cost, allowable depreciation hasn't caught up with the real decline in value. (Like the saying about your car being worth $5,000 less the moment you drive it off the lot.) In those cases, you would refer to the real economic worth of the assets.

Sometimes book value happens to be very close to real economic value, such as when the business and the assets are relatively new. Another case is when the company's tangible assets are replaced on a regular basis. But never assume that book value is the same as economic value.

Why book value departs from economic value:

Pricing a company at net worth (book value) does not accord any value to goodwill or profitability. Another way of saying this is that it doesn't consider unrecorded assets (those not listed on the balance sheet) including goodwill, customer lists, favorable leases, and the like.

In addition, it doesn't consider unrecorded liabilities, such as unfavorable contracts or leases. Those can significantly impact the value of the business, but they don't show up on the balance sheets. You should realize that book values, which are the basis of Net Worth, are usually misleading.

The book value of an asset has nothing to do with its true value to the average buyer out in the marketplace because the depreciation that's subtracted each year does not equal the real annual decline in value of those assets due to time and wear.

This problem is accentuated when "accelerated" methods of depreciation have been used in order to speed up the write-off of these assets.

On the other hand, some assets hold their value much better than others. In fact, they may even rise in value, due to inflation. Real estate is the classic example. The point is that traditional accounting methods do not produce balance sheet values that reflect true economic worth.

For that reason, lenders and buyers sometimes refer to a measure called "adjusted book value". However, that's really the same as "asset value" (defined in the last chapter.) It refers to the fair market value or liquidation value of assets, minus liabilities. It's not really "book value".

ഇൽ

For these reasons, book value is usually appropriate only when the business is unprofitable, or very risky, or when the only way the deal can be financed is through extensive borrowing secured by its resaleable assets.

Chapter 8

Capitalization of Income Stream Method

This method can be used with any business that shows significant before-tax earnings on an adjusted income statement (Chapter 3). It takes the net income of the company, and capitalizes* it at the average rate of return produced by other investments bearing the same level of risk. The company is valued as an investment opportunity.

The theory behind the method:

The most popular version of this method bases value on net operating income *before* interest, depreciation, or income taxes - reasoning that those expenses are a cost of owning the company, not a cost of operating it.

Depreciation* is a fictional annual expense. The real expense comes up-front when you actually shell out money to buy that item, but that's not considered an "operating" expense. The depreciation expense can also be misleading because the owner can elect different depreciation methods for any particular asset, which means enables you to manipulate net income. However, its effect on valuation is eliminated if you add back the depreciation deductions and instead subtract an amount that reflects the real annual decline in value of those operating assets.

We add interest expenses back for the same reason. You can set up a business with different kinds of loans, and the annual interest expense will vary accordingly. In addition, different types of business entities are each taxed differently. For that reason, we add back any interest expense and we always uses *before-tax* net income.

Note, however, that if you add back the interest expense, you still have to account for the liabilities that produce it. It's not like they don't exist. If you don't deduct the interest from net income, you have reduce your end-value by the liabilities that cause that interest. That approach is preferred because it seems to produce more consistent results.

Keep in mind that we are talking about Market Value, which implies a sale of the business. What happens to liabilities when the company is sold? Either the seller pays them off at settlement, or the buyer assumes them, but deducts them from the price. So either way you look at it, the liabilities must be deducted in order to show the actual net value to the seller.

Is there a sensible way use the current interest expense in your valuation, instead of deducting liabilities? Some appraisers try to predict the post-acquisition interest expense. They assume that a buyer will use the maximum possible amount of borrowing to finance the deal, but there are so many different ways to finance an acquisition that any interest expense you select is going to be speculative. That approach makes sense only if the valuator represents the buyer and knows the financing approach that will be taken.

Another approach is to look up the average "debt to equity" ratio or "liability to net worth" ratio for companies in that industry. Then you subtract the amount interest suggested by that "average" amount of debt. However, you still have to guess at all of the loan terms. The companies surveyed for that data may not have representative debt ratios. Considering all the guesswork involved, this doesn't seem very reliable. It seems better to take interest off the statement entirely, and instead deduct the liabilities from the end result.

Besides, our approach is consistent with the way most businesses seem to be sold these days - through a purchase of assets where the buyers come up with their own debt/equity structure - arranging new real estate, and equipment loans, new lines of credit, and so on.

Note that this is similar to the way investment real estate is valued. You figure out the operating profit (NOI) produced by the property, without any deduction for mortgage interest, because you are looking at the property as an investment purchased with cash, like stock. You also add back any deduction for depreciation. Then you divide the resulting NOI by a capitalization rate. If the buyer assumes the seller's mortgage, then you deduct it from the price paid to the seller. But usually the buyer arranges his own mortgage, pays the seller the full price, and then lets the seller pay off his existing mortgage with the sale proceeds.

This method appeals more to sellers than buyers because adding back the interest and depreciation tends to result in higher values, even after the liabilities are deducted.

Some buyers are uncomfortable with that because these items really do affect the bottom-line profitability of the company. But since those amounts can be manipulated, who's to say what the proper interest and depreciation deductions should be?

We have explained how we compensate for the lack of an interest deduction by subtracting the liabilities that would produce it, but we haven't explained how to compensate for the lack of a depreciation deduction. Surely the company's assets will gradually wear out and eventually need replacement. Isn't that a real cost of doing business that should be quantified as an annual expense? Yes - particularly since income capitalization is based on the assumption that the income stream produced by those assets will last indefinitely. However, the reality is that if the assets wear out, the income will disappear too.

The preferred approach is to estimate the real annual decline in value of those assets, and use that in place of actual depreciation.

Step 1(d) below tells you how to do that.

This method is related to the Discounted Cash Flow Method in that it uses the company's *income flow* as a measure of its value. However, this method is also related to the common, but often misleading use of "multiples"* - arbitrary numeric factors by which net income is multiplied to get a price. They're actually a shortcut of the Capitalization method. The theory behind the two techniques is similar: using a "multiple" of 8 times earnings is the same as dividing by a capitalization rate* of 12%. Likewise, a multiple of 10 is equal to a capitalization rate of 10%.

However, this arbitrary selection of multiples often produces haphazard results. In addition, those who employ this quickie technique usually apply it to a net income figure pulled right off the income statement, without making thoughtful adjustments.

The Steps:

1. Prepare an Adjusted Income Statement:

(a) See Chapter 3 for directions on preparing an adjusted income statement, and refer to Step 2 of Chapter 6 for additional comments.

Don't use a "pro forma*" income statement. A pro forma statement shows a higher level of sales than is currently being attained, as well as other very speculative assumptions. It shows "what could be", not what is. The object of an adjusted statement is just to give a clear picture of the current situation. All changes should be well-substantiated and made only to correct misleading impressions concerning the company's income and expenses.

If sales or income has varied significantly from year to year, then use a weighted average* of the last 3 to 5 years. On the other hand, if the trend is consistently rising or falling, you should use the last year instead of averaging.

(b) Add back any interest that has been deducted as an expense.

(c) Add back any depreciation that has been deducted as an expense.

(d) Deduct an amount that represents the real average annual decline in value of the fixed operating assets.

Think in terms of the average annual cost of repairing or replacing those assets. We aren't talking about improving them. We aren't talking about normal maintenance costs - such as cleaning, tuning, painting, lubricating, etc.. We are talking about fixing them when they break, replacing parts when they wear out, and replacing the whole item when it's finally shot. Consult management for the past history of those expenses.

This info is usually available for real estate and leasehold improvements. For machinery and equipment, it might be easier to get an estimate of how long those items actually last, and divide their cost by that figure to get average annual economic depreciation. Where there are many assets of the same type, and each has a relatively small value compared to the whole, then lump them together and treat them as a class. If there are expensive individual assets, you can deal with those individually.

Make sure you include any important intangible assets - such as patents or copyrights. Divide by the number of years they really provide a competitive advantage that results in added income.

2. Select a capitalization rate. Refer to Chapter 6 for instructions. When you pick your rate, try to stand in the shoes of an actual purchaser who is viewing the company objectively as an investment.

Note: Technically, if a company is carrying a lot of debt, you shouldn't use the same cap rate as a company that's carrying little debt. The more leverage there is, the riskier the endeavor, and that should be reflected in a higher capitalization rate. By taking debt out of the equation (not deducting interest), we can remove this factor from the equation, which permits a lower cap rate and thus produces a higher price. Buyers may not like this approach, but if the buyer increases risk by loading up on debt, that's his own doing, and he can't really ask the seller to reduce the price because of it. Why should the price for a company bought with cash be more than the price for a company bought using a big loan? That's the buyer's problem, not the seller's.

3. Divide net operating income before-tax (Step 1) by the capitalization rate selected in Step 2.

4- Deduct any liabilities that will be assumed by the purchaser. The result is the value of the company.

Note: If this method produces a *very* low value, that means the income is too low to result in goodwill* value for the company. In those situations, income-based valuation methods (such as this one) may give a lower value than methods that simply add up the value of the individual assets. In that case, make sure you use the asset-based methods outlined in Chapter 6.

ঙ০ৎ

Summary:

Net Operating Income (from adjusted statement)

+ Interest Expenses (from adjusted statement)

+ Depreciation Expenses (from adjusted statement)

- Estimate of real annual economic depreciation of   the operating assets

= Adjusted Net Operating Income Before-Tax

Then, . . .

$$\frac{\text{Adjusted Net Operating Income Before-Tax}}{\text{Capitalization Rate}}$$

(MINUS)

Liabilities

=

Value of the Company

Chapter 9

The Small Business Method

This is a technique used by business brokers to value smaller businesses. It's a variation of the Capitalization of Income method that considers some of the peculiarities of the smaller company.

However, don't limit yourself to this method. If other techniques in this book apply, use them, too.

What do we mean by "small"? That's hard to define precisely, since a firm doing $10 million in sales could have many of the same characteristics as a small, home-based business. But let's assume that we are talking about before-tax income (*including* owners salaries) of less than $200,000 per year before interest and depreciation are deducted.

Step 1: Calculate the adjusted Net Operating Income as follows:

(a) Follow the general instructions in Chapter 3.

(b) Make sure the following expenses are removed from the statement by adding them back into income:
- depreciation
- interest
- non-operating expenses

(c) Remove any non-operating income from the statement.

(d) Since most smaller businesses don't own their real estate, make sure the expenses include a reasonable amount of rent for the premises occupied. At the same time, if it they do happen to own the real estate, remove the real estate mortgage interest from the expenses and the realty from the assets.

(e) We are working with *before-tax* net operating income, so don't calculate and deduct taxes.

Reconstruct the income statement this way for each of the past 5 years.

Step 2: Based on those reconstructed statements, calculate the weighted average* of the "net operating income before tax" for those five years.

Step 3: Select a Capitalization Rate. (See the instructions in Chapter 5.)

Bear in mind that the cap rates for small businesses are higher than those of larger firms because they are typically less-resilient, and therefore riskier. Cap rates for smaller businesses can range as high as 100%. The higher rates seem to be supported by the reality of the marketplace - and you can't ignore what buyers are really paying for a small business. It's said that most small firms sell for a price that's one-to-five times their adjusted annual earnings, depending on the consistency of that income stream over the years. If five times earnings is the top end, that corresponds to a cap rate of 20%. One times earnings corresponds to a cap rate of 100%. If you are a seller, this may seem like a hard pill to swallow, but you might as well face reality up front.

Step 4: Divide the weighted average of those net operating incomes before tax (Step 2) by the cap rate.

Step 5: Add the economic value of any non-operating assets that will be included in the sale.

This would include investment securities, rental property, personal vehicles, and personal assets of the owners that are listed on the balance sheet - anything that isn't directly, substantially, and necessarily linked to the primary business activity of the firm.

Understand that the value of the operating assets, including inventory, is already included in the figure produced in Step 4. The theory behind capitalization is that the operating assets are inseparable from the earnings they generate.

The only time you would add something extra for operating assets or inventory is when jthe business has more assets than is normal for a business in that industry - but the stuff has to be readily useable or resalable, and its value must be ascertainable with reasonable certainty. Similarly, if operating assets or inventory are sparser-than-normal for that kind of firm, then capitalized value should be reduced by the amount needed to bring them up to par.

Step 6: Next, add the market value of any real estate that will be included in the sale.

Since most small businesses don't own their own real estate, this is considered an extra.

Step 7: If the buyer will inherit both the current assets* and the current liabilities, then add the "Net Working Capital".

This will occur if the business is sold by way of a transfer of stock, or if the contract specifically states that the buyer will take over these items.

For our purposes here,

Net Working Capital is defined as:

Current Assets* *not including inventory* (unless excessive, see in Step 5). Make sure you include cash, accounts receivable, and pre-paid expenses.

MINUS

Current liabilities* *not including amounts currently due on "long-term" liabilities*

Step 8: If the Buyer is assuming any liabilities of the business, these should be deducted from the total.

Most small businesses are sold as a purchase of assets, not as a purchase of corporate stock, so the buyer rarely assumes liabilities. The seller usually pays them off at settlement, so the value of the firm (to the seller) should be reduced by that amount.

When assets are retained by the seller:

The seller may chose to retain ownership of some assets. If these are operating assets that contribute to the earning of income capitalized in Step 5, then their economic value should be deducted from the end result. On the other hand, if they are non-operating assets*, they won't be among those whose value is added in Step 5. If the seller is retaining real estate, don't add its value in Step 7, and remember to include a reasonable amount of rent for the premises in the operating expenses in Step 1.

Owner's salary:

Many versions of this method remove the owner's salary from the operating expenses on the adjusted income statement. With this amount added back into net income, you get a value that's much higher. However, those versions should also be using a higher cap rate to compensate. Remember, the higher the cap rate, the lower the value. The cap rates used in versions that add back the owners salary tend to be very high - 50% or more. (That means "multipliers" ranging between 1 and 3.) These high cap rates don't really correspond to expected rates of return on an investment. It's a good idea to relate cap rate to the real rate of return, so we suggest that you stick with the procedure outlined in this chapter - leave a reasonable owner's salary among the expenses on your adjusted income statement and then select your capitalization rate in the normal fashion, as explained in Chapter 5.

As we stated earlier, this method is really just another version of the Capitalization of Income method. It doesn't just value the "goodwill" - it includes everything. If you buy a business based on an income-method valuation, then the operating assets are automatically included.

In addition, bear in mind that the seller often retains ownership of certain non-operating assets and real estate. And since these deals are usually structured as a purchase of assets (not a purchase of stock) the seller keeps the cash and working capital items, except for inventory. If they are transferred to the buyer, then he pays extra for them. This is reflected in Step 7.

As far as inventory is concerned, most small businesses run "lean and mean", unless inventory happens to be the main operating asset of the business (for example, in a retail store or parts supplier). So, in most cases, the value of a small business usually boils down to the capitalized value of its net operating income before tax, plus the value of any non-operating assets the buyer wants, minus any liabilities he is willing to take on.

Chapter 10

Discounted Cash Flow Method

This method holds that a business is worth the present value of all benefits flowing to its owner during the future.

In other words, the company represents a stream of monetary benefits that will go to its owners over the next few years - composed of the annual business income, plus proceeds from the sale of its assets at some point in the future. So we want to figure out the present value of those benefits in today's dollars.

This method is good for acquisitions that will involve high risk, or when the business will only be owned for a limited number of years (less than 10).

Many leveraged-buyouts* fall into this category, since they are often intended as short-term investments where almost all of the purchase price is borrowed and the company's assets are used as security for the loan.

Short holding periods are common in turnaround* acquisitions too. A troubled company is bought at a bargain price, put back on its feet, and then resold at a higher price that reflects its improved performance.

The theory behind this method:

This method is different from the Capitalization of Income Method since we *do* consider interest, depreciation, and income tax expenses. We adjust the income statement to show what these will be after an acquisition so that we'll know how much cash flow will be left after operating expenses (the cost of doing business), loan payments (the cost of owning the company), and income taxes (the cost of supporting Uncle Sam). We view the remainder as a lump sum that will be left over at the end of each future year, and we calculate its present value. We do this for each year of the projected holding period, then we total those present values. Finally, we project the present value of its net assets at the end of the holding period, and we add that in as well.

Buyers seem to like this method because it approaches valuation from their perspective. ("Just tell me the risk level, the cost to get in, the return, and how long it will take.") It's a healthy exercise because it forces them to assess the risk at several turns, and it forces them to realistically predict performance and costs for each year.

This is very similar to the cash flow study that buyers do when they attempt to predict the feasibility of an acquisition, so you can use your work here for that as well.

The hard part is forecasting the company's earnings, expenses, and capital expenditures for the next 5 to 10 years, plus the value of its assets and its liabilities at the end of that period. That involves a lot of speculation, so this method does receive some criticism.

 Steps 3 and 4 ask you to assume a ball-park purchase price right up front, so it's probably a good idea to perform any other applicable valuation methods first. That way you'll have an intelligent basis for that figure.

Brief Description of the Method:

Refer to the summary at the end of this chapter for an overview of the method. For *each year* of the projection, you should have a vertical row of figures corresponding to each step in that summary.

1. First, you predict the income and cash flow* of the company for X number of years into the future. Then you calculate the "present value"* of that cash flow for each year.

2. Then total the value of all of the assets you think will be present at the end of the holding period (the "residual assets"). Figure out the present value of that too.

3. Total the results of Step 1 for each year, and add the results of Step 2. Then *subtract* the present value any liabilities you expect to remain at the end of the period.

How to measure future benefits:

Variations of this method measure future benefits in different ways, referring to net income after tax, or net income before tax, or cash flow*. This author, and the majority of professional valuators, feel that *"net cash flow after tax" makes the most sense.* After all, we're really talking about the amount you can permanently remove from the business each year. That's net cash flow after tax, after debt service, after capital expenditures, and after any necessary additions to working capital.

The Steps:

1. Project Net Sales for each of the next several years.

How many years? Pick *the shorter of:*

(a) ten years,
(b) the term of the longest piece of debt that will be used to finance the acquisition, or
(c) the period within which the company will probably be resold.

When it comes to predicting future sales, be conservative and keep them in line with the level they're at now. Don't try to show more units sold. No matter how confident you are about growth, it hasn't occurred yet. Remember, a buyer pays for the company as it stands today, not for what might happen in the future.

If sales have fluctuated a lot during recent years, don't even use last year's figure. Instead, use a weighted average* of net sales for the last five years. After you pick the sales level for year one, increase it for each subsequent year by a conservative rate of inflation (4% to 6%).

Is there anytime you can justify higher sales projections? Yes, but very few companies qualify. The company must show a consistent trend of annually increasing sales and earnings for a very long period of time (say, 8 to 10 years). That growth must have occurred at a consistent rate (for instance, 10% to 15% each year) - and not in an unpredictable fashion (for instance, 5% in one year, 30% in the next, and -10% in the next). In addition, market demand for its product or service must be stable and proven over many, many years. It can't be something that's subject to constant change or improvement, such that any particular company could get left in the dust by an innovative competitor. (So high tech industries never qualify.) And the market must be relatively immune from exogenous economic conditions.

Generally speaking, only very mundane products can fill this bill, and even there, it's a stretch. The total market for mundane products grows very slowly, and each company's share of it tends to be firmly entrenched and very hard to steal away. This is reinforced by the conservatism of lenders, who usually assume that future revenues will correspond to a weighted average from the past. They might view the promise of rising sales as a good sign, but it usually won't affect the amount of their loan.

If you insist on projecting increases, at least compare those to the industry average to make sure they are reasonable. If profits are now 4% of gross sales, and that's close to the industry average, then don't fantasize that they'll go to 12%.

2- Determine the "Operating Profit" for each year of the projected holding period. Start by preparing an adjusted historic income statement (See Chapter 3).

Then, take the "percentage operating profit"* from that statement and multiply it by the net sales you project for each year of the holding period (from Step 1). That will give you an estimate of "Operating Profit" for each future year. In other words, if the adjusted statements show operating profit (before tax) of 9.5% of net sales, then assume that it stays at 9.5% for each year of your projection. If the percentage has fluctuated a lot over the past several years, then use a weighted average* for the period.

Get your operating profit percentage from an adjusted historical income statement. Don't take it from a "pro forma"* income statement.

A "pro forma" statement is a speculative prediction. Buyers generate "pro forma" statements for their own private reasons, to estimate the company's upside potential. Don't use them for valuation. They are discussed more thoroughly in Chapter 15.

3. For each year of the projection, adjust operating profit for any changes in future depreciation.

Depreciation is deducted as an expense when you figure the Net Operating Income. However, depreciation will be different after the company is sold, so you have to make adjustments for each year of the projection. How do you do that? Well, start by adding the old depreciation amount back into operating income. Then calculate the total amount of depreciation that will be deducted in each year after the acquisition, and subtract that instead. Do that for each year - replacing the old figure with the new figure.

If your valuation is an acquisition that will be carried out as a stock purchase, then the present depreciation schedule will be inherited by the new owner, so no adjustment is necessary. In that case, just go to the next step.

If the assets of the company are older and most of their original cost has already been written off, then the buyer will probably want to structure a deal that provides a fresh depreciation schedule. Now they can be written off all over again, which improves the company's cash flow.

A new corporation is formed to purchase those assets, and the old company will just consist of an empty corporate shell and the proceeds of sale. With no hard assets and no business, it just winds down its affairs and "liquidates" - distributing the cash to its stockholders. The new corporation divvies up the purchase price among the various assets, and that becomes the new depreciable basis for each.

The Internal Revenue Code defines the period over which you are allowed to write off each type of asset. That's called the "useful life" of the asset. Sometimes you can select from several options, but once you make your choice, you have to stick with it. For this discussion, let's just assume that the cost (tax basis) of the asset is divided evenly over the number of years in its useful life. That's called the "straight line method" of depreciation. To keep your calculations simple, you might consider grouping all assets of the same type together so you can treat them as one asset.

To illustrate, let's assume you paid $1000 for an asset, and tax law allows you to depreciate it. (Not all assets can be depreciated.) The law says you can depreciate it over 5 years on a "straight line" basis (equal amounts of depreciation taken each year). This means you can deduct $200 per year from your company's revenues when figuring taxable income.

So, go back to the adjusted historic income statement and find the amount deducted for depreciation. Add that amount back to the operating profit (Step 2) for each year of your projection. Then assume a ball-park purchase price for the assets and allocate it among them. Figure out the future depreciation for each group of assets, and deduct the total annual amount from the operating profit in each year.

It might seem ridiculous that you have to guess at the purchase price of the company in order to do a valuation, but that's the deal. Fortunately, accuracy is not as crucial now, because if you find that your end result is different than your initial guess, you can adjust and recalculate. We suggested earlier that you use some other valuation methods first so you will have something reasonable to base your guess on. Some people just use future book value*, or an industry rule of thumb, or they capitalize* net income from the adjusted income statement. That last approach can also be used to estimate the value of the residual assets.

Consult an accountant or an up-to-date tax guide for the depreciation rules, because they are complex and they change all the time. For example, most real estate is written off over a specific number of years, on a straight-line basis. However, you can only depreciate that part of the price that's allocated to building and equipment permanently attached to it (the fixtures). Land can't be depreciated, so the value of the lot must be subtracted before the calculation is made. Furthermore, there may be optional methods you can use, so you'll want some expert advice on what's best. It's a good idea to include notes in your valuation explaining the assumptions you have made so that your advisors can offer input before you make any decisions based on your conclusions.

Both buyer and seller are bound by the decision on how the purchase price is allocated, but the buyer usually has the more say on the issue. The allocation method is usually spelled out in the Agreement of Sale. Even if the company is very profitable, sellers usually have to accept little or not allocation to "goodwill"* because every buyer needs maximum depreciation to make an acquisition work, and goodwill is not a depreciable asset.

Buyers who plan on making capital improvements after the acquisition should  figure those into the depreciation. Most manufacturing companies need new equipment on a regular basis. Consult current managers and equipment dealers for guidance on that. Major capital outlays are common during the first 3 years after acquisition since sellers tend to neglect the need for improvements and repairs once they know they're selling. In fact, some people add these costs to the adjusted balance sheet as a liability for "deferred maintenance". Make sure you bone up on any new technology that will have to be acquired in order to stay competitive with the rest of the industry. If the company's capital expenditures have been

relatively consistent in the past, you may decide to use that historic average, but don't forget to increase it by a factor for inflation. Everything costs more each year.

These depreciation estimates can become very detailed. For example, in the third year after an acquisition, *total* depreciation might include the following:

- that year's depreciation on the original acquisition cost of the real estate, with increases to its basis for any subsequent capital improvements;

- that year's depreciation on the machinery and equipment originally purchased at acquisition, with each major category of assets calculated separately;

- that year's depreciation on trucks and vehicles originally acquired;

- that year's depreciation on new machinery and equipment purchased in the second year, with each major item, or group of items, calculated separately;

- that year's depreciation on new machinery and equipment purchased in the third year.

All of these different depreciation figures, one for *each* class of assets acquired in *each* year, are added up.

"Accelerated" depreciation methods are sometimes allowed by the tax law, and these will give the company more cash flow* in the early years, but they also involve certain disadvantages so consult an accountant before using them. Also note that you can't use different methods of depreciation for different items of property of the same class placed in service in the same year. A brief treatment of depreciation can be found in popular tax guides available at your book store. Since tax laws change constantly, never assume that the same rule will hold from year to year.

The result of all this is the "Adjusted Net Operating Income".

4- *Adjust the interest expense for each year of your projection by (a) adding back the interest that was deducted on the current income statement, and (b) deducting the amount of interest expense you actually expect in each post-acquisition year.*

To estimate those interest expenses, you'll have to assume a purchase price for the company, and then predict how it will be financed. You'll have to speculate on how much of the price can be borrowed. The most important factor affecting that is the quality and quantity of the assets, since they are the security for the loan.

Here are some rough rules of thumb for how much you can borrow using company assets as security:

Accounts Receivable:
  80% of its Book Value
  (100% if collection is guaranteed by the buyer or seller),

Machinery and Equipment:
  80% of its Liquidation Value

Real Estate:
  65%-80% of its Market Value
  (depending on how marketable it is),

Raw Materials Inventory:
  50% of Book Value

Work-in-Process Inventory:
  0-25% of the Book Value of, depending on the type of materials used

Finished Goods Inventory:
  85% of its Book Value

These percentages are called the "advance rates", and they vary from lender to lender, so make sure you verify them with up-to-date information.

If the assets have been recently appraised by an outside firm, you can use those figures instead of book value. There is hidden value in the assets if their current market value is greater than the value shown on the books. This is particularly true with real estate and with inventory accounted for by the LIFO* method (Last In, First Out).

See Chapter 13 for more detailed instruction on how to determine the amount that can be borrowed when the assets are used as security.

When you estimate the post-acquisition interest expense, work with a simple loan structure. Someone once noted that it's very *un*sophisticated to use a sophisticated financial structure to accomplish a small deal. Rather than borrow different amounts at different rates and terms, secured by different groups of assets, try to *combine* real estate with machinery and equipment as security for one term loan of 10 to 15 years. Then use your inventory and your accounts receivable to secure a separate "line of credit", which will provide the money needed to actually run the business (the "working capital").

On a more complex level, the following types of loans are commonly used to finance acquisitions:

Equipment Loan (a loan for a term of years, secured by the company's machinery and equipment). Usually for a 5 to 7 year term, at "prime rate" interest plus two points.

Real Estate Loan - a loan for a term of years, secured by the real estate of the company. For a 15 to 25 year term, at prime rate plus 1 to 2 points.

Working Capital Loan - a revolving line of credit secured by inventory and accounts receivable. It has an indefinite term, and generally you pay only the interest on the loan as long as there is still adequate security for it. Interest is often prime rate plus 2 or 3 points. The loan principal is repaid at the borrower's option, as excess profits exist for that purpose and it becomes desirable to bring the loan balance down. In some cases the loan principal is repaid gradually, according to a schedule set up by the lender.

Hopefully, the total amount advanced for secured financing will be enough to supply the entire purchase price. If not, the buyer must raise cash by selling stock to investors (who then own part of the company), or else the buyer must take on additional debt in the form of *un*secured financing. *Unsecured debt is difficult to obtain.* The lenders have nothing to rely on but your cash flow prediction, and without any collateral to secure the debt, they will ask for higher interest rates and personal guarantees. You can try to raise unsecured debt from individual investors. The investment instrument used to evidence unsecured debt is generally known as a "debenture". To sell this to an investor, you usually have to sweeten the deal by including a privilege to convert the debt to stock, or by attaching a "warrant", which is an instrument giving its holder the right to purchase stock later at a predetermined price. Warrants can sometimes be "detached" by the debenture holder and sold to someone else. These sweeteners offset some of the risk to the investor.

Interest rates depend more upon the type of lender than upon the variety of loan. In this book, we assume that the loans will come from a commercial bank. For a good discussion of the different types of lenders (commercial finance companies, insurance companies, etc.) and their expectations regarding return, you might want to find a book on leveraged buyouts or financing sources.

Preferred stock* is another way of raising equity, but the "interest" paid to the investor is really a dividend, so the company can't deduct it from income for tax purposes. Dividends are paid out of the *after*-tax income, so this is a more expensive way to raise money.

Most private acquirers prefer to finance the deal entirely with debt in order to avoid diluting their stock ownership.

There is also a chance that the seller may finance the deal, or that it may qualify for some kind of government loan program. However, don't assume that these money sources will be available, at least not at this stage.

Once you've made some informed guesses about the amount to be borrowed and the interest rates that will be charged, add up the total interest for each separate year of the projected holding period. Deduct that interest from Operating Profit to give Taxable Net Income for each year.

Paying down the acquisition loans:

You may plan to use your excess cash ("cash flow safety cushion") to pay down the revolving loan principal each year, or to retire debentures, or to redeem stock given to outside investors. In that case, only do one year at a time. You have to complete your calculations for each year before you'll know how much cash is left over to pay down the loans. Then, since reducing those loans will reduce the amount of interest that's paid in the subsequent year, you'll have to re-calculate for that next year based on the new loan balances. However, don't use *all* of your excess cash to pay off debt - you still need to keep a sizeable cash reserve on hand. Also keep in mind that lenders often charge a fee to revise the loan payments if you don't want to stick with the original amortization schedule. You don't want to plunk down an extra $50,000 in loan principal along with your 13th scheduled payment, only to find that your required monthly payment stays the same.

By the way, there are many hand-held calculators and computer programs that figure out the interest and principal payments on a loan, and they make this process a lot easier than using loan tables.

Remember: Interest is an expense that's deducted on the income statement. Therefore, when you adjust the income statement, you have to add back any interest from debts that won't exist after the acquisition.

Interest isn't usually listed as an "operating expense" - it falls under "other expenses", so look for it there. Only add back interest that has been deducted before arriving at oper-

ating profit. Also remember that only the interest portion of loan payments is deducted as an expense, not the part that goes to repaying part of the loan principal.

Your result at the conclusion of these last 2 steps is the Net Taxable Operating Income.

5- For each year, calculate federal and state income tax and deduct them from the result in step 4 to give you the Net Operating Income After Tax.

Make sure you are using the latest corporate income tax rates. Remember - tax laws change constantly, so seek out the latest rates, and find out if different ones apply to later years of the projection. State income taxes are usually deductible on the federal return in the year paid, so some people estimate state tax at about two-thirds of its stated percentage rate. In other words, they assume that you get about a third of it back

because it's deductible on the federal return (the federal corporate tax rate has been around 34% on taxable income over $75,000). This will vary as the rates change. Otherwise you have to figure the state tax first and then calculate the federal tax based on a different amount of taxable net income. The value of a deduction (in federal income tax savings) is generally the amount of the deduction times your federal tax rate. In other words, a deduction of $1000 for a taxpayer in the 34% bracket will save $340 in federal taxes, so the actual cost of the deductible expense is really only $660 - which is about two-thirds. So, if the state tax rate is 10% and the federal rate is 34%, then a very rough short cut would be to assume you have a combined tax bite of 34% + two-thirds of 10% (6.6%) = 40.6%. Different rates apply to different levels of income, and there may be tax surcharges on income over a certain amount, so check the current tax code.

6- Find out if an Investment Tax Credit (or similar incentive) is available under the current federal tax law. If so, add that amount back to the Net Operating Income After Tax.

At the time of this writing, the investment tax credit has been repealed, but it seems like very year there is a proposal to reinstate it. By the time you read this, it might be available. If so, consult a current tax guide or your accountant on how to take this credit.

If available, it will allow you to reduce your federal income tax by a percentage of certain types of capital expenditures - usually capital improvements such as machinery and real estate. A credit is usually worth more in tax savings than a deduction because it reduces your taxes dollar-for-dollar. So, if you spend $100,000 on new machinery in a year when a ten percent investment tax credit is available, then your federal tax is reduced by $10,000. On the other hand, the actual tax savings from a deduction is only equal to the amount of the deduction, multiplied by your tax rate. So if your effective rate is 34%, then a $10,000 deduction is worth $3400.

At times in the past, this credit has also applied to the initial purchase of the company assets. (Another big incentive to acquire the company through a purchase of assets, rather than by purchasing its stock.) However, there was a limit on the total amount of the credit allowed for the purchase of *used* property, and some types of property did not qualify at all. Again, make sure you consult your accountant for all these conditions.

7- Add back the amount of any Depreciation deducted earlier.

While depreciation is deducted from income for tax purposes, you don't really shell out cash each year to pay it. Assets that wear out over time are paid for all up front, in their year of purchase. But if a depreciable asset will last ten years, then the IRS insists that only one-tenth of its cost is deductible each year. The annual depreciation expense is a fiction, so we add it back to operating income to show the true cash flow for that year. However, any real capital expenditures must be deducted from cash flow in the year spent (Step 9).

8- Add back any Interest expense deducted in Step 4.

Why do we do this? Because in a later step we will subtract the full amount of all loan payments from the Net Cash Flow available after tax. Those loan payments include *both* principal *and interest*, so you don't want to subtract the interest portion twice. For that reason, we add it back now. We only deducted it earlier so we could include it in the tax deductions when we figured out the tax bite.

Your result after this step will be the amount of Net Cash Flow After Tax available for capital expenditures debt service, and additions to working capital.

9- Now subtract the anticipated Capital Expenditures for each year.

These are items that are not written off entirely in the year purchased. That usually includes new equipment, improvements to real estate, and anything else needed to keep the business running that must be depreciated over a period of years according to the tax code. Sometimes the code allows you to "expense" a capital item (deduct its entire cost in the year purchased), so those should not be included.

10- Subtract the amount that will be added to Working Capital in each year.

As sales increase, the company's working capital must increase. "Working capital", for the purpose of this calculation, is considered to be total inventory, plus accounts receivable and cash reserve, minus accounts payable and other current liabilities. In order to predict the working capital needed in each year, we have to *separately* project each of these items for *each* year. Your accountant may be able to give you some quick estimates, based on experience.

If you decide to project the working capital needs yourself, then follow these instructions:

a) Inventory Projections:

First, use your adjusted financial statement and adjusted balance sheet (see Chapter 3) to calculate the "inventory turnover ratio":

$$\begin{array}{ll} & \text{Percentage Cost of Goods Sold} \\ X & \text{Net Sales Projected for that Year} \\ & \rule{4cm}{0.4pt} \\ = & \text{Cost of Goods Sold} \end{array}$$

(This is from the adjusted income statement. "Percentage" means percent of the amount of Net Sales in that year. In other words, take the dollar amount of that item and divide it by the dollar amount of net sales.)

$$\text{Inventory Turnover Ratio} = \frac{\text{Cost of Goods Sold}}{\text{Total Inventory at Year's End}}$$

Example: If your Adjusted Income Statement says that Cost of Goods Sold is 58.6% of Net Sales, and management says that the inventory level should be about $1,500,000 to support Net Sales of $6,000,000, then your Inventory Turnover Ratio is:

$$\frac{.586 \text{ X } 6{,}000{,}000}{1{,}500{,}000} = 2.344$$

Assume that this same ratio will apply to each year of the projection, and plug your projected annual net sales figure into this formula:

$$\text{Inventory} = \frac{.586 \text{ X Net Sales}}{2.344}$$

Note: Before doing this, ask the company's accountant what the inventory turnover ratio *should* be at certain sales levels. You may wish to alter your ratio in view of that feedback. Don't be bashful in asking for information.

Make sure your inventory figures include raw materials, packaging materials, work in progress, and finished goods - all at cost.

b) Accounts Receivable Projections:

To calculate these, use your adjusted income statement and adjusted balance sheet to find the Average Collection Period (ACP) Ratio:

$$\text{ACP Ratio} = \frac{\text{Accounts Receivable}}{\dfrac{\text{Projected Sales}}{360}}$$

Example:

$$\text{ACP Ratio} = \frac{500,000}{6,000,000 / 360} = 30$$

So, for each year:

$$\frac{\text{net sales}}{360} \times 30 = \text{Accnts. Rec. for year}$$

Use this method to separately predict the accounts receivable for each year. In the first step, make sure you are using an accounts receivable figure that corresponds to the level of sales reflected on the adjusted statement. The company's accountant can help you verify that.

c) Accounts Payable Projections:

First, calculate the ratio know as "Accounts Payable Days" (APD):

$$\text{APD} = \frac{\text{Accounts Payable}}{\text{Annual Materials Purchases} / 360}$$

The annual amount of materials purchases should be included in the detailed breakdown of "Cost of Goods Sold", which is part of the income statement. If the company hasn't provided those details, ask for them.

Example:

$$\text{APD} = \frac{\$280,000}{\$1,200,000 / 360} = 84$$

Next, calculate the following percentage:

$$\frac{\text{Annual Materials Purchases}}{\text{Net Sales}} = Y\%$$

Next, assume that the same APD ratio will apply in each future year, and calculate accounts payable as follows:

$$\text{Accnts Payable} = \text{APD Ratio} \times \frac{Y\% \times \text{Net Sales}}{360}$$

Example:

(1) Assume APD = 84 from example above.

$$(2)\ Y\% = \frac{\$1,200,000}{6,000,000} = .20$$

$$(3)\ 84 \times \frac{.20 \times \text{Net Sales}}{360} = \text{Accnts. Payable}$$

So, if annual sales for year 2 are predicted to be $6,360,000, then:

$$84 \times \frac{.20 \times 6,360,000}{360} = \frac{\$296,000}{\text{payables in year two}}$$

d) Projecting "Other Current Liabilities"

Probably the easiest way to do this is to assume that current liabilities will grow each year at the same rate that net sales grow. Consult with management to make sure the number you start with (in year one) makes sense for that level of sales.

e) Cash Reserve

Every company should probably keep a size-able cash reserve on hand, and it should grow as sales levels grow. To determine the amount of cash reserve, you can refer to books on key financial ratios published by companies like Robert Morris Associates (Philadelphia). These include data on the average cash reserve maintained by companies in the same industry, grouped according to sales volume. If you can't find this information at the library, check with your accountant.

f) Calculate annual Additions to Working Capital, for each year of the projection:

(1) Use the figures from the previous steps to complete the following formula:

Accounts Receivable
+   Cash Reserve
+   Inventory
     <u>minus</u>
     Accounts Payable and
         Other Current Liabilities

=   Total Working Capital

Do this for each year of the projection.

(2) Subtract the total amount of Working Capital needed from the total amount needed in the year before. This will tells you how much must be added to working capital in that year.

A shortcut you can use is to calculate the "current ratio" for your company and compare it to the current ratio for the average profitable company in that industry. That will tell you how much working capital to add in the first year. After that, assume that total working capital must increase each year by the same percentage that net sales increase each year.

g) Subtract the Additions to Working Capital from the Net Cash Flow After Tax. This will give you Cash Flow Before Debt Service.

11- Subtract total annual Debt Service from Cash Flow Before Debt Service:

Look back to the work you did for Step 4. Add up all loan payments for the entire year. Include both the principal and the interest portion of each payment.

On a revolving loan, remember that you normally pay only the interest due. We assume that you won't be repaying part the principal unless you have excess cash available and you voluntarily choose to do so. Many companies do use part of their excess earnings each year to pay down their loans, but those earnings could also be used to pay off some subordinate debt or non-amortizing debt, such as debentures. Just don't use all of your excess earnings this way, because you still want to maintain an adequate cash reserve. Beyond that, you don't have to leave the money in the company - you can distribute it as dividends to the stockholders.

Also, don't worry that you will reduce your final valuation figure if you use the excess cash flow to pay down loans, because the final value is reduced by the amount of any liabilities anyway.

12- The amount left is your Cash Flow Safety Cushion.

Lenders want you to maintain a reasonable safety cushion in your cash flow - generally 20 to 50 percent of the Cash Flow Before Debt Service. Look at how much cash flow is left after you've made all the deductions in the prior steps. Make sure it's at least 20% of the total amount you estimated in Step 8. If it isn't, then go back and determine whether you can cut back on some of the items deducted from cash flow in steps 9 through 11.

This cushion is available for capital recovery or reinvestment. You can use it to reduce the principal of a revolving loan, or to reduce subordinated debt, or to redeem stock. When stock is sold to outside investors to help finance an acquisition, that dilutes the stock ownership of the real players, so many buyers use their excess earnings to buy back (redeem) stock sold to others or to redeem debentures that are convertible to stock.

Remember that if you decide to use part of the cash flow cushion to reduce your debt, the loan amounts in succeeding years will be less, so you will have to re-calculate the loan payments for those years, including the interest part of those payments. Both will be less than before.

13- Determine the present value of the remaining Cash Flow Cushion for each year, and add those present values up.

The theory behind "present value" is that an amount received in the future is worth less than the same amount received today. This is because you lose out on the investment income you would otherwise earn in the meantime. (Inflation also decreases the value of money over time, but that's not taken into consideration in present value conversions.) The rate you use to determine this lower value is known as the "discount rate". The discount rate must reflect a risk-free rate of return, plus an additional premium for the extra financial risk inherent in your particular company. To arrive at that, ask yourself what kind of return a typical investor will expect in exchange for sinking money into a company with the same risk profile as yours. For highly leveraged deals, the discount rate is fairly high, perhaps 20%-35%. See the chap-

ter on choosing a capitalization rate for more information on this.

Even if excess earnings are not distributed to the owners, we still view them as a benefit received by the owners at the end of each fiscal year because they increase the owners equity and the overall value of the business by reducing the liabilities and outstanding stock.

To find present value, you can use a calculator programmed with the present value function, or the tables contained in the Appendix of this book.

14- Next, determine the present value of the assets you believe will be present at the end of the projected holding period.

This represents the residual value of the company at the end of the projection period - an estimate of its sale price at that time. We base it on the economic value of the assets, including any intangible assets that can be resold separately.

If you have a consistently profitable company in a consistently profitable industry, you could estimate future value by using the Capitalization of Earnings Method (shown in Chapter 8). You might also use an industry rule-of-thumb, or simply capitalize* the net operating income projected for the last year of the holding period. Whatever method you use, make sure the number makes sense in light of your other figures. Liabilities are deducted in the next step, so don't subtract them here.

Liquidation value of the assets is the traditional basis for estimating the future sale price of the company in this step. It assumes that the business will be terminated and the assets sold piecemeal. If you are certain that the company will be saleable at the end of the holding period, then it seems reasonable to use *fair market* value instead of liquidation value, but don't attribute any value to goodwill. *Refer to the Glossary and to Chapter 6* for input on how to arrive at liquidation value or market value.

15- Add the amount determined in Step 14 to the total amount from Step 13. Then deduct the present value of any liabilities you expect to remain at the end of the projection period. The result is the present value of the company.

ഇൗരു

 As you can see from these final steps, this valuation method is best for situations where the purchaser only plans to own the company for a limited number of years. However, even if the method doesn't apply well to your situation, you can use it to demonstrate the financial feasibility of the acquisition to lenders and investors by just taking your analysis through Step 12. The figures can be used to show that an acquisition can safely pay for itself and meet everyone's expectations on investment return.

ഇൗരു

Variation: The Discounted Future Earnings Method

This is another version of the method. Essentially, you take the results of Step 6 (Net Operating Income) for each year of the projection, and then you discount them to present value (See Step 13) and add them up. The technique focuses exclusively on earnings. It by-passes the difficulty of trying to predict the value of the company ten years from now by assuming that its residual value is included in the other figures. Since Net Operating Income is always going to be much larger than cash flow after actual expenses, this assumption may be reasonable, but some see it as too big a leap. If you use too short a holding period, it certainly seems to lose validity. We prefer the "cash flow" approach outlined in this chapter.

Summary of Discounted Cash Flow Method:

For *each future year*, calculate the following:

Projected Net Sales (as a percentage of Projected Gross Annual Sales) (Step 1)

X   Operating Profit Percentage (Step 2)

=   Operating Profit (as a percentage of net sales)

Then, adjust the depreciation for that year by...

(adding)   Depreciation amount used on the adjusted income statement
                  (Step 3)

(subtracting)   Depreciation actually projected for this year (Step 3)

Then, adjust the interest expense by . . .

(adding back)   Interest expense used on the adjusted income statement

(subtracting)   Interest Expense projected for this year (Step 4)

Result   =   Taxable Net Operating Income

                  (minus)   Income Taxes (Step 5)
                  (plus)   Investment Tax Credit (Step 6)

Result   =   Net Operating Income After Tax

                  (plus)   Depreciation projected for this (Step 7)
                  (plus)   Interest projected for this year (Step 8)

Result   =   Cash Flow After Tax (Step 8)

                  (minus)   Projected Capital Expenditures (Step 9)
                  (minus)   Projected Additions to Working Capita (Step 10)

Result   =   Cash Flow Before Debt Service

Result   =   Cash Flow Before Debt Service (Continued)

(minus)   Debt Service on term loans   } Total debt
(minus)   Interest on revolving loans   } service
(minus)   Interest on unsecured debt   } for that
(minus)   Dividends on preferred stock   } year   (Step 11)

Result   =   Cash Flow Safety Cushion (Step 12)
               (sometimes called "excess earnings")

Do this for each year of the projected holding period.

Then . . .

Calculate the *present value* of the cash flow safety cushion for each year, and add them up. (Step 13)

Add the present value of the assets you expect to be present at the very end of the projected holding period. (Step 14)

Deduct the present value of any liabilities you expect to be present at the end of the projected holding period. (Step 15)

Final result = the value of the company.

ಏಂಡ

Chapter 11

Excess Earnings Method

This method can be used for any company that produces significant earnings. It holds that a business is worth the value of its assets, plus a premium for goodwill* if those earnings are high enough.

Brief Description of the Method:

Add the following two items together:

1- The value of the company's profits, but only to the extent they exceed the minimum return an owner would demand from her investment in those assets

+ PLUS +

2- The *net* value of the company's assets (the value of its assets, minus its liabilities)

Part 1 is thought to represent the value of "goodwill" and other *intangible* assets, as opposed to the *total* profits from utilization of the company's *fixed* assets. (This is also called excess earnings.) In other words, an investor buys a bunch of tangible assets and expects a certain *minimum* rate of return. In this method, we assume it's equal to the cost to finance the purchase of those assets. Anything earned above that is excess earnings, which we attribute to the *intangible*

assets of the business. To place a dollar value on the flow of excess earnings, we divide it by a capitalization rate.

Some appraisers don't like this method because Internal Revenue Ruling 68-609 says we shouldn't use "capitalization of excess earnings" to determine the value of intangibles if there's better evidence available concerning value. "Better evidence" might be recent prices paid for the same kind of intangibles in an active secondary market, or a special, well-accepted method for valuing a particular type of intangible asset. Fine, except that very few intangibles fill that bill. If we assume that most profitable businesses have goodwill and other intangibles, yet there is no special way to place a value on them, then it seems appropriate to use a method that lumps them all together and values them as a whole.

Steps to the method:

1. Determine the actual market value of all Tangible (fixed) Operating Assets.

This refers to tangible items of property (fixed assets) necessary to run the business, including real estate, machinery, equipment, fixtures, the unamortized portion of leasehold improvements, tools, and so on. Make sure you exclude any goodwill or intangible assets shown on the balance sheet, since the point of this exercise is to separately calculate the earnings value of those intangibles. However, any transferable intangible assets that can be readily sold in a secondary market can be included here - such as an assignable franchise agreement, a liquor license, or an assignable lease. You want to *exclude* non-operating assets* - things that don't have much to do with the primary business activity of the company, such as investment securities or rental property.

See Chapter 3 for instructions on how to adjust a balance sheet to reflect "economic value" instead of book value. The value shown on the company's balance sheet is known as "book value". It's arrived at by subtracting tax depreciation from its original cost. Obviously, that figure can be significantly different from the real economic value of the asset. A very valuable piece of property could have a book value of zero. What we want here is "market value": the price at which something is likely to change hands in an arm's length transaction between a willing buyer and a willing seller, neither being under any particular compulsion to act, and each having full knowledge of all material facts. Still, in practice we use different measures for different assets:

- For Inventory use "cost"
- For Real Estate, use "market value"
- For Equipment, Fixtures and Vehicles, use liquidation value or replacement value.
- For cash, leasehold improvements, transferable pre-paid expenses, and current accounts receivable, use book value

The most reliable way to find the market value of assets is to have them professionally appraised.

There are specialized appraisal firms that deal only with business assets. Don't use an appraisal prepared for insurance purposes, because it's probably out of date, and it's probably based on "replacement value" (the cost to replace each asset from scratch).

Appraisals require physical inspection of the property so that its condition and existence can be verified. That's one reason they don't come cheap, but they are very important and can be well worth the cost. Buyers will usually arrange for an asset appraisal as a prerequisite to closing the deal, in order to verify that the company is at least worth a certain amount, and because their lenders will require it eventually anyway. Owners who are planning to sell should consider doing an asset appraisal ahead of time so they know what they're selling.

Who should take responsibility for arranging the appraisal - buyer, or seller, or lender? It generally falls on the party who initiated the deal. But keep in mind that appraisers exercise a certain amount of personal discretion when they estimate value, and many suspect that the appraiser subconsciously exercises that judgment in favor of the party who's paying his bill. For instance, lenders prefer more conservative figures, and to make sure that any subjectivity is exercised in their favor, they usually insist on hiring the appraiser and paying him directly. However, an appraiser is supposed to be impartial, and most probably are.

All of the following should be covered in an asset appraisal: land, buildings, inventory (raw materials, work in process, finished product, packaging materials), furnishings & fixtures, machinery & equipment, vehicles, and any other fixed assets necessary to run the business. Things like accounts receivable, notes receivable, and intangible assets are not tangible operating assets, so they are excluded. Note: Chapter 3 gives some short-cuts that are sometimes used to make rough-estimates on the value of assets, but those are no substitute for formal appraisal methods so you take your chances if you use them.

2. *Project the amount of Working Capital needed to run the firm properly. Add that figure to the total economic value of the tangible assets.*

This will probably be different from the amount of working capital now used by the company. You can estimate the current adequacy of working capital by comparing the company's "current ratio" to the industry average. You can get the industry average from your accountant or from reference sources at your library (look for books on key financial ratios for private companies, published by Prentice Hall or Robert Morris Associates.)

To help put this in focus, let's refresh our memory on what "working capital" is. In order to produce a return from a group of tangible assets, the business also needs some money to run the day-to-day operations. That's working capital. It pays the salaries and bills, but it's more than just cash. It includes accounts receivable and inventory that will soon be converted into cash, so that the cycle can be repeated. Working Capital is defined as:

Current Assets: Inventory
                    Accounts Receivable
                    Cash Reserve
                    Pre-paid Expenses
        (minus)

Current Liabilities, such as Accounts
        Receivable

So, when a company is purchased, the new owners receive part of the working capital from the seller in the form of inventory, accounts receivable, and pre-paid expenses, but they must come up with the rest themselves.

3. *Determine the bare-minimum return an investor would probably demand for investing in the tangible assets and working capital of this company.*

One popular benchmark is the cost of borrowing those funds. For that perspective, the commercial lender is an investor whose lending rates reflect the minimum acceptable rate of return. However, lenders assume less risk than true investors, and their rates reflect that. That's because they finance the safest portion of the investment - they only loan a portion of the most conservative estimate of value. They rarely finance "cash flow", intangibles, or other speculative aspects of the deal. Yet they demand recourse to all of the assets as loan security. If working capital is financed, it's secured with accounts receivable, which are relatively liquid. So it might be misleading to refer to lending rates as the minimum rate of return required by investors.

Some versions of this method apply different rates to the fixed assets than to the net working capital. For instance, they might apply a 15% rate of return to the investment in fixed assets, and a 10% rate of return to the working capital. However, the approach in Chapter 6 will give you a single rate for the combined investment in both fixed assets and working capital. You decide.

4. *Add the value of the fixed operating assets (from Step 1) to the net working capital (from Step 2), and multiply the total by the rate of return from Step 3. The result is the investor's "basic return".*

5. Prepare an Adjusted Income Statement. See Chapter 3 for instructions.

Make sure you explain your adjustments in notes attached to the valuation so others will know what you've done. If annual sales have fluctuation a lot, use a weighted average from the past five years. Don't use a pro forma statement that a higher level of sales in the future.

6a. Next we want to substitute real economic depreciation in place of the artificial figure that has been used for tax purposes.

So, add back the depreciation expense to the adjusted statement. Next, try to estimate the real annual decrease in the value of the company's tangible operating assets, and subtract that in its place. The easiest way is to divide the total economic value of those assets by their average remaining useful life. For example, if you think the company's assets have a current resale value of $220,000, and they will wear out in 5 years, at which point you can sell them for $20,000 scrap value, then you should deduct $40,000 for real annual "economic depreciation".

6b. Next add back the interest expenses on the adjusted statement.

7. Subtract the result of Step 4 from the result of the last step. This gives you the company's "excess earnings" - the earnings attributable to goodwill and other intangible assets, as opposed to earnings produced by the fixed assets.

Many businesses don't produce Excess Earnings. In that case, the business is worth the market value of its tangible (fixed) assets plus current assets minus liabilities. Don't try to attribute significant value to trademarks, customer lists, or other intangibles if there aren't any excess earnings.

In practice, most valuators find that the intangibles of small companies have only nominal value, so they exclude them unless they can readily be converted to cash (for example, accounts receivable).

If the figure for Excess Earnings is negative, then we assume that the value of the company's assets is greater than its value as a going business.

8. Divide Excess Earnings by a "Capitalization Rate" that reflects the risk and attractiveness of an investment in that company (the same rate you used in Step 3). The result is the value of the excess earnings, commonly referred to as "goodwill value".

9. Add the following together:

The total value of the
tangible fixed assets (from Step 1)
 PLUS
The total value of "current
assets" to be transferred.
 MINUS
Any liabilities
 PLUS
The excess earnings
calculated in Step 8

RESULT = The value of the company.

Finally: Any liabilities to be assumed by the purchaser must be deducted from the final value.

These include accounts payable, accrued liabilities, current liabilities, long-term debt, accumulated unpaid stock dividends, obligations on employee benefit plans, and any other obligations. If ownership of the business is transferred by a purchase of stock, all of the company's liabilities will normally go to the new owner, so those amounts must be deducted from value. Make sure you look into the possibility of unrecorded liabilities and potential liabilities that have not yet surfaced.

Alternative Approach:

Step 1 - Look at income statements for the past five years to see if earnings are rising, falling, or fluctuating. If there is an upward trend, find the weighted average* of the pre-tax operating income. If the trend is stable or downward, refer only to the last year.

Add back any interest expenses shown on the statement, and then adjust the depreciation to what it would be after an asset acquisition. (See last chapter for details for how to adjust depreciation.)

Step 2 - Next, go to the balance sheet. Look at Operating Assets (the tangible fixed assets necessary to run the business) and estimate their current market value. Multiply this value by the rate of return you would demand from an investment in those assets. Make sure you *multiply* by that percentage - don't "capitalize" by it (i.e., don't divide by the percentage).

Step 3 - Subtract the return on assets (Step 2) from the pre-tax operating income (Step 1). The result is "Excess Earnings".

Step 4 - Divide this by a capitalization rate that reflects the expected risk and return from an investment in this company. This gives you the "Value of the Excess Earnings".

Step 5 - Add the value of the Excess Earnings (Step 4) to the current market value of the tangible operating assets. The result is the value of the business.

This version seems more streamlined, but it's very similar to the first way.

Summary of the Excess Earnings Method

Total Market Value of Tangible Assets: (Step 1)
  Land and building
  Inventory
  Equipment & machinery
  Vehicles
  Furnishings & fixtures

PLUS
  Additional Working Capital Needed to run the business (Step 2)

= Total amount to be financed

  X minimum % return demanded from that investment (Step 3)

= Minimum return on fixed assets (Step 4)

Then,
  Net Operating Income Before Tax (from adjusted income statement) (Steps 5-6b)
MINUS
  Minimum return on fixed assets (Step 4, above)

= Excess Earnings (Step 7)

  (divided by) Capitalization Rate (Step 8)

= Value of the Excess Earnings

  (plus)   Total value of Tangible Fixed Operating Assets (from Step 1)

  (plus)   Value of any Current Assets that would be transferred to a new owner

  (minus)   Any liabilities to be assumed by the buyer (Step 9)

= Total Value of the business

Chapter 12

The Internal Revenue Service Approach to Valuation

When a business is sold, there's usually some taxable profit to the seller because of the increase in value during the ownership period. If the buyer and seller aren't related in some way, we can usually assume that negotiation has been conducted at "arm's length", so there's little reason to question the validity of the reported price. In that case, we assume that the seller has tried to get the highest possible price, which is reported in due course to the tax authorities.

In other situations the IRS might question whether the company has been transferred for the full amount of its value. One red flag is when the business is transferred between parents and offspring. Most of these transactions take advantage of the gift tax laws, which allow some tax exemptions by utilizing "annual gifting" programs. But let's say you try to base the underlying value of the company on book value, despite the fact that the company is extremely profitable. Book value might have little validity in that case, so the IRS could successfully challenge your gift tax return.

Similarly, if the owner dies before the company has been completely transferred, estate taxes will come into play. A technique known as an "estate freeze" has been used in the past to help reduce taxes, but it has come under increased regulation lately.

Another type of transfer that is subject to a high level of IRS scrutiny is the Employee Stock Ownership Plan (ESOP). Employees can use this vehicle to buy the company from its owners on a tax-deferred basis. Each ESOP must be approved by the IRS, including an initial appraisal to make sure the company is being sold at its fair market value.

The IRS may challenge you on all sorts of issues. These include the allocation of purchase price, depreciation deductions, recapture of tax benefits,  buy-sell agreements, lapsing rights, retained interests, transfers in trust, the impact of leverage, and so on. For this reason, we feel that whenever there is a significant tax implication, it would be wise to include the IRS method in your study and make sure you follow the rules laid out in the tax code. Life is short, and any minor monetary advantage someone might possibly gain by short-cutting the tax code would never be worth the hassle of an IRS challenge and the potential repercussions involved. If you have a honest, reasonable argument for using an certain tax treatment, and it happens to save you some money, that's different.

The Internal Revenue Service has its own approach to the valuation of a business. In fact, to some extent, many of the other valuation methods are derived from IRS and Tax Court rulings. If you are involved in any dispute involving gift tax, estate tax, or the like, then understanding the IRS viewpoint will be essential to its resolution.

Where taxes are in issue, a well-prepared and thoroughly documented valuation report based on other methods will often be accepted by the Service as indicative of value, but its weight in resolving the situation is strengthened considerably when the IRS method is also included. Despite wide general acceptance of the other valuation methods, there's a good chance that the IRS approach will be deferred to in these situations. In addition, keep in mind that the price you get with the IRS method might be lower, which would actually save you some taxes.

 Remember that tax laws change constantly, so *always consult your accountant* when tax matters are involved.

Brief Description of the Method:

The Treasury Department first promulgated its valuation formula with ARM 34 and 68 (Appeal and Review Memorandums). Since then, its policy has been more clearly set forth in a series of Revenue Rulings and Revenue Procedures. Those are reproduced in the Appendix, but newer or more obscure ones may apply to your particular case, so make sure you do additional research. The following provide the basic framework for the IRS approach:

ARM 34 and 68 - Discusses the formula for valuing goodwill (quoted in Rev. Rul. 65-192).

Rev. Rul. 65-192 - "The general approach, methods and factors outlined in Revenue Ruling 59-60,... are equally applicable for income and other tax purposes."

Rev. Rul. 59-60 - Its purpose is "to outline and review in general the approach, methods, and factors to be considered in valuing the shares of the capital stock of closely held corporations for estate and gift tax purposes."

Rev. Procedure 66-49 - Deals with how to report valuations to the Internal Revenue Service.

Rev. Rul. 68-609 - Discusses return on tangible assets and capitalization rates for intangibles, when the IRS income approach is used. (Clarifies and expands on ARM 34.)

Rev. Procedure 77-12 - Describes the method for allocating a lump-sum purchase price to inventories.

Various sections of the current tax code will also be relevant to your transaction, including (but not limited to) sections 2700 through 2704. Some new valuation rules have recently been included in Chapter 14 of the Internal Revenue Code as well.

Always read the entire ruling, code section, or regulation, research more recent developments, and consult your accountant or tax attorney. Tax rules change constantly!

The tax law also evolves in response to court decisions, so make sure you review the Recent Developments chapter on that subject!

ઠ૦૦૨

The IRS method adds the value of the Net Tangible Assets to the capitalized Value of the Excess Earnings ("goodwill"). A large number of estate tax issues revolve around the value of goodwill, so regard that subject carefully.

Steps to the IRS Income (Excess Earnings) Approach: (Summarized)

1- Using balance sheets for the last five years, determine the *average* value of the Net Tangible Assets during that period. (Net Tangible Assets = Total Assets (minus) Identifiable Intangible Assets (minus) Liabilities). Averages may be weighted* to consider trends.

2- Determine the company's Return on the Net Tangible Assets by multiplying the figure from Step 1 by a percentage that corresponds to the normal rate of return on assets for that particular industry. Use a lower rate if your business has attributes that give it less risk than average.

3- Determine the average Net Profit Before-Tax from the last five years.

4- Subtract the figure from Step 3 from the figure in Step 2. The result is the company's Excess Earnings (earnings in excess of what a "typical company" would produce from those tangible assets).

5- Capitalize* the Excess Earnings from Step 4 at an appropriate percentage rate. (In other words, divide Excess Earnings by that percentage.) Consult the Revenue Rulings and Chapter 5 of this book for guidance on selecting an appropriate capitalization rate. The result is the value of the "Goodwill" of the business. (You can also think of this as the value of the intangible assets.)

6- Add the result in Step 5 to the value of the Net Tangible Assets determined in Step 1. The result is the value of the business.

This is just a summary of the usual procedure. Make sure you consult the full text of these and more recent Revenue Rulings and Revenue Procedures whenever they apply to your case.

The ones referenced here are reproduced in the Appendix.

ઠ૦૦૨

Revenue Ruling 59-60 deals with some factors that have a strong bearing on value, including the company's earning capacity, the outlook for that industry in general, and the financial history of the business. The author's personal opinion is that this ruling places importance on factors that aren't relevant or reliable in most cases, including book value of the stock and the stock prices of publicly-held companies in the same business.

In earlier chapters (particularly Chapters 6 and 7) it was explained that book value can be a very misleading indicator. We also don't like methods that base value on the sale price of other companies, since the task of gathering the data, and assessing, quantifying, and implementing appropriate adjustments to the price of each company is so cumbersome and subjective that the results ultimately become convoluted and unreliable. However, the IRS disagrees. Therefore, when taxes are in issue, it's a good idea to use the comparable sales method. Then, if you think the results are dubious, argue that point accordingly. Chapter 16 should help you in that regard.

If less than all of the stock is being transferred, an adjustment for "minority discount" or "control premium" may be in order. Consult Chapter 21 for more advice on those issues.

Again, IRS Rulings take the position that the stock prices of publicly-held companies are relevant indicators of value. The Price-Earnings Method is derived from the Comparable Sales Method, but that approach has its weaknesses too. Nonetheless, it would be good to put some thoughtful effort into comparing the performance of your business to that of public companies in published financial reports. Fortunately, the IRS does acknowledge that no single approach is determinative in reaching a value conclusion.

Special Considerations in Estate Tax Valuations:

If the success of the business is due to the efforts or talent of someone who is leaving after the acquisition, then the company will probably be worth a lot less once they are gone. Make sure you point that out, and distinguish it from a company with a broad management team, where responsibilities are distributed among a number of well-trained people.

It has been stated elsewhere in this book that valuations conducted in preparation for the sale of a company often anticipate future profits to some degree, but this author feels that practice is not appropriate. This goes for estate tax valuations as well. Valuation should never be based on conjecture concerning something that has not yet occurred. In some ways valuation takes the future into consideration - for instance, in the selection of capitalization rates, or in the adjustment of historical income statements to show how expenses might look under different ownership. But in general, valuation should be based on the company's present situation, as indicated by its most recent past, and not on expectations of better results in the future.

ಬೋಲ

Once again, remember that *all* transactions can have important tax consequences, so make sure a qualified tax professional reviews your assumptions before you rely on them.

Chapter 13

The Ability to Pay Method

This is one method that all buyers should probably use. It's based on the idea that the company's own cash flow should be able to pay for its acquisition over a reasonable length of time, with a healthy margin left over for safety.

Like the Discounted Cash Flow Method, this technique requires you to estimate a ball-park purchase price before you can actually do the calculations - so you should probably use any other applicable methods first, in order to come up with a reasonable opening estimate.

If the company can't pay for itself over a reasonable length of time, then it's considered a bad investment, no matter how low the price may seem.

This method is designed to produce a price that makes the deal is feasible when financed in the conventional manner. In that regard, it is very similar to the Discounted Cash Flow Method. If more buyers would use it as soon as they get a sense for the seller's minimum price, they could avoid wasting time on deals that won't work out.

Sellers should also use this method, in order to verify whether their asking price is consistent with what most buyers will be able to pay. It's just a matter of facing up to the fact that most acquisitions require substantial borrowing. Companies are rarely purchased with cash.

That may seem absurd, but it's exactly what you have to do. You actually "back into" your value by taking an educated guess, then you finish the rest of the steps to see if they verify that figure. If they don't, then you adjust the initial assumed price up or down, according to how far off you were, and then try the calculation again. You may have to do this several times to narrow the gap sufficiently. It's actually easy if you use spreadsheet software to do your calculations. Even if you do it manually, it's not hard to get to get reasonably close.

For example, let's say you assumed a price of $4,000,000, yet your end result is a value of $6,000,000. Obviously, you guessed too low - so try it again, setting the assumed price somewhere in between - at say, $5,000,000. You can usually narrow it down after a couple of tries.

This method is ideal for someone who is buying a business solely for its income. It's essential for any buyer who expects the company to be stand on its own financially. It also makes sense for situations where there isn't any special synergy between the subject company and some other business owned by the buyer.

This method "backs into" the price. First, you figure out how much after-tax cash flow is available for debt payments. You reserve 20% to 50% of this as a safety cushion, and the rest is available for loan payments. Then you determine how large a loan this payment corresponds to, and that gives you the price.

If you are wondering what we mean by corporate synergy, it refers to special advantages that result from owning a company and combining it with existing operations. The concepts of vertical and horizontal "integration" are based on the creation of synergy. Those benefits can include capturing a supplier, gaining new distribution channels, or tying down needed support services for other operations. However, adding more to the product line, providing additional sales staff (they'll probably be combined anyway), or adding production capacity doesn't normally produce the kind of advantage that justifies a higher price. You can't assume synergy will result if you don't know who your buyer is, so you can't let that possibility affect the valuation you do for the seller. Market value is supposed to reflect the most likely price, not the long-shot.

The reason for the cushion is to make sure the company can always safely make its loan payments, and to insure a reasonable profit from the business. If the buyer takes on a load of debt with no net return left over in the end, then the investment has very limited value. Don't depend on growth predictions to provide the upside - that's just speculation. Base it on what's happening now, and make sure there's an adequate return for all the time, effort, and financial risk.

Assumptions you can make:

•   Most active acquirers believe a business should pay for itself over 8 to 10 years, as long as there is an adequate investment return during that period. Lenders also seem to like 10 years as a loan term.

•   For the interest rate, use the prime rate plus 2 to 4 points, depending on how much risk is associated with the business.

•   Assume that the buyer will be able to borrow about 80% of the purchase price (75% to 85% is probably average), but loan terms fluctuate all the time so you should get an update on what's being offered these days.

Steps to this method:

1. Predict Net Sales for each of the next ten years (or whatever period you've decided to use) and find the average.

If you project an increase in sales or profits: Buyers like to speculate on the possibility of higher sales and earnings when they evaluate a company, but those figures should not be used for the valuation. Lenders won't regard them seriously, even though they want to see that you have improvements in mind. It might be feasible to increase profits by instituting tighter financial controls and cutting costs, but it's just too speculative to rely on.

The company must stand on its own as it is now, and the deal should be structured so that post-acquisition improvements are not essential to its success. The company is assumed to be operating at maximum efficiency, especially if current management is staying. So stick with present sales volume, increased at most by a conservative rate of inflation each year (3% to 4%). If sales have fluctuated a lot in recent years, then use a "weighted average"* of annual sales for the last five years.

Is there anytime you are justified in assuming higher sales? Since a company is valued "as is" (not prospectively) you really

aren't supposed to do that. However, some people might argue that it's permissible if the historic sales trend has been consistently upward for a significant number of years, at a steady and predictable rate. There can't be any known instabilities in the market or in customer demand. The market must be immune to changes in economic conditions demographic patterns, and other uncontrolables. The product or service can't be subject to rapid change, due to variable consumer tastes or the potential for developing better technology. This is quite a tall order, and very few companies qualify. That doesn't mean improvements won't occur. Why would anyone buy the company otherwise? But that's something you predict for your own purposes. The chapter on Proforma Cash Flow Analysis treats that subject separately.

2. Determine the Operating Profit* before tax.

• We use the net operating profit from the last full year for which we have financial statements. Again, be careful about trying to tighten up the operating expenses. That's really speculative. Many acquisitions premised on belt-tightening have failed when it later turned out that the company couldn't operate on such a lean diet. In addition, if a buyer acknowledges the feasibility of certain improvements, the seller might try to use that to justify a higher price. But you can't run a business on a shoestring. The changes that bring about improvements are more likely to cost money than to arise from cost-cutting.

• Sellers can adjust expenses to eliminate excess salary and perks, but expect plenty of resistance on that issue.. Adjusted Income Statements are treated more thoroughly in Chapter 3.

• Determine the percentage of pre-tax operating profit to net sales. (Net Operating Profit divided by Net Sales.) Then multiply the sales figure from Step 1 by this percentage. That will give you the average annual amount of net operating income that can be expected during the period you have selected.

If Operating Income has fluctuated a lot over the past, then calculate these percentages separately for each of the past five years and use the weighted average*. Next, find the weighted average of Net Sales from those same years. Finally, multiply the average percentage times the average Net Sales, and use that as your Net Operating Profit. See the Glossary for instructions on how to calculate a weighted average*.

3. Calculate Net Operating Profit After Tax.

Now you have to figure out your tax deductible expenses for those future years, including interest and depreciation. Subtract those from the Operating Income determined in Step 1 to get the net taxable income for each year, then apply the corporate income tax rate to the result. That will give you the after-tax net operating income.

a- To determine your interest deduction, you first have to assume a ball-park purchase price. Having familiarized yourself with today's corporate lending terms, you should know what loan amount will be offered. For an example, let's assume that your loan will be 80% of the purchase price, for a 10 year term, with interest at prime rate plus 3 percent. That means the remaining cash must come from the buyer's pocket or from outside investors. We'll assume that outside investors will put up the cash in exchange for Preferred Stock*, on which they will receive an annual return of prime rate plus 4% to 6%. That's considered a "preferred dividend", so it should be included in the amount available for loan payments.

To find the annual loan interest, you can either calculate each year separately, or just use the average annual amount over the ten year period. To find the latter, add up all the loan payments for the ten year term, and subtract the principal amount of those loans. That gives you the total amount of interest. Divide by 10 to get the average annual amount. Don't forget to include "interest only" loans, such as Lines Of Credit. Don't add any preferred dividends because those are a distribution of earnings, not interest, so they aren't deductible for tax purposes. (Take that into consideration when you determine how to capitalize the company.)

Anticipate Additional Expenses!

- On top of the basic purchase price, buyers should consider their acquisition expenses.

- In addition, a new facility might be needed if a lease is lost.

- Inventory that has been allowed to deplete before settlement will also have to be replenished, and there will be other new working capital needs as well.

- It might also be prudent to build up the sales and marketing program after the acquisition because competitors will probably take a run at your customers, trying to take advantage of all your distractions during the transition period.

All of these items should be included in the borrowing requirements, which may involve several different types of loans. Step 4 of Chapter 10 discusses loan structure in more detail. The single-loan approach is often best, but it may be too simple for your situation.

b- Next, figure out how much Depreciation* can be deducted. Depreciation is already reflected on the income statement as an operating expense. However, if the company is transferred by way of a sale of assets, then the amount of depreciation will change. A new corporation will be set up to purchase those assets and carry on the business. The total purchase price will be allocated among those assets, and that will become the basis for the new depreciation schedule.

Most privately-held companies are sold as a purchase of assets, because that enables the buyer to increase depreciation, which increases cash flow. The existing corporation has already depreciated the original cost of those assets, so that's probably all used up by now. An asset purchase allows you to beef them up again, which increases cash flow so there's more cash to make loan payments with. There are a few disadvantages for the seller in an asset deal, but those are usually offset by the fact that it enables the buyer to pay a higher price.

Formerly, when a company was sold by transferring ownership of its *stock*, the buyer had to retain the old depreciation schedule, even if it was depleted. However, the present tax code might allow you to step-up the depreciable tax basis anyway, so check out the current law (start with Section 338) to see if you are now allowed to do that. See your accountant for details.

To adjust depreciation, take the ball-park purchase price from Step 3a and divvy it up among the various assets. (See "Allocation of Purchase Price" in the Glossary). Remember that any allocation to "goodwill" is usually small or non-existent because it cannot be depreciated. Make sure you base the new depreciation schedule on the current income tax law.

Once you figure out the annual depreciation for each class of assets, add it up. Now substituting that figure for the amount of depreciation taken in the past. The result should be the Taxable Operating Income.

c- Subtract Corporate Income Taxes (Federal and State): Use the corporate income tax rates. Get them from your accountant, the IRS and state tax authorities, or an up-to-date tax manual.

d- If a federal Investment Tax Credit is available under the current tax law, add that amount back. Congress has fluctuated on the availability of this credit, so it might be available when you are reading this. Step 6 of Chapter 10 discusses it in more detail.

e- At this point, you have the average Net Operating Income After Tax for those future years.

4. Add back the Interest and the Depreciation (deducted earlier in Step 3) to get Net Cash Flow After Tax.

Depreciation is added back because it's a non-cash operating expense. In other words, it's deducted on the income statement, but you don't really shell out money to pay it. (You did that up front when you first bought the assets, but weren't allowed to deduct the entire amount in that year.) This will increase cash flow.

The interest is added back because in a later step you're going to deduct the *total* amount of debt-service, including both principal and interest. This insures that you don't subtract it twice.

5. From the amount in step 4 (Net Cash Flow After Tax), deduct the Capital Expenditures you expect each year during that period.

Find out what the company has spent on capital expenditures in the past. Any expense you can't write off *entirely* in the year it's paid is usually considered a "capital expenditure".

New equipment and improvements to real estate are the most obvious examples.

Watch out for deferred capital expenditures that may have accumulated. That includes needed investments in plant, repairs, improvements, or equipment that should have been made but weren't. Dealing with these can really jack up your expenses during the first few years after the acquisition. The same will happen if rapidly developing technologies require you to make an investment in new processes or equipment just to remain competitive. If the company hasn't kept up with these things, then you better add their cost to your capital expenditures for the first couple of years.

If you plan to use an average of the company's capital expenditures for the past several years, remember to increase it by a factor for inflation (4% to 6%) every year into the projected period.

Add up the anticipated capital expenditures for each year, and then determine the average. If deferred items can't wait, then those should be added to the average for the first couple of years. Subtract the result from Net Cash Flow After Tax (step 4). This will give you Net Cash Flow Before Debt Service.

6. Subtract an appropriate Cash Flow Safety Cushion from Net Cash Flow Before Debt Service.

Investors and lenders will demand a safety margin of 20 to 50 percent, depending how much risk they perceive in the deal. As a result, only 50 to 80 percent of the cash flow is really available for debt payments. Try to be objective and conservative in determining the required cushion.

Deduct the cushion from the cash flow, and divide the result by 12 to give the amount available for monthly loan payments.

7. Figure out the loan amount corresponding to that monthly payment.

- For this example, we assume a ten-year loan term and an interest rate of prime plus 2 or 3 points, depending on the risk involved in the deal.
- For simplicity, we are assuming that a single term-loan will be used to finance the entire purchase price, even though several different types of loans (or "layers" of financing) may actually be used.
- You should also figure on a working capital loan (revolving line of credit) so you have some cash to operate the company.
- We assume the monthly interest payments on that line of credit will also be paid out of the cash flow. (With most line of credit loans, you only have to pay the accrued interest on the debt. You can repay the principal if you have excess earnings. This assumes your lender has confidence in the underlying security for the loan and the reliability of the borrower.)
- Preferred stock dividends and payments on unsecured debt must also be paid out of the cash flow, so include those too.

Note: Traditional "loan tables" can be used to determine the "loan amount" corresponding to the available monthly payment, but it's easier to use a financial calculator with a loan amortization function. Texas Instruments and Hewlett-Packard make some nice models, and they also perform the present value calculations required in the other methods.

8. Step 7 gave you the loan size the cash flow can support, and hopefully your lenders will extend that much. From this, you can figure out the total purchase price, based on the lenders loan-to-value ratio.

For instance, if you can borrow 80% of the entire purchase price, then you would divide the amount calculated in step 7 by .80 to get the total price.

ගාය

Caution: This method is very imprecise, and it should not be used to validate the company's ability to meet debt payments or other obligations. For that, a year-by-year analysis of cash flow should be done in conjunction with the advice of qualified accountants. See Chapter 14 in that regard.

Summary of Ability to Pay Method:

Average annual Net Sales expected during the projection period (Step 1)

X   Operating Profit Percentage (Step 2)

=   average annual Net Operating Profit expected during the period

(plus)   interest deduction used on adjusted statement

(minus)   average annual Interest Expense expected (Step 3a)

(plus)   Depreciation deduction used on adjusted statement

(minus)   future Depreciation expected (in the case of an asset deal (Step 3b)

=   Taxable Net Profit

(minus)   projected Income Taxes (Step 3c)

=   average Net Operating Profit After Tax expected during the projected period

(plus)   Depreciation (Step 4)

(plus)   Interest deducted above in Step 3a (Step 4)

=   Net Cash Flow After Tax

(minus) Average Annual Capital Expenditures (Step 5)

=   Net Cash Flow Before Debt Service

(minus)   20% to 50% Safety Cushion (Step 6)

=   Net Cash Flow Available for Debt Service

Then, divide this amount by 12 to give the available monthly loan payment, and determine the loan amount it will support.

Chapter 14

Can the Acquisition Pay for Itself?
(Proforma Cash Flow Analysis)

This chapter is an adjunct to the last chapter. The Ability To Pay Method arrives at a company's value by combining information about its past history with certain assumptions about its future ownership. This chapter goes one step beyond that.

Here, we are trying to help a particular buyer figure out if the acquisition will really work, in light of the way it will be financed and things that will be done to improve it. It involves a lot of speculative financial projections that really aren't legitimate for valuing the business. This chapter deals with feasibility as a separate matter.

Most buyers have to finance their acquisitions with borrowed money, and they expect the company's' cash flow to provide the monthly payments.

No matter what the valuation formulas tells you, if the company's cash flow after expenses isn't adequate to make the acquisition loan payments, then the price is too high.

This isn't just a concern for buyers. Sellers need to consider it too, because almost every potential buyer will have to look at the acquisition this way. Very few buyers are able or willing to finance a purchase with cash out of their pocket. Even if they *are* able, they are rarely willing, unless there's some extraordinary benefit from owning that company.

In valuation, we only look at how the company is performing now. But a Proforma is an attempt to base an investment decision on how the buyer thinks the company might perform after certain post-acquisition changes are made.

We can't base *valuation* on better performance in the future, because that would give the seller credit for improvements made by the buyer. This kind of futuristic analysis is only for buyers who are confident about what they can do, and who are able to bear some risk. Buyers who are more conservative, less certain, or less able to tolerate loss should avoid this kind of speculation. But both types of purchaser should verify all assumptions carefully, get lots of outside advice, and test their final conclusions before they "go at risk" on the deal.

The first step is to prepare a "pro forma" income statement and balance sheet. This is similar to the "adjusted" income statement discussed in Chapter 3, except that it also anticipates the financial effect of changes the buyer plans to make after the acquisition.*

Those predictions can be difficult to make, and with so much on the line (particularly for lenders and cash investors), every assumption should be backed up. This is no place for wishful thinking and guesswork. Translating improvements into dollars without undue speculation isn't easy. It demands a lot of research, and it's always wise to seek input from advisors who have experience in that particular type of business. They can red flag any faulty assumptions and miscalculations. If they feel your projections are realistic, they might offer an opinion letter to that effect, which will add credibility to the proposals you make to lenders and investors.

Preparing the pro forma will require lots of detailed consultation with management in order to determine places where costs can be cut, where costs will increase, how new efficiencies can be created, and where revenues may be improved. The pro forma should be quite detailed, especially in the expense categories. All deviations from present performance should be explained in the "notes" to the statement. Once again, this is not a time for optimistic speculation. As it turns out, your pro forma may not differ much from the normal adjusted statement. You may even conclude that things have to get a lot worse before they get better.

Cash flow pro formas usually project financial results for about ten years into the future. Each number will change every year - so don't just plug in the same assumptions year-after-year. You have to detail the specific changes and results for each year. You should summarize these results in spreadsheet form so they will be easy to compare from year to year.

After you have prepared your pro forma statements for each year, refer to Chapter 10 to prepare your cash flow analysis. Do each year separately, following the instructions there through Step 12, and using the figures from your pro forma instead of from an adjusted statement. At the end, you'll have a Pro Forma Cash Flow Analysis, in a format corresponding to the "Summary" at the end of Chapter 10. This is different from the format used by most accountants, but it will give you similar results.

This analysis requires you to make assumptions about the purchase price and the loans you'll take out to finance the deal. See Chapter 10 for guidance on how the deal might be financed. Also try to get current input from some real lenders.

In order to do a proforma, you need to assume a purchase price. If you've gotten this far in the book, you probably have the results from at least one valuation method, and you probably know what kind of price the seller has in mind. Hopefully, you have already used the Ability To Pay Method. At this point, you might just be checking to make sure the company's income will support the anticipated price.

Every year of your projections should include a cash flow safety cushion of 20% to 50% *after* loan payments.

Remember: Just because the cash flow seems adequate to service a certain amount of debt, that doesn't mean the company will qualify for a loan of that size. There are a lot of other requirements - including an adequate amount of collateral (loan security) in the form of resalable company assets. These days, it's unusual for a lender to loan more than a predetermined percentage of the "secured loan" value of the assets. Very few lenders will extend funds purely on the strength of cash flow, even when its proven by past perfomance.

For example, let's say you want to purchase a business, and to accomplish your plan and produce the cash flow predicted on the pro forma, you need $1 million in loans for the purchase price, the working capital, and new equipment. Your projections show that the company will produce enough income to safely make the payments. But there's only $800,000 in securable assets - so unless you can find a lender willing to advance you more than 75% of the secured loan value, then you won't get more than $600,000 in loans. In that deal, you'll have to come up with the remaining $400,000 in cash by yourself.

In the interest of safety, lenders seldom loan more than 80% of the purchase price or 80% of the value of the securable assets, whichever is lower. Many times it's substantially less. One reason is to make sure they'll get their money back if the borrower defaults and end up foreclosing on the assets. If the value of those assets drops, or if they overestimate their worth up front, then they come up short after the auction. Another reason they limit the loan amount is to make sure the buyers will have lots of their own cash at stake - which offers increased assurance that they'll try harder to make the business work.

Refer to Chapter 18 (on secured loan value) to figure out how much can actually be borrowed.

Chapter 15

Popular Methods to Avoid

There are several valuation methods in common use that have serious drawbacks:

1. Replacement Cost Method
2. Comparable Sales Method
3. Price/Earnings Ratio Method
4. Rule-of-Thumb Pricing Methods for small businesses

Each is discussed below. We give you the basic procedure, but we also tell you why we don't like them. If you've heard of these techniques and are tempted to use them, go ahead and read on. Otherwise you can skip the rest of this chapter.

Exception in the case of tax disputes:

Despite our objections, if you are doing a valuation for purposes related to taxation, you may want to include the Comparable Sales and Price/Earnings Methods in your analysis. We think these methods are difficult to carry out in a reliable way, but the IRS and the Tax Court supports their use, so you should probably use them if you're involved in a dispute over taxes. You should also refer to Chapter 12 regarding the IRS approach to valuation.

The Replacement Cost Method:

This approach is rarely used for anything other than insurance claims, where the property has been insured at "replacement value". It would have to reflect the value of recreating that *entire business* in terms of its tangible assets. That would not normally include any intangible assets and it would not take into account the earning power of the business. Therefore, it overstates market value in some ways and understates value in other ways. The *net* result could be over or under. In most cases it would not be realistic to duplicate a business in this way, except for a brand-new "start up" that hasn't developed much business yet.

Comparable Sales Method:

This method uses the average purchase price of similar companies that have recently been sold. What could be a more reliable indicator of "market value" than the actual sale price of similar goods? Those recent sale prices are called "comparables", and you should limit your data to companies that are involved the same (or a very similar) line of business. Each price is translated into a "multiple of after tax earnings". In other words, the sale price, divided by the earnings (net operating income) of the company, gives you a number called an "earnings multiplier".

You figure out the multipliers for several recent sales, and average them. Then you can multiply the earnings of your subject company by that number in order to estimate its value. The average multiplier is called the Price/Earnings Ratio.

This is acceptable in theory, but in practice the technique usually proves to be less manageable, unless all of the companies are remarkably similar to begin with. Comparable sales data is great for valuing real estate, but there are lots of complicated adjustments to be made in the case of a business. That procedure is extremely cumbersome and very speculative. It usually gets short-cut, so the results become even more unreliable.

The reason you have to make those adjustments is because no company or sales transaction is truly comparable to another. Businesses that seem similar are always different in many ways. For this method to be reliable, you would have adjust the sale price of *each* business in the sample for *each and every way* it differs from the subject business. You have to compare apples and apples, not apples and oranges. You just can't do that without a lot of speculation.

To help make the point, consider the variety of ways in which companies and transactions differ:

- Physical facilities and location
- Type, amount, and quality of assets
- Operational differences regarding the type and quality of management, policies affecting earnings, existence and terms of labor contracts, and so forth.
- The form and terms of the transaction. (See Chapter 19 for more on how this can affect price.)
- Differences in operating expenses that affect profitability (differing local wage scales, state taxes, local utility rates, etc.)
- Differences in method of purchase price payment. (Cash, stock, notes, earn-outs, installment sale).
- If stock of the purchasing company was

traded for stock of the selling company, you also have to go back and value the buying company in order to know what its stock was worth at that time.
- Differences in the prevailing interest rates at the time of sale, which determines the rates of return used in the valuation, as well as the amount each buyer could finance and thus afford to pay.

You would have to calculate the impact (in dollars) of each of these factors on the sale price of each company in your comparison, and then adjust those prices accordingly. Whew!

 Even if you were up-to-the-task, you'd first have to get your hands on detailed information about each company and each transaction. Problem is, nobody wants to release those facts, particularly in the kind of detail you need. Even if you could locate the data, how would you translate each difference into dollars? Remember, you are trying to adjust the sale price of each company in the sample to show what that price *would* have been if the company was just like your subject company. Otherwise you are comparing apples to oranges. These are complex, difficult, and time consuming calculations to make. And the great subjectivity involved in the process makes the result inherently less reliable.

You also have to do this with a sufficiently *large* sample of companies, so that you end up with an average of many transactions. This is to help smooth out the aberrations you just can't account for. Most of the time, you'll be lucky to find detailed info on more than a couple of deals. Most of the available data is for *publicly-held* companies. Information on privately-held companies is closely guarded and there are no public disclosure rules that require its release.

So why not use the public companies? Well, for one thing, public companies are operated differently than private firms. The objectives of management are different, and they also use different accounting methods. To use the comparable sales method, you would have to somehow conform each public company's income statement to the same accounting methods used by your privately-held company, translating each difference into a dollar impact on the sales price.

Furthermore, ownership interests in a public company are transferred by different methods than a private company. When a publicly-held company is acquired, a control premium is usually paid over-and-above the current trading price of the stock. This reflects the additional value that a majority interest has over a smaller interest. In addition, there are usually big costs attached to the transfer of public stock interests. All of this has a huge impact on the P/E ratio for those deals, so they really don't equate well with private firms.

Despite the disadvantages, it still can be enlightening to check out "comparable sales" if you can find the information. If companies in that industry have been selling at a certain multiple of net income on a consistent basis, that might shed some light on realistic price expectations. However, try to get the details so you can distinguish those transactions from the company you are actually dealing with.

One could take the position that a consistent pattern of sales at a certain multiple is indicative of true market value. However, if the P/E ratios vary all over the place, then this argument is worthless because there's no consistency. You can't just use the average. Regardless, anyone can pick the comparison apart by pointing out significant ways in which each company in the sample is different from the subject firm.

You can't escape the fact that comparables can only serve as value indicators to the extent that the companies and the transactions are truly comparable. Because of that, comparable-based valuations are easy to shoot down.

"Offers" to purchase a company are never reliable indicators of value because they haven't been fully negotiated at arms length. Offers change dramatically while going through the negotiating process that leads to the final acquisition agreement. The price a seller thinks he's getting will suffer adjustments prior to, at, and even after settlement. No one should accept these as valid negotiating ammo.

If you insist . . .

Despite its weakness, you might still want to take a crack at the comparable sales approach. Many argue that it's the most objective method, since in its simplest form it calls for relatively few judgement calls by the appraiser. In theory, the method makes a lot of sense because it bases market value on sales that have actually occurred. What could be more valid than that? But it does cut a lot of corners.

It's vital to adhere to a strict standard for what you consider comparable. You can't just use any "equally desirable substitute company". You'll never find a company that's an exact duplicate, but that doesn't mean you can use comps from different industries, and it doesn't excuse you from having to adjust your figures to account for the individual differences. If, despite the caveats, you still want to try this method, here's how it's usually done:

Step 1 - Gather Recent Comparables.

Locate information on companies in the same line of business that have changed hands during the past year or two. For instance, if you are valuing a company that fabricates metal parts for industrial machinery, you would not use just any old manufacturing company as a comp. You would limit it to metal fabricators. That doesn't mean you have restrict it to companies making exactly the same products, but the closer the better.

Normally, you find the SIC# (Standard Industrial Classification Number) of the business. This is available in the business reference section of most libraries. Then try to limit your search to that classification.

Comparable sale information is not easy to come by. You can buy it from a commercial source, or you can do a lot of digging on your own. Here are some firms that sell the information:

- W.T. Grimm & Co. (Chicago, IL) - Has data on acquisitions in 40 different industry classifications.

- Cambridge Corporation (Ipswich, MA) - Does an annual review summarizing acquisition activity during that period.

- "Merger & Acquisition Sourcebook" (Quality Services Co., Santa Barbara, CA). An annual volume of information on large company acquisitions.

- "Mergers & Acquisitions" (Philadelphia, PA) - Does quarterly summaries of acquisition details and has a data base of several thousand transactions that can be accessed via your computer modem.

- Institute of Business Appraisers (Boynton Beach, FL) Data is available only to members. Seems mostly limited to small businesses (retail shops, restaurants, professional offices, and other service businesses) but the information is intelligently organized and translated.

Another way to find this information is to call lots of business brokers and intermediaries and ask them to share information on the sale of similar companies. This can be a frustrating process, since few will have recently brokered a business like the one you're valuing. Even if they have, they may not be willing to disclose the details. Information about private deals is usually treated as confidential. Besides, people have better things to do than dig through old files for someone they don't know.

Don't use old information. Usually, you limit the search to deals that have occurred within the last two years, but there's some flexibility there. If significant changes in economic or market conditions have occurred, you should be more careful. That can make even one-month old data unreliable. On the other hand, if economic and market conditions have been remarkably stable for the past 5 years, then 4-year old data might be acceptable.

However you get your information, you need an adequate number of comps to constitute a statistically significant sample. Three or four isn't enough. Ten or fifteen might be acceptable, but they must be closely comparable. Keep in mind that when lots of comps are available, you can't kick out the ones you don't like. You are obligated by good faith to include all of them.

You can discard comps only if they are too old, or if the companies are too dissimilar to the subject company.

Step 2 - Choose the "financial ratios" you will use in making your comparison. Then separately calculate these for each company in your sample.

This method compares companies on the basis of their financial ratios. These ratios show mathematical relationships between the sale price and the earnings of the company. The following ratios are typically used:

1- Ratio of stock price to annual net earnings - called the "P/E Ratio".

2- Ratio of selling price to gross sales. Called "Price/Gross Ratio".

3- Ratio of selling price to book value. ("Price/Book Ratio")

Example - If a company has . . .

- gross annual revenue of $5,000,000
- net earnings of $700,000
- and a sale price of $6,500,000

That means . . .

- P/E Ratio = 6.5MM divided by 700,000 = 9.2
- Price/Gross Ratio = 6.5MM divided by 5MM = 1.3

Both figures in the ratio must be determined as-of the same date. In other words, if you are using a P/E Ratio, and you get your earnings figure (net operating income) from a quarterly financial statement dated April 30th, then you have to use the stock price from April 30th, too.

There are other financial ratios in use and some might be meaningful to your situation. You may include them in your analysis if you can find the information needed to calculate them, but good luck on that. Complete financial statements are almost never available.

Alternate method: Divide the market value of the company's total capital (all stock plus all long-term debt) by the company's earnings.

Some versions of this method use the weighted-average* of earnings (before interest, depreciation and taxes) from the last five years. That is a good approach when you are referring to a return on both equity capital and debt.

Step 3 - Find the average (mean) ratio for all companies in your sample.

In other words, if you regard eighteen companies as good comps, then figure out the P/E Ratio for each one, add those together, and divide by eighteen to find the average P/E Ratio.

Step 4 - Look at the range between the highest and the lowest ratios in the sample.

Is there a big spread between them? Or are the ratios in your sample grouped closely together? The narrower the range, the more reliable this method will be. If the ratios are spread out all over the place, then it's harder to make any hard-and-fast conclusions. Consistency implies validity.

Also look at the "median" or mid-point between the high and low ratios. For example, assume your sample gives you the following P/E Ratios:

9.2 13.1 6.8 8.5 8.7 9.4 7.4 9.5

The mean or average is 9.1
The lowest is 6.8
The highest is 13.
The range is 13.1 - 6.8 = 6.3
The median is 10.0

Common sense tells us that if lots of ratios are bunched up in a very small "range", then an average from that group is going to be fairly reliable. On the other hand, if the range is very wide, the results won't mean much because for any given company the ratio could be almost anything. We are looking for a consistent pattern, where the range is fairly narrow.

Our example here has a fairly broad range (6.3). That suggests unreliability. But you will also notice that most of the ratios are clustered closely in the middle of the range. That suggests that the highest and lowest ratios are oddballs - aberrations. It wouldn't be unreasonable to discard them if they are inconsistent with the group as a whole. The range of the remaining cluster of ratios is only 2.0 and that's narrow enough to be regarded as a reliable overall pattern. It makes sense, therefore, to refer to the average of that subgroup (7.5) as a reliable mean. In this case, that would be a better number to use than the overall mean of 9.1.

A more sophisticated way of looking at consistency would be to calculate the "standard deviation" and divide it by the mean to produce the "coefficient of variation". However, unless you are a financial analyst and already understand what that means and how to do it, stick with the approach outlined here.

Step 5 - Pick the most reliable of the ratios, based on your analysis in Step 4.

In other words, if the range of Gross/Price Ratios is narrow, and the range for P/E Ratios is very wide, disregard the P/E Ratio data and base your price on the Gross/Price Ratio data. The ratio with the smallest coefficient of variation is the most reliable.

Step 6 - If Steps 4 and 5 seem to produce consistent data, then go ahead apply the average (mean) ratio to the company you are valuing.

In our example, we have a mean P/E Ratio of 7.5 - so,if the company you are valuing has earnings of $500,000, then:

$$7.5 = \frac{X}{500,000} = Price/Earnings$$

X equals value, and you find it by multiplying 500,000 by 7.5. This gives you a value of $3,750,000 for your subject company.

Remember to use current earnings - from a recently updated income statement - not a forecast of what the company might be doing in the future. The buyer is purchasing the company as it stands now. Don't expect him to pay a price based on earnings that don't exist.

Price/Earnings Ratio Method (Multiple of Earnings Method):

This method is similar to the Comparable Sales Method, but instead of looking to *past* acquisition prices for "comparable" companies to get an average P/E (price/earnings) multiple, it looks at the *current market price* of publicly traded stocks for comparable companies. In other words, instead of using data from private companies, it uses publicly-held companies as "comparables" and their stock exchange price as the "price". The technique suffers from the same limitations as the Comparable Sales Method, plus a few more when applied to a non-public company.

In this method, you try to find publicly-traded companies that are similar to the company you are valuing. For each one, you get their most recently published income statement, and then you look up their closing stock price on the same day. You divide the stock price by the annual "earnings per share" from the income statement. That gives you the Price/Earnings Ratio for that company. You average the P/E Ratios from all the companies in your sample, and use that to calculate the market selling price of your subject company:

$$\text{P/E ratio for the stock of a publicly traded company} = \frac{\text{the stock's current traded price}}{\text{Net Income per share}}$$

Then multiply that P/E ratio times *your* company's net income to get the Market Value of your company

The P/E ratios of public companies are published by the US Census Bureau ("Quarterly Financial Report for Manufacturing, Mining, and Trade Corporations") and by Dunn & Bradstreet. The "price" is the public stock price, and the "earnings" are from the published quarterly results (but check to make sure they are "annualized").

The stock of larger companies tends to trade at higher P/E's than that of smaller companies. That's because, generally speaking, larger companies have proven to be more stable and reliable in their earnings. So a large company with the same "earnings per share" as a smaller company will trade at a higher price. In addition, the stock of a larger company is usually traded at a premium because its more marketable. For that reason, the P/E ratio of a larger publicly-held company must be discounted before you apply it to a smaller closely-held or privately-held situation.

By using this method for a privately-held company you are taking a huge leap. Namely, you are equating the value of stock in your private business to the value of stock in the average publicly-held business in that industry. That is a pretty rash assumption. It's difficult to see how this method can be valid for anything except other large publicly-held firms with wide distribution of ownership (control not concentrated in a small number of individuals). The method just doesn't seem appropriate for small, closely-held companies - and the main reason is because a public company's stock price is affected by factors other than financial performance. The behavior of the "market" as a whole has a huge impact on its price. It can jump all over the place based on nothing more than rumors. In other words, it's affected by factors that have nothing to do with earnings. That's why the price of public company's stock (the "value" of that company) can vary tremendously from day to day. It forces you to guess at what the price of your subject company's stock would be if it were publicly traded.

Another problem is that publicly-traded shares represent fractional minority interests, so they are not comparable to a 100% interest in the company being valued. A majority interest always carries a per-share premium.

In addition, as mentioned earlier, different companies use different accounting methods, which affects their reported earnings. To use another company as a comp, you must conform its accounting methods to those of the subject company. That means you have to recast its financial statements in all sorts of ways - depreciation, bad debts, inventory, and so on.

Public companies usually have several other classes of stock in addition to the common voting shares you see on the exchange, and this complicates the question of how the company is really performing on a per-share basis. In addition, net earnings are often not distributed to the shareholders. That makes you wonder what really determines the price of that stock. You have to somehow estimate and subtract any appreciation resulting from supply-and-demand pressure in the market. Well, how the heck do you do that? Some might argue that no adjustments are necessary because all these factors reflect the expectations of the market concerning future earnings of that company. Even so, valuation is supposed to be based on actual current earnings of a company, not on future expectations.

Nonetheless, it doesn't hurt to have some information on the P/E ratios of "similar" companies that are publicly traded. The data might prove valuable in bolstering some other point you're trying to make during price negotiations. It could also be helpful in valuation disputes with the tax authorities, since they tend to view the P/E Method as appropriate evidence of the value of a company.

A note on comparability between companies:

When looking for companies you feel are comparable to your subject company, the particular industry isn't always the most important consideration. What's most important is whether they are subject to the same economic and market influences. Those tend to be the same for companies in the same

industry, but that's not always the case. For instance, you might have a food processing company that makes sausage under its own label. Yet that firm will be subject to different market influences than one that makes sausage for its own chain of restaurants, or one that packages the sausage under the label of different companies. In each case, there will be differences in growth, profitability, and consumer preference trends.

One way to help mitigate these variations is to use a weighted average* when you calculate your average ratio. In other words, if some companies in your sample are *more similar* to the subject company than others, you can weight those more heavily when computing your average. (See Weighted Average in the Glossary for instructions on how to do this.)

Rule-of-Thumb Methods:

Over the years, many little short-cut formulas have evolved for valuing small businesses. Most of these are based on the P/E method. They are called "rules-of-thumb" and some are useful, but they should be employed with caution.

Their obvious weakness is that they take so little into account. Nonetheless, these simple formulas can provide you with a helpful point of reference for comparing a number of different deals in the same industry. Their primary use seems to be as an initial screening device. However, if the rule is well-established and widely used, in an industry where most businesses are organized and run in about the same way, then the rule-of-thumb will have more validity. One reason is because it represents the collective opinion of people who are very experienced in that particular type of business - people who know what they are usually worth. They have evolved around the peculiar realities of owning that kind of business. They have been refined over the years - customized by people who know that business inside and out.

These formulas also gain validity simply by being widely used. If it seems like everyone in that industry uses the formula, then it's probably the most reliable indicator of market value, no matter how broad a brush it seems.

Here's the thing: market value refers to the price the market is likely to pay - and if the market uses the rule-of-thumb, then that tells you your market value right there, like it or not.

You might object if your company is somehow atypical of that industry, since these formulas usually presume that your firm is within range of the norm. (But, of course, everyone wants to think their firm is special.)

Most rules-of-thumb employ some form of multiplier, or gross revenue capitalization. The net income (or the average gross sales) for a specific period (several months to a year) is multiplied by a numeric factor that has found acceptance in that particular industry. For example:

- 4 to 6 times gross monthly sales for a restaurant

- 10 to 12 times gross monthly sales for a retail clothing store

- 1.5 times annual commissions for an insurance agency

The formulas are usually based on gross sales because they're used by people who immediately know much of gross is consumed by operating expenses. They've already factored it into the formula. Gross sales is all they really need to know.

Many of these formulas exclude the value of inventory. That's added to the end result, based on original cost. Since these formulas are based on income or gross revenues, they are most appropriate for service businesses that have few assets or retained earnings. Most are for small retail or service businesses, and hardly any apply to large, asset-heavy firms like manufacturing companies.

If you use these rules-of-thumb, make sure you also employ at least one of the more comprehensive valuation methods. In addition, rules-of-thumb can change over time, and they even vary from region-to-region based on differences in local market demand, income, and expenses. Check around to make sure you are using the right version.

To find a rule-of-thumb, contact the national trade association for that particular industry. Another source might be the large "business brokerage" chains, since they often supply their local offices with the formulas used for smaller retail and service businesses, which is the bulk of their trade. These formulas aren't trade secrets - they are common knowledge. (Obviously, they would have no validity as indicators of market value if they weren't in free, wide-spread use.)

Below are some examples. In many cases there is more than one accepted method, so these are offered for illustrative purposes only. Note that there is often a *range* of multipliers, due to variation in the relative strength or weakness of the business at hand.

If the rule of thumb refers to "net earnings" or "net income", that usually means *after* deducting the employment cost of all the people needed to produce and sustain those earnings. So if the buyer is someone who will be working in the business, then the expenses should include his/her salary.

Often the buyer must purchase existing customer lists or accounts. A certain portion are lost each year, but you can assume that attrition is already factored into the formula.

Advertising Agency	75% of annual billings
New Car Dealer	50% of net earnings, plus inventory, fixtures, and equipment
Clothing Store	15-20% of net earnings, plus inventory
Bar (Tavern)	4 times monthly gross sales, plus inventory
Day Care Center	75% of gross sales, or a flat dollar amount per child enrolled (varying from $600 to $1000)
Dental Practice	1 to 1.5 times annual net earnings, plus inventory, equipment and fixtures
Medical Practice	1.5 to 3 times annual net earnings, plus fixtures, equipment and inventory
Law Practice	0% to 100% of annual fee revenue, depending on how much client business is likely to be retained after the selling attorney(s) depart
Dry Cleaning Plant	100% of annual gross sales, plus inventory
Gift Shop	30% to 40% of annual gross sales, plus inventory
Hotels	7 to 8 times net operating income
Real Estate Agency	20% to 50% of gross annual commissions
Restaurant	35% to 50% of gross annual sales, plus inventory
Radio Station	2 to 6 times annual gross revenues

Accounting Firm	50% to 175% of annual billings
Insurance Brokerage	80% of gross annual revenues
Public Relations Firm	1.5 times gross annual revenues
Food Brokerage	1.5 to 2.0 times gross income

ഇരൗ

 Stay away from formulas that are supposed to apply to many different types of companies. For instance, there are people who believe that most businesses should sell for between 8 and 10 times their annual earnings, no matter what industry they're in. That's their valuation formula. Fascinating. The 8-to-10 part is supposed to correspond to the average return an investor should expect from an investment with similar risk. It doesn't take into account the particular industry involved (which, naturally, vary in relative profitability and risk), individual differences in the company, differences in market and economic conditions, and so on. They just apply a multiplier of 8 to 10, depending upon how successful the company seems to be. What makes matters worse is that those who use this kind of formula often apply it to an *un*adjusted net earnings figure taken right off the income statement. Anyway, it should seem obvious by now that a valid rule-of-thumb could never be this broad.

Chapter 16

Tips on Valuing Specific Types of Businesses

The information in this chapter is based on input from numerous experts in each particular industry. Their advice has been condensed and paraphrased here for your benefit.

Retail Stores

Retailing is a very competitive field in which the successful formats are constantly changing. What works today usually won't work two years from now. You have to stay ahead of the game by sensing new trends long before they really take off. You have to exercise this foresight a year or more in advance, trying to predict the product mix, location, and presentation that will appeal to future consumers. Customers are capricious and loyalty is rare. In most cases, you'll get their business only as long as you do the best job of satisfying their everchanging needs and fickle tastes. They expect you to do that in a convenient manner, and at a cost that's less than the perceived value of what you are selling. When you fall short, the market share that took years to build can be stolen by more insightful competitors in a matter of weeks.

With so little to count on, people in retailing have their work cut out for them. You might gain a head start if you purchase an existing business, but your success will still depend on what you make-of-it after that. The store might look like a gold mine today, but in this industry, nothing stays the same for very long.

For that reason, retail businesses rarely sell for much more than their asset value. Most of the value lies in inventory, location, franchise rights, and any operational systems already in place. The store's "concept" might have some transitory value. But anyone considering the purchase of an existing retail business should determine whether there really is an advantage to doing so. It's often better to just start something from scratch. Here are some factors that affect value:

Location - Success in retailing often hinges on location. You have to be where the market can see you and get to you conveniently. The customer's perception of this is more important than the reality. The best concept in the world will fail if it's located wrong - which can mean the wrong side of the right intersection. Some locations are so good that almost anything will work there, provided the rent isn't too high. The difference between a good location and a bad one is often a matter of a few feet.

The right location can also change over time. Try to think like the customer on this issue. What seems like a decent spot to you might actually be perceived as inconvenient by the rushed consumer. The differences can be subtle and not within your conscious awareness. It can depend on how far the building is from the road, the number of curbcuts leading onto the property, and the walking distance from the car to the door. You also want to be very close to other stores frequented by your target consumer. If the goods you offer are usually bought on impulse, rather than as a planned purchase, then you need to locate in a spot where your customers have to walk past you in order to get into their destination stores. Just driving past isn't good enough. Being on the far side of their destination store also doesn't work. The only exception might be where the property is extremely inviting, in and of itself - such as a waterfront festival center.

Most successful retailers won't commit to a particular location for a long period of time, unless they are themselves a destination store. Don't delude yourself on that issue just because you know of some customers who go out of their way to get to you. Walmart is a destination store. You probably aren't, so avoid a long-term lease unless it allows you to lock-in a very low rent. A lease in a great location at a decent rent is a terrific asset. In fact, it's sometimes the only thing that makes a business work. But if you get stuck paying high rent in a shopping center with low traffic, you're dead. These mistakes are very easy to make, so try to retain some flexibility.

Most retailers want to use their working capital for inventory rather than tie it up in real estate equity, so they lease their stores rather than buy them. For that reason, the value of owned real estate is usually excluded when valuing a retail business. Deal with that separately. Instead, include a reasonable rent in the income statement expenses.

If the location isn't good but the lease expires soon, you'll be able to move to a better spot. In that case, adjust the income statement to reflect the higher rent for the better location. However, be careful about projecting higher sales yet, since that's still the speculative part. Of course, your gamble will be that an increase in sales will more than offset the higher rent.

Within the same shopping center, some spots are better than others. You might be located in the busiest center in America, but you'll still die if you get stuck at the wrong end. Don't pay Malibu rents if you aren't on the beach.

Operating Systems - Point-of-sale computer systems are fairly standard these days. They offer instant feedback on inventory level and daily sales performance, and they help prevent employee theft. For merchandise managers, the data they produce is the mainstay of successful buying decisions.

Franchise Rights - These can have significant value if there is high consumer recognition of the name and lots of support from the parent organization. On the other hand, if they really don't contribute much, then they are just costing you money. Many franchise programs get you started with a concept, but do little else after that. Another issue is transferability to a new owner. In many cases, the franchisor reserves the right to approve any subsequent buyer of the franchise, which imposes a contingency on your deal that you can't avoid.

Management - Luck might get you started, but success in retailing depends on whether you have good planning and management ability. You'll need talented people in certain critical areas. Salespeople are fairly easy to replace, but it's not easy to find an insightful merchandise buyer, a good floor designer, or a controller who can constantly monitor the numbers and link them to what works and what doesn't.

Inventory - This is the largest asset for most retailers. The buyer of a retail business normally purchases the inventory at its original cost, minus any hard-to-move, outdated, or unsalable merchandise. The acquisition contract should provide for a last minute inventory audit just before settlement, with a corresponding adjustment to the price.

Buyers should find out the average number of inventory turns produced each year by successful retailers in that field, and compare that to the subject business.

Accounts Receivable -

Scrutinize these carefully. In most cases, anything older than 60 days should be discounted for lack of collectability, and anything older than 120 days should not be given any value at all. (Unless the store normally offers credit beyond 30 days.)

In-store financing is often part of a retail business, and it provides a separate profit-center. Look into the credit terms granted, and find out how much of it turns into bad-debt each year. Discount the accounts receivable accordingly. For example, a chain of retail jewelry stores provides financing for a large portion of their customers, and they routinely experience 30% bad debt. They compensate for that by maintaining very high mark-ups on their merchandise, and by charging very high interest rates for the financing. They cover their cost for the merchandise with the cash down payment, and then gamble on the upside.

Most retailers should question whether it's really necessary to offer credit directly to the customer. By simply accepting bank credit cards, you can usually fill the customer's need for credit and avoid the unnecessary risks. For larger purchases, let the customer find a leasing company or bank to arrange a lease or financing. They manage those risks for a living. A retailer's main job is making the sale. To help clean house before putting their business on the market, a retailer would be wise to eliminate in-store credit unless it's really a big profit center.

Fixtures, furniture & equipment - The

FF&E has value only if it still gives you an up-to-date presentation. Buyers should avoid acquiring anything that's outdated or in need of replacement. Leading retailers often give their stores a complete facelift every 2 or 3 years. Unless you're going for a quaint image, most customers are turned off by worn or dated presentation.

Trade Name -

If the business hasn't done well in the past, then the existing name can actually be a detriment. It has little transferable value unless the business has been quite successful and has loyal local patronage. One exception might be where customers expect reliable follow-up service after the sale. In that case, the familiar name might imply greater reliability and inspire more customer confidence, which can help you make sales.

Customer Base -

Let's face it - many retailers want to think they have a group of loyal, steady customers, but there's very little loyalty out there. Those customers are gone as soon as they find a better deal or an easier way to buy. Any seller who tries to attribute added value to his customer base is facing an uphill battle.

Theft Control Systems -

The wages paid to retail employees don't top the national pay scale. Yet, at the same time, these people handle a lot of money and valuable merchandise. The temptation is great, and they frequently succumb to it. Employee theft, even in food service, can turn a profitable company into a losing venture.

Advertising and Promotion Budget -

Don't underestimate these costs. Contact retail associations to find out how much successful retailers in your category spend on this each year. A corresponding amount should be included on the adjusted income statement.

Putting the deal together - Sellers view confidentiality as very important, but they often worry more than is necessary. Customers are rarely scared off by rumors a sale, unless returns or service after the transfer of ownership are an issue. A more realistic concern is the possibility of losing employees who become worried about the continuity of their jobs or the added hassles of working for a different employer. Sellers should communicate with them up front, or some may look for job security elsewhere.

Lenders consider retailing a risky venture, so finding a loan for the purchase of a retail business will be difficult unless you already have a great track record in that field, or unless you are buying into a successful, nationally-known entity. You usually can't borrow more than a percentage of the liquidation value of the assets. You can also forget about bank financing if you can't demonstrate experience in retailing. In most cases, the seller finances the deal.

Rules of Thumb for Retail Businesses

Please review our warning about "rules of thumb" in Chapter 15. These formulas reflect a lot of hearsay and can be awfully misleading, so be careful if you use them. We list them here for those who are curious.

Clothing Store	15% of annual earnings, plus inventory
Convenience Store	With beer and gas: 28% of gross annual sales Without: 10% of gross sales
Deli	30% to 50% of annual gross sales, plus inventory
Independent Drug Store	25% to 75% of annual earnings, plus inventory and FF&E; Or 80 to 120 times average daily sales
Flower Shop	25% to 40% of Grossannual sales, plus inventory.
Gift Shop	30% to 40% of annual gross sales, plus inventory
Garden Center	10% of annual earnings, plus inventory and FF&E
Hardware	35% of gross annual gross sales; Or 25% of annual gross sales plus inventory

Home Center/Lumber	Market value of assets (real estate, saleable inventory, equipment) - plus premium of $50,000 to $100,000 if earnings are 5% of sales, or up to 8 times earnings if earnings are greater than 5%.
Liquor Store	25% to 30% of annual gross sales, plus inventory and market value of liquor license
New Car Dealerships	100% of average annual earnings plus new inventory at cost, used inventory at NADA book value or negotiated price, and FF&E at liquidation value. Variables include: how modern, well-located, and physically attractive the dealership property is; transferability of franchise rights; demographic trends in community; the presence and quality of sales, parts, and service managers; popularity of brand sold; quality of support, market protection, and dealer relations from manufacturer.
Video Stores	1.5 to 2 times annual earnings, plus book value of inventory.

(Unless otherwise stated, "earnings" refers to the net operating income before tax. The expenses should include reasonable wages for all necessary workers and managers, including the owner's salary.)

Valuing Medical Practices

Medical practices are occasionally placed on the market due to the retirement, death, relocation, or disability of a practitioner. When group practices break up or reorganize, a valuation is usually done so that departing members can be bought-out. Often, when new "physician associates" are recruited by a practice, their contract includes an option to buy-into the practice under pre-arranged terms. This requires an estimate of value at the time of buy-in. In addition, hospitals and other practitioners often purchase these firms as a way of expanding their market ("catchment") areas. By capturing providers, hospitals can expand their patient base, and offer a wide mix of specialties to help keep referrals under their own roof. The practice might be brought into the hospital, or operated as an independent satellite. Managed care plans, such as HMO's, also acquire existing practices as captive providers.

Group practice makes sense today, more than ever. Administrative complexity has increased to the point where doctors need full-time personnel to manage their firms, giving them the time they need to actually practice medicine. The cost of that is more feasible if a number of practitioners join together to create overhead efficiencies. Then they can afford to hire professional office administrators to handle the everyday business concerns.

Every practice, regardless of size, must have the in-house capability to handle and respond to certain matters, including:

- Cost-containment measures imposed by Medicare and third-party payors
- Complex requirements for record keeping, pre-authorization, claim resolution
- Effective procedures to reduce malpractice risk
- Stringent regulations regarding occupational safety and medical waste disposal

- The restructuring our health care delivery systems through various trends and legal mandates
- Competition from HMO's, PPO's and other new provider formats
- Wage and training costs of personnel
- The need for local practitioners to lobby regulators and third-party payors on their own behalf
- Continuing education for physicians

It's no wonder that doctors who sell their practice want to be compensated for all this. A profitable, competitive practice with a steady referral base and an established administrative team is worth a lot more than just its equipment and furniture.

Specific Valuation Methods

There are several approaches to valuing a medical practice. Remember, in each case, we are looking for fair market value, which is an estimate of . . .
- the most likely price at which that business will change hands . . .
- within a reasonable period of time . . .
- in that particular area. . .
- between a willing buyer and a willing seller. . .
- in an "arm's length" transaction. . .
- where both parties are motivated but neither is under any particular compulsion to act.

Bear in mind that if the success of that practice depends upon the unique talents, reputation, or relationships of the departing owner, then its value will be much lower after that person leaves. In that event, the only way to preserve some of that value is by arranging a gradual transition to the new owner, during which the seller remains actively involved and the buyer has a chance to inherit some of those qualities and relationships.

The value of a practice won't be the same to every prospective buyer. It depends on the particular advantages and disadvantages to each party. It depends on how the practice will be managed, how the purchase will be financed, what changes will be made, and how much client attrition will be experienced. When the buyer is a hospital or an established group practice, client retention is likely to be higher.

Discounted Future Benefits Method:

Refer to Chapter 15 for instructions on this method. It's based on the idea that a purchaser shouldn't pay more than the cost to duplicate the firm's income stream from scratch. In other words, how much more net income does this firm produce than you could generate by starting from scratch? Capitalize that amount, and then bring it back to present value. Assume that the start-up firm will have the same format and an equivalent location. Factor-in the cost for the latter.

If you are looking at a specialty with few practitioners in that particular market, then your projections might indicate that a brand new practice will be equally successful after a year or so. On the other hand, if there is a glut of doctors in that specialty, or if this firm is one of the best-known in the area, or just has a great location, then an acquisition will be more attractive.

Remember - to project future revenues, don't increase the current amount by more than a factor for normal fee inflation. You should also adjust for the patient attrition that is certain to occur when physicians leave the practice. And keep in mind that your expenses will increase annually. You can get estimates of those increases from medical associations.

In some versions of this method, you predict the income of a start-up business for several future years. Then, taking one year at a time, you subtract that amount from the current income of the subject business, and calculate the present value of the difference. Finally, you add up the present values. We believe this approach is sound, but a little more cumbersome than the one outlined for you in Chapter 15.

Excess Earnings Approach

This method is also commonly used. See Chapter 11 for details. It's based on the idea that the practice is worth the fair market value of its tangible assets, plus the capitalized value of its "goodwill". This figure automatically takes into account the value of any intangible assets.

In both methods...

• The operating expenses should include the salary of a doctor hired to replace the owner-practitioner. Get that figure from executive recruiters in that market area who specialize in medical personnel.

• Both methods involve the use of a capitalization rate or discount rate. Refer to Chapter 5 for directions on how to select that rate, and make sure you consider the following factors:
  • The future outlook for that particular medical specialty, in light of:
    - Trends in professional regulation,
    - Foreseeable developments in treatment and pharmacology,
    - The evolving reimbursement policies of third-party payors.
  • Size of the existing patient base, patient age mix, payor mix.
  • Demographic trends, demand for services, and competition from other practices in that market area.
  • The location and quality of the office facilities and equipment.
  • The desirability of the firm's hospital affiliation, staff privileges, and call rotations.
  • Availability of physician back-ups.
  • The firm's malpractice record, and the quality of record keeping to date
  • Credentials of the remaining physicians and support staff.

- The established office hours, credit terms, and policies that patients will expect to continue.

Ability To Pay Method

This method helps you set an upper limit on your price by checking whether the firm's net cash flow can support it. To do this, you project the firm's post-acquisition revenues and expenses. Follow the instructions in Chapter 13 and 14.

Buyers should also try to project post-acquisition (proforma) net income in order to estimate the net result of the changes they plan to make. Don't base the purchase price on this, since you don't know whether those changes will really come to pass, and since you don't pay the seller for improvements you make yourself.

Comparable Sales Approach

This method bases value on the recent selling prices of other firms. It sounds great in theory, but the data is difficult to obtain. To have any validity, you need an adequate number of comparables, but you probably won't find more than a couple. In addition, no firm is truly "comparable" to any other, since that means . . .

- Having the same specialty and clinical approach
- Being present in the same market area, with equivalent office locations
- Having staff of the same qualifications
- Having an equivalent patient base and referral network
- Having the same payor mix and patient age mix
- Having the same fee schedule and operational format (which also implies equivalent operating costs)
- Having an equivalent admitting hospital

This really narrows things down. To the extent that any practice in your sample differs from the subject firm, you have to make some very subjective adjustments to the sales price in order to compensate. In the process, the figures can become so convoluted that they are useless. For that reason, many reject this "market survey" approach to valuation.

Rules of Thumb for Medical Practices

Read Chapter 16 regarding Rules of Thumb. These often amount to a shot in the dark, so we don't really encourage their use. However, to appease your curiosity, here are a few we have heard of:

Human medical practice	1.5 to 3X annual net profits, plus equipment, supplies, & furniture Or: 20% to 60% of gross annual fee revenue
Dental practice	1-1.5 X annual net profits, plus equipment, supplies & furnishings Or: 20% to 50% of gross annual fee revenues Or: One year's net profit before tax, plus owner's salary, plus equipment, supplies and furnishings.
Veterinary medical practice	60%-80% of gross income + value of building at $30-40/square foot (with land, other improvements and fixtures deemed to be included.) Or: Capitalize adjusted net income at 22-29% + real estate as above. *Note:* If buying out the existing owner while working in the practice, make sure that valuation date is when you started work there. Since your own efforts have built the practice since then, you don't want to be *paying for yourself* as well. Consult AVMA *Economic Report on Veterinarians & Veterinary Practices* for comparative performance data.

Other Health Care Businesses

Methods similar to those above can be used to value any other business providing in-office healthcare treatment. However, this section deals primarily with at-home treatment providers, which have multiplied in recent years as a result of pressure to lower the cost of health care.

Initially, these cost-saving efforts were focused on expanding the out-patient treatment of hospitals. The next step was to develop smaller, satellite treatment facilities without overnight accommodations. Both approaches eliminate the costs associated with overnight stays, but the patient must be ambulatory, and the cost of developing and staffing those facilities was often equal to hospital treatment. As a result, the cost-saving advantages are often minimal, and the real motivation for building these facilities is competitive. Rather than trying to lure all prospective patients to one central location, they can capture more business by building small satellite locations all over the community, particularly if those locations are more convenient than those of the competition. These small facilities are also less imposing than big hospitals, so skittish patients are less intimidated from seeking treatment.

At-home care, on the other hand, really does result in significant savings to insurers and consumers, so there is plenty of incentive to use it. It allows patients to be discharged earlier from the hospital, or avoid visiting the hospital altogether. Also, disabled patients can avoid the hassle of traveling to get treatment. At-home care includes infusion therapy, nursing, physical therapy, respiratory care, and a growing number of other treatment services.

Valuation considerations:

- Since these are service businesses, the focus is on intangible assets, particularly quality of the patient base and referral base.

- In addition, where skilled treatment services are involved, the quality of the firm's personnel is paramount. Whether these people are employees or contractors, they must be well-trained, experienced, reliable, available, and plentiful. The quality of the personnel is everything, particularly with at-home nursing services. However, during certain periods, the competition for qualified employees can be intense, since hospitals often pay signing bonuses for new hires when employees are scarce, so much depends on the firm's ability to attract these people and keep them on board. Buyers should make sure the personnel file of each skilled employee includes verified information on training, experience, and certifications.

- Scrutinize labor costs carefully. If competition for good employees is stiff in that market, something is wrong if labor costs appear lower than expected.

- Make sure all licensing and board certifications are in order.

- Check out the firm's liability coverage and history of prior claims. Search for undisclosed potential claims. Buyers should take every possible measure to avoid inheriting the potential liabilities of the prior owners.

- Gain a thorough understanding of the payor mix - in other words, what percentage of the revenues come from Medicare/Medicaid, from private insurers, and from self-pay by patients.

Government programs have strict limits on the amount they will pay for any type of treatment (called DRG's). Private insurance companies pay according to the terms of the policy, which often limits coverage to a percentage of the customary and reasonable fee (UCR) for that service in that particular region - something they usually estimate on the low side. If the patient refuses to pay the difference between the fee and the reimbursement, the firm must eat the different. In theory, a high percentage of self-pay patients is the best situation, if you have an effective fee collection system. Fee collection also depends on local demographics, and the bill-paying culture of that particular region. For example, in conservative, high-employment, non-urban areas of the mid-west, fees are more likely to be paid in-full and on-time. Conversely, certain areas of the east coast require very careful decisions regarding credit, and very aggressive collection policies in general.

- A related subject is how the company handles the shortfall between the fees billed and the amounts that are actually received. The difference must be accounted for somehow on the income statement as a deduction from operating income. Some firms seem to routinely bill higher amounts than they actually expect to be paid by third-party payors, in order to counter-balance unrealistically low UCR's, and to help maintain the pressure to raise them. Buyers need to find out whether this is being done so that they can understand the real extent of the shortfall.

- The market value of any medical equipment may differ significantly from its book value. Sometimes the existence and condition of equipment is hard to verify because it's located in the homes of patients. Some former patients might have equipment they refuse to return. Also, keep in mind that equipment located in a patient's home is subject to more rapid deterioration. For these reasons, you should be very careful when estimating the value of those assets. Also remember that health care technology changes rapidly, so this equipment becomes obsolete very quickly.

- A new technological advance can make your entire treatment program (and inventory) obsolete overnight, particularly when pharmaceuticals are involved. However, since the approval process for new drugs is very lengthy, there should be plenty of warning.

- Health care is subject to a great deal of governmental regulation. Reforms aimed at reducing the cost of health care will change the way these services are delivered, and the profitability of many firms will change as a result. This regulation will occur on both the state and federal levels, so pay attention to the legislative wind at all times.

- Learn who your competition is. Health care is a local business with a long development curve. Some national firms have made inroads quickly in local markets by spending a lot of promotional money, but it's still hard to come in and become a success overnight. The heavyweight competition is more likely to come from local hospitals that acquire related businesses. With a large number of skilled employees already on hand, a huge referral base, and an established local image that inspires confidence, they can pump up that business quickly.

- Burn-out is common in the health care business. Buyers should interview the employees and managers to estimate potential turnover. They should also look into the relative availability of replacements in that market.

The valuation methods for these firms are income-based. See Chapter 5 for guidance on selecting a capitalization rate. An asset approach is appropriate only if the business is brand new or only marginally profitable.

When using an income-based method, you should consider the cost of replacing any outdated treatment equipment. That will involve expensive capital investment that can't be deferred.

You might want to avoid using Rules of Thumb for this young industry, since the formulas haven't had much time to evolve yet.

Also be careful about using a Market Data or Comparable Sales method. You can try to work up a logical system for adjusting each company in your sample, pruning them down to their common denominators, but your rationale for doing that may only have validity in your own mind. It's totally subjective, and each appraiser, left to his own logic and devices, will make those adjustments differently. There's no universally accepted system for doing it, and there never will be, so this approach will always generate dubious results unless the number of comparables in your sample is very large, and unless the companies are all fairly similar to begin with.

Valuing an Accounting Firm

First review the chapter on valuing a service-type business.

Discounted Future Benefits Approach

This may be the most appropriate method, since most of the value lies in the client base. Follow the directions in Chapter 15. Generally, you consider future income for a period not longer than five years. In reducing the income for each of those years to present value, you can use a fairly low discount rate because the income stream enjoyed by established accounting firms is usually quite stable. Many use the buyer's "cost of capital" as the discount rate. That's the interest rate a buyer would expect to pay when borrowing funds to purchase the firm, blended prorata with the rate of return lost by that buyer on any cash invested in the business.

Capitalization of Income Approach

Again, follow the instructions in Chapter 15, and use a fairly conservative capitalization rate.

Rules of Thumb

Accounting firms are capable of performing very sophisticated valuations, but most firms still seem to be sold according to a loose rule of thumb:

1. Start with a base price equal to the firm's gross annual revenues

2. Then add a premium if it produces higher than average (>50%) profitability, or has a very high-profile reputation, or a great location in a growing community, or a unique specialization that draws higher fees. That premium can be up to 50% of the gross billings.

Seller financing:

Banks rarely loan money for the acquisition of a personal service firm, so these deals are usually financed by the seller. The buyer is purchasing the client base, which generates the fees used to pay the purchase price, so this is often called an "earn out". Conventional lenders are scared off because of the fragile nature of client relationships and the hazards of malpractice liability. Since seller financing is the norm, sellers can't really pump up the price to offset the risk of carrying that debt, but they should be willing to discount the price in order to get all cash at settlement. The seller financing is for same period of time as the future income projections - usually five years.

Other contract terms:

- The seller usually guarantees that the client base will generate a minimum amount of annual gross revenue in the first year after the settlement, otherwise the price is adjusted. That amount is usually close to the current annual revenues. After that, it's up to the buyer to maintain revenues and minimize client attrition.

- The firm's clients may be apprehensive about dealing with a new accountant, so arrangements should be made for a gradual transition to the new people. Often the change is characterized as a merger between the buying and selling firm, and the selling principals gradually step out of the picture over a couple of years, indicating that the practice is being purchased by the "remaining" partners.

- A covenant restricting competition by the seller is usually included in the agreement. It should state that it survives settlement. It should be very specific in terms of the geographic area covered, the type of activities that are restricted, and the period of time involved. Sometimes its coverage is limited to existing clients of both the subject firm and the buyer's firm. In any case, in order to be enforceable, it must be reasonable in terms of time and size of the geographic area involved. It should also stipulate the remedies available in the event of breach, and the seller should be protected in a similar manner in case the buyer defaults.

Valuing a Manufacturing Company

Manufacturing companies are considered desirable acquisition targets because a large proportion of their value is attributable to fixed, securable assets in the form of equipment, inventory, and real estate. That means its easier to borrow money to finance these acquisitions. Service businesses, on the other hand, use very few fixed assets to generate their profits, so those loans are secured primarily by cash flow. Lenders don't  like this as much, since cash flow isn't something they can seize and sell at auction if the buyer defaults.

Preparing the adjusted balance sheet:

Refer to Chapter 3 for guidance on this important step. Pay particular attention to inventory, making sure that all obsolete material is subtracted. If feasible, hire an equipment appraiser to estimate the real market value of the manufacturing equipment. You might get away with using its depreciated market value, as installed. That amount is roughly equivalent to the cost to go out and buy the same piece of used equipment from a dealer, and then have it trucked to the plant and installed. It's about the same as replacement value. Buyers and lenders tend to be more conservative. Since most used manufacturing equipment is sold at auction, you should probably lean more toward liquidation value. Don't include anything that's obsolete or not really used in the business anymore. Find out if the company has the kind of equipment and facilities it needs in order to be competitive, since the cost of upgrading those things can send the working capital requirements through the roof during the first few years after acquisition.

Manufacturing plants usually have specialized floor plans and mechanical systems. It's unlikely that a different company can move into the same space without making a lot of expensive changes to the building. For that reason, the market value of industrial real estate is usually lower than its book value. You may want to consult with brokers and appraisers who can estimate what the property would bring if placed on the market and sold within a reasonable period of time.

Find out if customers have deposits on product that hasn't been delivered yet. These may be included in the "cash" amount listed on the asset side of the balance sheet, but an equal amount should also appear on the liabilities side. They shouldn't appear as sales (on the income statement) until the goods have been delivered.

Keep an eye out for hidden potential liabilities such as the cost to clean up environmental contamination, product liability suits, employee accident claims, OSHA noncompliance, warranty claims, and so on.

Keep in mind that the company is worth more than its liquidation value only if it is reasonably profitable. With that in mind, you prepare an adjusted income statement so you can compare its performance to the industry averages. The statement should show the net operating income before income taxes. Don't forget to remove any non-operating income, discretionary owner expenses, unusual income events, expense events, interest, and depreciation.

Sales contracts - Depending on the nature of the business, you may want to verify any contracts the company claims as the basis for future revenues. Scrutinize those documents thoroughly, especially if most of the income comes from a few big deals. Investigate the reliability and credit of those customers as well, and make sure the customers don't have kickout options. Verify whether the company actually has the capability to produce the goods contracted for. Look at warranty terms, especially if it involves a new, unproven product.

If these big sales depend on the special abilities of people who are leaving the company, then don't use capitalization of income to value the firm because that method assumes that you've captured the source of the income indefinitely. Instead, calculate the net income you expect from any valid contracts, and reduce that to present value. Then add the residual value of the assets.

Make sure these sales will be profitable at the prices that have been promised. Just because the company has contracts for $10 million, that doesn't mean they will produce the same percentage of operating profit experienced in the past. The owner may have contracted those deals at impossibly low prices.

Product Obsolescence - How much technological change occurs in this industry? Does the company have a product development team? If the industry is revolutionized overnight, will the company be participating in that, or will it be left out in the cold? Consumer products are especially vulnerable to rapid change. Today's craze is tomorrow's overstock. In some ways it's like starting from scratch every morning. You can never rest on your laurels.

Suppliers:

Does the company use materials that are difficult to obtain, or whose cost is subject to wide fluctuation? Is the company locked into long-term supplier contracts when cheaper sources are available? If the raw material costs shown on the income statement are reasonable, will those same prices be offered to the new owner?

Union workers:

The success of a acquisition will depend on your ability to control the operating expenses. When workers are represented by a union, prospective buyers should check out the details of any labor contracts so that scheduled wage increases don't catch them by surprise. Pay attention to the expiration date of the existing contract, too, because that's when it all turns into a big issue again. It may be a good idea to eliminate those future unknowns by renegotiating the contracts in advance.

Generally, unions are viewed as a wild card that can add a significant amount of risk to an already-risky acquisition. Business survival depends on maintaining constant work flow and control over your operating costs, so union disruption can be fatal to a fragile business. If a union is involved, it would be wise to meet with union representatives in advance to discuss the situation, and try to gain whatever concessions you need in order to preserve the company and the jobs it provides. If union officials express a lack of cooperation on these issues, you might achieve better results by appealing directly to the workers, but labor laws restrict what you can do or say without damaging your rights, so make sure you consult with a labor relations attorney first. There are lots of technical requirements to satisfy, so do everything by the book. Sometimes workers will recognize when a union is working against their real interests, in which case they may vote to decertify (throw out) the union. If that comes up, be prepared for a bitter battle because the union reps will lose lots of dues income, and perhaps their jobs, if the decert goes through.

Other techniques have been used to get rid of a union, such as closing down the business for a period of time and then starting it up from scratch as a new entity, using the assets of the old company. Some of these tactics are made illegal, so make sure you consult a labor attorney before planning anything of the sort. In general, the union climate is weaker now than it was in the past, so union reps are more likely to work with you.

Organized workers are not always a problem. Their cooperation has occasionally helped bail out sinking companies and make unworkable deals happen, but it's nothing to count on. Humans, by nature, are rather selfish, short-sighted, and non-empathetic, and labor unions have helped create an attitude of entitlement among many workers. As a result, many workers expect obsolete jobs and wage scales to be preserved for them even after the subject industry has died. They can't conceive of moving to another area or retraining themselves to qualify for a modern career, so don't expect much sympathy when you request a simple wage freeze. Many entrepreneurs are willing to take on a faltering company and try to make it work for a few more years, risking everything in the process, but the workers feel cheated if concessions are needed to make that happen, so don't expect that saving their jobs will be an instant motivator. Any concessions will involve an uphill battle.

Selecting a Capitalization Rate:

In order to set the cap rate, you have to learn as much as possible about business conditions in that particular industry. You should start with the trade magazines and any projections published by the U.S. Department of Commerce. Then talk to anyone who knows anything about that industry. There might be stock market analysts who study that specific industry, and they can be extremely valuable sources of input. Some advisors claim that most mid-sized manufacturing companies ($1 million to $50 million in sales) sell at cap rates ranging between 15% and 25%. (That's not a rule of thumb - just an observation.) This assumes stable economic and lending conditions, and financial ratios that correspond roughly to the industry averages. Once you feel like you understand the risk/reward situation, refer to Chapter 5 for guidance on selecting the cap rate.

Remember that risk increases if a small number of customers account for a large portion of the company's sales. Start worrying when one customer represents more than 20 percent, or when a handful of customers account for half of its business.

Valuation methods to use:

Consult Chapter 4 for guidance on this. The most widely-used techniques for profitable manufacturing companies seem to be Capitalization of Income, Discounted Cash Flow, and Excess Earnings.

The Acquisition Contract:

The seller of a manufacturing company should be willing to warrant certain things, including:

- the accuracy of the financial statements
- the condition of equipment
- known liabilities
- saleability of inventory
- disclosure of material facts or forthcoming events that may affect the company

Highly-leveraged acquisitions were common during the 1970's and early 1980's. Today, lenders rarely seem to loan more than 60 to 80 percent of the purchase price, even with lots of securable assets. Obviously, it pays to ask the seller to finance at least part of the price.

For more information on negotiating an acquisition contract, see Chapter 20.

Valuing Golf Courses

A golf course is valued in one of two ways: as an income-producing business, or according its land value for development, whichever is higher.

If the course has been in existence for a while, the surrounding community may have grown up around it, in which case the value of the land for development may exceed the value of the business. New courses are only feasible on cheap land - which usually means way out of town. The exception might be where local zoning permits this type of use on rural or agricultural land, which may be relatively inexpensive even when it's close to town or has good highway access. Another affordable land option is when zoning permits the golfing use in a flood plain, or in the green area that must accompany other development.

Never base your price on the projected success of a real estate development project. In other words, don't assume you can afford to pay a certain price because of the projected return from a speculative development plan. Development is fraught with unforeseen costs, expensive delays, and unpredictable market response. There's no way to tell what's really going to happen, so if you over-pay for the land based on proforma results, you'll never get your money back out if the project folds and you have to resell the property.

Today, many view golf courses simply as an amenity for land development projects. They are used to create a certain atmosphere and attract people to purchase expensive homesites. The cost of the golf course is passed through with the lot prices, and the real profit comes from the lot sales and development fees paid internally. Often, ownership of the course is passed to the homeowners association - or else they individually buy shares in the course when they purchase their lots, gradually taking the developer out. At that point, they carry the risk, and the developer gets a long-term contract for course management. Pretty slick.

Some view a golf course as a way to bank land for future development. This can work, if you keep the place simple (low operating expenses) and if your projected revenues will at least cover the debt service on the loan used to purchase it. However, it's difficult to get a loan for raw land, so most deals like this involve seller financing or a cash purchase. You get enough golf income out of the land so it doesn't cost you anything to own, and then wait for the ground to rise in value as the community grows. Then you develop it.

The firms that specialize in selling golf courses often take a commercial real estate approach to appraising them. That compares the value according to three different angles: market approach, replacement cost, and income value.

For the market approach, you need data on the recent sale prices of other golf courses. Try to limit that to courses with the same number of holes, same amenities, same season length, same condition, and same number of rounds played per season. To the extent these factors differ, you adjust your comparables. There are some generalizations you can make concerning these adjustments, but the hard part will be getting hold of the data. Few firms keep track of it, and those that do either want to be hired to do the valuation, or want big bucks for the information.

Replacement value is usually not a feasible approach. Land cost for equivalent locations may have gone through the roof. Facilities may have been overbuilt. There may be a large number of older existing courses in the market that can afford to charge lower

fees than a newly-built course could. If this method is useable for your case, you can't equate brand new with old - the calculations must include deductions for depreciation (wear, obsolescence, limited useful life). Golf courses require periodic renovation - don't assume they're stable as long as the grass grows.

Income-based valuation methods for a golf course usually capitalize net income before income taxes, depreciation, and interest. The income statement should be adjusted beforehand. There will be add-backs for owner perks and unusual expenses, and add-ons for the cost of better maintenance and management. The point is to be on a par with the costs of running a competitive, professionally-managed course.

Your analysis will be better if you can find out whether the operating ratios are in-line with the industry averages for other courses in markets of equivalent size and climate. You will need to determine why the course performs the way it does before you can speculate about unrealized potential. Prospective owners often assume they can increase income through advertising and improved amenities, and brokers may encourage this in order to make the deal. The truth is that most courses are already very close to their maximum revenues. The theoretic "maximum operating capacity" may be much higher, but that doesn't mean the players will come.

Important information for comparing different courses includes the type of golfer attracted (tourist, resident, membership), variety of income sources (greens fees, cart fees, lessons, driving range, equipment, food), and number of rounds played per year (take the average of several years, due to annual variations in weather, economy, and demographics). Analyze the location very critically, particularly with regard to the competition. Courses located several miles from the communities they serve are often poorly patronized except at peak times when golfers can't get on a course closer to town. Distance from the population density isn't the only consideration. A lot depends on the customer's perception of how convenient it is to get to the course, so scrutinize the road access. Industry associations, such as the National Golf Foundation, sometimes put together estimates of how much local population is required to support each 18 holes of golf in a given climatological area. Golf may be overbuilt in your area, or it may be considered underbuilt, according to these criteria. However, don't view these formulas as guarantees of success or failure.

Wholesale & Distribution Companies

There are no special methods for valuing these firms, so just follow the general guidelines in Chapter 4. However, you should always check out the Economic Value of the Assets Method, since it often gives a higher figure than the income-based methods. Compare the company's financial performance to the "industry averages", paying particular attention to before-tax profits. (This information can be found in reference books on key financial ratios*, published by Robert Morris Associates and others.) If you detect lower-than-average profitability, that lends support to the asset value approach.

Make sure you check out the following ratios as well:

*   Number of "inventory turns" per year (total cost of inventory for the year, divided by average amount of inventory).

*   Current ratio and quick ratio

*   Return on assets (before-tax profit divided by total assets)

*   Sales divided by working capital

*   Sales divided by total assets

Again, compare these to the industry averages so you can get a sense for the risk level and pick an appropriate cap rate. Other factors bearing on risk will include:

*   The size and quality of the sales force.

*   The number of major accounts served. If a high percentage of sales (20% or more) come from a single customer, or if 50% of sale are from a handful of customers, then the situation is deemed more risky.

*   The history of accounts receivable collection. If the customers aren't creditworthy, then the company is weaker and riskier.

*   Size up the company's ability to place new product lines on the market quickly.

*   Look for computerized systems that track inventory, payables, receivables, orders and shipping.

*   The size and growth rate of the particular market served is also very important.

*   Does the company depend on a single manufacturer? If so, that ties your success directly to that of the companies you represent, and having all your eggs in one basket makes you very vulnerable. The business will be more stable if you represent a variety of manufacturers.

- Look at the quality of the real estate. Fortunately, the buildings used for wholesale and distribution companies tend to be wide-open, single story, "general purpose" structures, with high ceilings, lots of loading docks, and great accessibility to major highways. This makes them very saleable, compared to most manufacturing plants. However, if the building lacks these characteristics, it won't be as attractive to buyers, and its value will suffer as a result.

Asset values:

Most of the asset value will lie in inventory, trailers, trucks, and real estate. This makes the asset-based valuation of this type of business relatively simple, compared to that of a manufacturing company. Information on the market value of these assets should be readily available and fairly reliable, compared to the specialized machinery and customized buildings used by manufacturing companies.

In fairness, the real estate should be valued separately from the business, because most companies lease their facilities. In addition, the real estate can throw off the valuation if it's located in an area where property values have zoomed, or if the property has been rezoned to a more valuable category. You want to focus on the business value, so break out the real estate value separately.

Valuing a Restaurant Business

It's been said that restaurants have the highest failure rate of all businesses, and that 20% of all restaurants are for sale at any given time. Whether that's true or not, it certainly is a tough business to succeed in. You need a lot of skills:

- You need a keen eye for what makes a good location, and you must secure that property at a feasible cost.
- You must create an appealing entertainment "concept" - through interior design, service, and menu.
- You need financial skills to monitor and control your costs scrupulously.
- You must be a savvy promoter.
- You must be creative.
- You must be able to tolerate an unusual and demanding work schedule.
- You need a talent for managing people.
- And you must sustain your enthusiasm for all of these roles, day-in and day-out.

Since these refer to personal qualities of the managers, that makes it hard to predict whether a restaurant will have more than fixed asset value under different management. You are supposed to value a business as it stands today, on the assumption that an equally qualified person will be running it after it's sold. However, if it's obvious that the success of that business is due to the particular talents and personality of the current manager, who will leave after the sale, then the price should reflect that. The truth is that most restaurants are sold for liquidation value of the assets.

Real estate and geography:
- Your food concept and prices must be appropriate to the particular market. What attracts crowds in a big urban market often doesn't work in the suburbs.

- Your particular location in the market is extremely important. You must know the mindset of your target customer and how they will assess your location in terms of convenience, safety, and so on. Even when you're on the right side of town, your exact position is crucial. If your building is set back too far from the road, or stuck in the slow end of a shopping center, that is enough to kill you, unless your business is a true destination.

- Position is especially crucial for "fast food", where picky details like the angle of the parking spaces and the position of the curb cuts all affect your customer's perception of how convenient the place is.

- The physical appearance of the property must be consistent with the "concept" you are projecting.

- Remember what a restaurant sells - it's not just food. It's entertainment - sometimes that's the main thing. It's also consistency, cleanliness, convenience, value, and entertainment. Your property should project those themes inside and out.

- The cost to outfit restaurant space often runs beyond $200 per square foot. But don't spend money on details that no one will notice. Those ceiling frescos are a waste of money if no one ever looks up.

- Except for fast food, restaurants are identified with their location, so it's risky to move one to a new place. Besides, the cost of removing and reinstalling the mechanical systems often makes the project unfeasible, especially after you add the cost of complying with the latest health department regs. Existing properties might be grandfathered under the old rules, but once you start changing things, the newer, stiffer requirements often click in.

- Find out whether your rent or occupancy costs will remain stable and reasonable throughout the foreseeable future. For most restaurants, these are said to be 4% to 6% of total sales, even though the actual rent might vary from $3 to $20 per square foot per year. A small, efficient operation might be able to afford a rent as high as 10% of total sales. But on average, total occupancy costs (rent, insurance, taxes) range from 5% to 8% of total sales.

- Read the lease. Don't assume that today's rent will last forever. After the lease expires, the landlord may demand a higher rent that will squeeze that otherwise-profitable business to death. If the seller owns the property, and it's value has appreciated, you might not be able to afford what he can sell it for separately. In that case, you have to figure out whether it's worth trying to relocate the business elsewhere.

- Consider staying in the same location but downscaling the size of the space. Many restaurants have become much more profitable by renovating into a smaller, more efficient space.

Is the restaurant concept obsolete?

We use this term to refer to the atmosphere and the theme of the menu. The traditional full-menu restaurant and family restaurant has become obsolete in many markets. To a large extent, dining is entertainment, and entertainment is a trendy enterprise, so today's successful restaurant concepts are always changing.

These days the emphasis seems to be on shorter menus and lots of novel daily specials. But most managers are just playing it by ear and "doing what works".

Alcohol consumption - once making up more than 50% of restaurant sales - is way down. The dining rooms are compartmentalized and cozy, but bright and informal. But by the time you read this, those trends may have changed.

Yet, anytime you buy a restaurant for a price greater than its asset value, you are paying a premium for its concept, on the assumption that it has a few years left in it. One expert tells us that the average restaurant has a lifespan of 5 years before its concept is worn out. At that point the business either fades out, or starts over again from scratch. Few places are such a tradition that they can hang on to the same theme year after year.

Sales and Profitability:

Restaurant sales are said to range from $70 per square foot (for the lower quartile) to $250 (for the upper quartile). Companies owning several restaurants tend to produce the highest total net income and the highest net income per seat, but not necessarily the highest total gross revenues. That means you can sell lots of food but still lose money if you don't control your costs. You should become familiar with the following industry averages, and find out how your subject restaurant stacks up by comparison:

- Number of table turns per day: .6 to 2.5 (lower and upper quartile averages, respectively.)

- Average check amount

- Employee turnover (1.5 to 2.5, with a median of 1.7)

- Total sales per employee

- Productivity index = Total sales per employee divided by average payroll per employee. (The industry average seems to be around 3.6)

Below are some more industry averages to be familiar with. These are only estimates, and they vary based on geography - you should get updated information from restaurant associations. They are stated as a percentage of total sales.

- Food cost: 30% to 35% (This includes liquor, if served.)

- Payroll: 28%

- Total Occupancy Costs (rent or mortgage payments, taxes, insurance): 5% to 8%

- Maintenance & Repairs: 1% to 3%

- Net Income Before Taxes: 1% to 3%

If you put together a projection of post-acquisition financial performance, make sure that at least 12% of the total cash flow is available for debt service, taxes, and bottom line profit.

Adjusting the Restaurant's Income Statement:

Add back any optional or discretionary expenses, such as the owner's auto lease. If the owner is also the manager, you'll probably want to adjust the salary to between $35,000 and $50,000, depending on what hired managers are usually paid in that area. The owner's draw will come from the bottom-line net income.

Favored Valuation Methods:

When most restaurants change hands, they reopen with a new concept, so asset value is the basis for most sale prices. However, market value of assets may not be the appropriate measure. This is because restaurants are very expensive to furnish and equip, yet the investment is only worth its ability to generate sales and earnings. Liquidation value may be the appropriate measure.

The value of the underlying real estate is often the major element of value. For that reason, asset methods should exclude the real estate value.

The Market Data Comparable Sales Approach is not a meaningful basis for determining value unless you are dealing with a franchised product. In that case, you take out the value of the underlying land, but not the building, if owned. Adjust the income statement for each restaurant in your data sample, and then calculate its purchase price as a percentage of its adjusted income. Then find the average of those percentages, and multiply it by the adjusted net income of your subject business.

If you are dealing with a franchised restaurant that is not identical to other units (except for location and net income), then the market comparable approach may prove unreliable since there are so many variables involved. Trying to quantify them all is a very speculative endeavor.

For open, profitable establishments where the existing concept will be retained, the method of choice seems to be capitalization of net income before tax. Follow the instructions in Chapter 8, and add back the interest and depreciation before you divide by your capitalization rate.

Picking a capitalization rate:

Cap rates for restaurants tend to range between 20% and 35% of net income before taxes, interest, and depreciation.
- This suggests that 30% might be considered the median cap rate for the average established, independent restaurant in need of moderate renovation.
- Similarly, 20% might be closer to average for a hot national franchise with a great record of sales and earnings. The property would be relatively new, with little or no upgrading needed, and the concept would be very fresh.
- 25% might be the typical cap rate for a stronger-than-average independent in a modern property, established by a savvy local restauranteur who can read the emerging tastes of customers in that

market, or at least imitate the successful national chains.
- 35% might be a better choice for an older independent restaurant with an out-dated concept located in a property that needs major renovation. In any case, asset value might be higher.

Think this through for yourself, for these rates reflect a lot of opinion and speculation. We suggest that you seek out the advice of a restaurant management consultant before deciding on a particular rate.

If you are considering a higher cap rate, then make sure you compare the resulting price to the net asset value. In that case, the place probably needs a lot of changes, but if you drastically redesign it, you are actually starting a new restaurant, so it might be smarter to just purchase the location at market value and the useable equipment at liquidation value. Once you change the concept or design, even loyal past customers will view it as a new business.

Other factors to consider:

- Is it located in a seasonal market?

- Is local labor readily available?

- How much competition exists?

- How much time does the current owner invest each week to produce these results?

- Are you sure the expenses in your projections will remain stable?

Rules of Thumb for Restaurants

Despite the availability of formal valuation methods to help set the price, it's rumored that restaurants that include the underlying real estate tend to change hands at a rule-of-thumb price equal to the previous year's gross sales. It would seem wise to also discount that amount by 10% to 20% in order to offset the cost of renovation and lost sales during the transition. Here are some other rules of thumb we've heard:

Taverns	40% to 60% of annual gross sales, plus inventory; or 100% to 150% of annual net income, plus inventory (both include the liquor license)
Diners	33% to 45% of annual gross sales, plus inventory; Or 1.5 to 2 times annual net income, plus inventory
Delis	33% to 50% annual gross sales, plus inventory
Fast Food	100% to 150% annual net income, plus fixtures, equipment, inventory, and any realty (includes imputed value of franchise rights)
Ice cream	42% to 50% annual gross sales, plus shop inventory Or 100% to 150% of annual net income, plus inventory, fixtures, equipment.
Pizza Shop	33% to 36% of annual gross sales, plus inventory Or 150% to 200% annual net income, plus inventory, equipment, fixtures
Full or Limited Menu	33% to 50% of annual gross sales, plus inventory; Or 100% to 150% annual net earnings, plus inventory, fixtures, equipment (if very profitable)

Chapter 17

Special Considerations For the Service Business

A business that sells a service (instead of tangible products) usually doesn't have a lot of hard assets, so the "asset-based" methods don't apply well if the firm is profitable.

For profitable firms we use methods that calculate the value of an annual flow of income, and this is deemed to include the value of all the assets that produce it.

With this kind of business value derives from...
- a pre-established foothold in the business

- trained employees (management and sales staff)

- business systems that are up and running

- a group of likely repeat-customers or referral sources

- a recognized business name

- and perhaps a good office location.

Since these elements are difficult to isolate and appraise, their values are all lumped together under a more nebulous concept referred to as the "value of the income stream".

Capitalization of Income Method:

This technique is detailed in Chapter 8, but a variation is commonly used for service businesses:
- You start with last year's gross income, taken from an adjusted income statement.
- Then you subtract the normal operating expenses (including the owner's salary) and income taxes.
- The result is the "net operating income after tax". If sales or income have fluctuated over the past several years, then use a weighted average.
- Next, divide the net operating income after tax by the rate of return an investor would currently expect from an investment of equivalent risk (see "cap rate" - Chapter 5).
- Reduce the resulting figure by the amount of any liabilities the purchaser would assume. The result is the value of the business.

Discounted Future Benefits:

A service business can be viewed as a group of intangible assets, and this method assumes that the most important of those is the steady customers it has established over the years. It bases value on the net profit those customers will bring to a new owner, discounted to present value. (Hence the name, "discounted future benefits.")

Most businesses lose a certain portion of their existing customers every year, especially when a new owner takes over. This is called the "rate of attrition". Therefore, when using this method, you have to factor-in the normal rate of attrition expected by firms in that industry.

You can discover the rate by talking to experts from the trade association, consultants for that industry, or someone who has recently purchased that type of business. After deciding on a rate, reduce the projected net operating income for each year by that percentage. Then bring the results back to present value*.

For example, let's say you are dealing with a business that now produces net operating income (NOI) of $100,000, and reliable sources have told you to expect 20% annual customer attrition. That means that 20 out of every 100 customers will probably be lost every year regardless of how you manage the business. On that basis, you would expect that the NOI produced by that group of customers will drop to $80,000 in the first year after acquisition, $60,000 in the second year, $40,000 in the third year, $20,000 in the fourth year, and down to zero in the fifth year. Therefore, you would pay the seller for four

years of business, based on this naturally declining scale. He would not get credit for any new business established by the new owner after the acquisition.

We are dealing with *net* income, instead of gross income, so these projections should also reflect any annual increase you expect in the cost of doing business. In other words, let's say the trade association tells you that the cost of operating a typical firm increases by 15% each year. At the same time, those firms have only been able to increase their hourly fees by 10% each year. The result is that the net income will decrease by the net difference between those two (5%) each year. Therefore, in that case you would reduce the NOI by another 5% each year.

In fairness, some new customers will come to the business each year just by virtue of the fact that it's a familiar local entity, or through referral from existing customers or other established sources. Since this is part of the current business momentum, the owner should be compensated for it, but it's difficult to estimate what it amounts-to each year. You don't include new business developed by the buyer.

Since dollars received today are worth more than the same amount received in the future, you have to reduce the projected NOI for each year to present value*. Use a financial calculator or the present value tables included in the appendix of this book. For our example, let's assume you select a discount rate of 15%. On that basis, the present value of $80,000 expected in year-one is about $70,000 in today's dollars. Likewise, at the same discount rate, the $60,000 expected in year-two is worth about $45,000. And so on. So while the existing customers may bring in $200,000 (face value) over the 4-year period, it will be worth about $153,000 in terms of present value.

We are thinking of this as a "passive investment" unless an owner's salary is included in the operating expenses. In other words, we are comparing this to a self-amortizing investment that provides annuity-type payments and an annual return of 15%. With that kind of investment, you just pay your money up front and wait for the checks. With each payment, you get part of your money back, plus a return of 15%. You don't have to do any work. But if someone buying a business has to donate their own time and effort in order to realize that income, then the *operating expenses* must include the value of those services. Base that on the salary you would have to pay an equally capable replacement, hired to carry out those same duties, but only the portion corresponding to the time needed to deal with existing customers still remaining in each year. Don't deduct 100% of it.

In our example, since 20% of the original customers will leave each year, then only 80% of the employee's time will be spent with that group of customers in year one. In year 2, it drops to 60%, then 40%, then 20%. So, in each year, you deduct that percentage of the manager's salary as part of the operating expenses. Therefore, if the salary, hiring costs, employment costs, and benefits for that manager average out to $35,000 per year over the 4-year period, then in year-one, you would deduct 80% X $35,000 = $28,000. $80,000 net profit - $28,000 salary = $52,000 adjusted net profit. Then find the present value of $52,000. At a 15% discount rate that's about $45,000. That's what the existing customer base is worth for that first year. Do that for each of the four years and added them up.

This method also adds the liquidation value of any equipment that will be included in the deal, and the "cost value" of any non-obsolete inventory. The total of these three figures would then be regarded as a fair estimate of the value of the business.

෨෬

These methods are commonly used for dental practices, medical practices, law practices, insurance and investment brokerages, property management companies, and any other service business that tends to have a large amount of repeat business each year. The rate of attrition you select will depend a lot on whether the present owner's shoes can be filled by someone else. If most of the business comes to the firm as a result of special talents, technical knowledge, or personal relationships of the current owner, then all of those clients will probably leave when the owner quits.

Business valuation always assumes a sale of the business - and if the person primarily responsible for producing the income would no longer be present after the sale, then there's no income stream left to value. The value of that business is simply the liquidation value of the fixed assets.

For this reason, it's common for sole proprietor service businesses to have no transferable value. On the other hand, if the owner has trained a staff of people who are qualified to carry on and maintain that business with the same effectiveness and volume after his departure, then that owner has something significant to sell besides filing cabinets. For those suing in divorce court, this means you are wasting your time trying to claim a large sum of money based on the value of your ex-spouse's professional practice. Both theoretically and practically, no ongoing business value can be attributed to the income he or she currently produces. You can't modify the central principles of business valuation to avoid that reality.

It's usually difficult to find a bank loan to finance the purchase of a small service business or professional practice. For that reason, when a deal is made, it often involves some form of "owner financing" whereby the seller receives his purchase price over time. This, of course, is risky for the seller because the new operator might not be as talented or dedicated as the current one. Without his own cash at stake, or any responsibility for a formal bank loan, the new owner probably won't have as much motivation to do a good job. If he screws up the business and loses all the customers, it's relatively easy for him to just walk away from the whole thing. In that case, the business usually falls back into the seller's lap - only now it's been run down to nothing, so the seller loses both his business and the unpaid portion of his sale price.

For this reason, sellers usually feel they are better off taking a lower price in order to get all cash at settlement. If you have the time and patience, another route is to make the buyer a partner who will then buy you out over time. This is a great approach for those who want to retire, but feel anxious about making a sudden transition, plus it allows you to keep drawing a salary for a while. You have a chance to "train" the new owner to operate the business successfully, while you gradually ease out the door, making sure the transition goes well so things don't go all to hell in a handbasket. Since some customers may be hesitant about doing business with the new owner, this gives them a chance to warm up to the new owner gradually, lessening the chance that they will jump ship as soon as the seller leaves.

Rules of Thumb:

See chapters 15 and 16 for some popular short-cut methods of valuing certain types of service businesses. Before using them, make sure you also read the caveats that are included in those chapters.

Chapter 18

Secured Loan Value

Secured Loan Value tells you how much money you can borrow by using the company's assets as collateral.

This is a major factor in determining purchase price.

Most lenders only loan a certain percentage of the asset value, and if you're lucky, that will be enough to cover most of the price. The wider the gap between asking price and secured loan value, the smaller the field of buyers, since no one wants to put up lots of their own cash to do a deal. Therefore, the price you come up with by other methods will have to tempered by secured loan value. Most buyers qualify their deals on the basis of how much of the price they can borrow, so they are more attracted to companies with lots of valuable, securable assets.

Of course, having lots of collateral isn't the only factor in the lending decision. Equally important is the company's ability to generate the cash flow needed to make the payments. Therefore, the business must appear financially viable in its recapitalized, post-acquisition form. No lender is interested in financing a potential bankruptcy.

What if it's a very profitable service-business, with few hard assets? It's much harder to borrow against cash flow, no matter how healthy the company might be. You usually can't borrow more than the secured loan value unless earnings are exceptional, sales trends are upward, and future prospects for that industry are very promising. For example, if there was enough cash flow in each of the past five years to *safely* make all of the proposed loan payments, then the lender might consider making the loan without adequate collateral. Absent that, however, the lender will limit the loan amount based on the nature, value, condition, and quality of the collateral assets.

The lender's main concern is how much money it can recover if forced to seize the assets and sell them quickly. They don't want to be bothered with trying to get the highest possible price. They want their money back yesterday, so the assets will be liquidated at auction. Therefore, they peg secured loan values at somewhat less than auction or liquidation value. This reflects their uncertainty on how much they'll really recoup, and the costs of conducting such a sale. For this reason, secured loan values are usually defined as a percentage of "orderly liquidation value" or "forced liquidation value". The former usually refers to an orderly sale of the assets within a six-month period, so it's closer to "market value". The latter term refers to the amount the lender will probably recoup if the assets are disposed of at an auction held within 60 days of seizure. Lenders don't want to be saddled with the responsibility of locating the very best buyer. They don't want to care for the assets or insure them any longer than necessary, so the auction route is usually preferred. That makes forced liquidation value the usual measure.

It's difficult to estimate secured loan value without an outside appraisal of liquidation value. In that case, "book value" is often used as a substitute. It's usually less than liquidation value, so it's even more conservative.

You don't get a loan for the full liquidation value of the assets, only a percentage of that. The percentage is called the "advance rate", and it varies for different types of assets, based on the lender's degree of confidence in your company's future, the expected cost of conducting a liquidation, the relative liquidity* of the particular type of asset, and the risk of a decline in value.

After the loan is made, the lender will ask for periodic reports to monitor the continued presence and condition of the collateral. For instance, let's say the company has a revolving loan for working capital, secured by inventory. In that case, the lender wants to know if inventory levels drop significantly, so it can call-in that portion of the loan.

How to Determine Secured Loan Value

Lenders apply a different advance rate to each different type of asset. The rate used by the lender will also depend on the value, condition, desirability, and quality of the particular assets being offered as security. In addition, different types of lenders will use different rates. The only way to find out is to ask. The following is a typical rate schedule. The assets are listed in order of their desirability as security.

Type of Asset	Advance Rate	X	Measure of Value
Accounts Receivable (Not including doubtful accounts)	80%-90%	X	Book Value
Raw Materials Inventory	50%	X	Book Value
Finished Goods Inventory	25%-30%	X	Book Value
Work-In-Progress Inventory	0%-25%	X	Book Value
Machinery & Equipment	60%-80%	X	Liquidation Value
Real Estate	80%	X	Appraised Market Value

The lender might impose additional restrictions with regard to certain classes of assets. For instance, obsolete equipment or equipment designed to perform a specialized process is often excluded from eligible collateral.

Computers and other high-tech equipment become obsolete very fast, so they are rarely accepted at the same advance rate as other equipment. Intangible assets are generally excluded altogether because (1) they are rarely worth anything once separated from the business, (2) there usually isn't a secondary market for their resale, (3) their value is difficult to estimate, and (4) even if you can pin-down their value, it's usually too nominal to be worth the effort.

Using Accounts Receivable as Loan Security:

Receivables are often used as security for revolving loans to finance working capital. Those older than 90 days are usually disqualified (unless 90 day terms are standard practice in that industry). In addition, any past-due receivables from a particular customer can disqualify all receivables from that customer. This can be disastrous for some companies.

Ineligible receivables are sometimes included in the advance if the seller will personally guarantee their collection. Sellers are often willing to do this because it can get them a higher price to that extent.

Using Inventory As Loan Security:

Inventory advances are hard to predict because there are so many variables. It all depends on the particular product being made. For some companies, the liquidation value of inventory is close to zero because the goods have no value to anyone but a scrap dealer. This is frequently the case with work-in-progress. Lenders don't care if "WIP" can be turned into finished goods quickly. They base the loan on the inventory as it stands today. They don't want to get involved in the complication of converting the stuff to finished goods before they can get their money back. On the other hand, raw materials that are widely used will have considerable value. An example might be sheet metal in standard sizes and gauges.

The advance on finished goods depends upon the market for that product. It also depends on the company's normal percentage of standing orders. Some companies pile up finished goods in quantities that are far out of proportion to the number of orders on hand. Sellers who want a higher price can agree to buy back any inventory that remains unsold after a certain date.

Note: If the company uses the LIFO* method of inventory accounting (last in, first out), there will probably be lots of old inventory on the balance sheet, carried at prices that are less than what it's worth now. This hidden value can result in a higher advance rate.

Inventory is often used as security for revolving loans, where the loan principal isn't paid back unless the security diminishes. Only the interest is paid. The security for these is usually a combination of accounts receivable and invent- ory. However, inventory is less desirable as loan security, so any amount advanced against inventory might have to be amortized* (repaid over a set period of time). Again, it depends on the lender's confidence level concerning the quality of the security and the company's future.

Machinery and Equipment As Loan Security:

Equipment is used as security for short term loans (less than 5 years). To get a longer term, you have to combine the equipment with real estate.

The value of machinery and equipment is

based on its forced liquidation value because there isn't usually a big market for it. If the stuff is really specialized and hard to sell, you have to assume an even lower price. In many cases, you'll get your best price by selling everything together as a fully-equipped facility. But that's a tall order to fill, and lenders aren't that patient, so equipment is almost always sold at auction. Anyone who has purchased equipment through a used equipment dealer is familiar with the savings involved. Their stock has been purchased at auction and marked up, so you can imagine how low the auction prices are.

There are several factors to consider when estimating the advance rate and eligibility of a certain piece of equipment. Equipment that's obsolete or subject to rapid technological change will probably be excluded. As mentioned earlier, equipment that is designed to perform a specialized function is also worth less. And the advance rate for expensive items is slim too, since their are fewer potential buyers.

Another factor is whether the item can be easily detached and moved from the property. If it's costly or complicated to do that, the advance rate will be lower. Lenders also consider the vitality of the industry to which the equipment pertains, since this affects resale demand.

Lenders may ask you to provide a recent appraisal by an independent, professional appraiser. Fortunately, appraised values are often higher than balance sheet values, due to the effects of depreciation and inflation. Most appraisers can estimate value on the basis of a complete description of the asset: type, model, cost, age, depreciation taken, and condition. However, they prefer to conduct a physical inspection in order to verify their existence and condition.

If you don't already have a recent appraisal, don't go out and hire one, since the lender will want to use an appraiser of its own selection. If you have a replacement value appraisal, conducted for insurance purposes, that won't be acceptable. Lenders want market value and liquidation value.

Real Estate As Loan Security:

Much to the surprise of most borrowers, real estate is the least attractive form of security for an acquisition loan, due to its unpredictable marketability. Real estate demand fluctuates constantly, largely based on availability and the cost of real estate financing at any given point time. If the economy is slow, demand will be down, and values will be depressed. These are uncontrollable factors that can greatly influence on company value.

The problem with industrial buildings is that there's a very slow, limited market for them. They tend to be designed around very specific needs, which really narrows the field of buyers. Even if it could be leased as a income-producing property, it still isn't attractive security because lenders don't want to get involved with leasing, maintenance, and property management.

For these reasons, lenders don't like to inherit real estate. Consequently, if there is any doubt about the company's post-acquisition prospects, the lender may refuse to advance anything at all for the real estate. Nevertheless, the lender will still probably demand that it be included in the loan security. They may tell you that your loan amount is based on the value of all of the fixed assets, according to some undisclosed formula, but you don't really get any advance for the real estate. They just want you to throw it in as extra security.

Real estate is often used as security for seller financing. Sellers have a lot more confidence in the value of their real estate than the typical asset-based commercial lender does. Things that bother commercial lenders aren't a big problem for the seller, who is often better equipped and more willing to handle those disadvantages. Sellers often become the real estate lender by taking back a note secured by a first mortgage on the property. Alternatively, a buyer can purchase all of the assets of the company except the real estate, whose title remains with the seller. Then the seller leases the property to the buyer, with or without an option to purchase it at some future date. Someone selling his own private company is more likely to agree to this arrangement than a corporate seller.

Sometimes, for tax purposes, a individual buying a company will purchase the property separately, and then lease it to his newly acquired company. In that case, the personal credit of the buyer is just as important as the credit of the tenant company. In other words, this may be an attractive financial option for the buyer, but it complicates the lending arrangements.

Real estate is generally appraised at market value by a certified real estate appraiser. Before states started requiring real estate appraisers to take specialized courses and proficiency exams, many lenders would only accept commercial appraisals from an MAI-certified appraiser. However, in states where all appraisers must have advanced training, many lenders don't make the distinction any more. Some lenders will even settle for an average of several market value estimates provided by local real estate brokers. Brokers will often help you out as a gesture of goodwill, in the hope that you'll remember them later when you need the services of a broker.

Important Limit on Secured Loan Value:

Once you've calculated the total collateral value of the assets, you still have to figure out whether the company can generate the cash flow needed to make the loan payments. For instructions on this, see Chapter 14 (Cash Flow Analysis).

If necessary, see Chapter 10 for details on how to predict the type and amounts of loans that are used to finance an acquisition.

Chapter 19

Putting It All Together

Range of Value:

By this point you've used several different methods to estimate the value of your company, and each one will have produced a different figure. That gives you a *range of value* for the firm. This a very appropriate way to look at the value of a firm, because there is no single, correct number.

Nevertheless, you should still try to narrow it down, particularly if the range is fairly wide. This is a fairly subjective process, and it's only an estimate, but you still have to support your conclusion with logic. This chapter will give you advice on how to do that. Pay particular attention to the last two sections.

Unfortunately, you can't just average the results from different methods. There is a point lying somewhere in that range that represents the most appropriate figure, and it's not necessarily in the middle. As Revenue Ruling 59-60 says, "no useful purpose is served by taking an average of several factors."

It's important to be realistic and objective.

This is a sensitive topic, and sellers should try to face it honestly. Owners frequently seem to have the impression that there are plenty of rich corporate buyers out there who are just dying to pay too much for acquisitions. If you think that way, you will really do yourself a disservice.

First of all, acquisitions are big deals, and each one is very carefully studied, so they don't happen at prices that aren't realistic. If anything, the prices tend to be conservative,

because buyers know that there are other ways to enter any particular business. There are checks and balances throughout the entire process, imposed by parties who have an interest in making sure the deal is sensible: accountants, lenders, equity investors, appraisers, attorneys. Each one has their neck on the line, and each one is capable of putting the brakes on the whole deal if it doesn't look safe. So if you go into this with unrealistic price expectations, then the whole  thing will become a big waste of everyone's time. It's amazing how many hours are consumed in just the preliminary stages of an acquisition, and it's all spent in vain if the price is too high. In addition, a seller with unreasonable expectations will lose credibility in the business community as word gets around (and it will). Sellers should also avoid the bogus attitude that "anything's for sale if the price is right." That usually has the same effect. Either you want to sell and you have a realistic asking price, or you don't want to sell.

Another problem is that, when a company is priced too high, it's going to remain on the market for a long time. Everyone eventually hears about it, and after remaining unsold for a while it will seem like shopworn merchandise. That implies that there's something seriously wrong with the business. In addition, the delay might carry you into a period where the company just isn't performing as well as before, or when the economy hits a downturn, or the whole industry falters, or interest rates zoom up. All of these will lower the price you can get. If you're ready to sell, don't jerk around.

Sellers need to stand in the shoes of their prospective buyers. Try to view the company just like an outsider considering the purchase. If this business belonged to someone else, would *you* pay that kind of price? It's hard to be objective about something you are close to, but it's important to be honest with yourself. There once was a business brokerage that induced owners to sign up for their services by running an ad campaign claiming that most sellers give their company away by setting the price too low. In fact, it's just the opposite - owners are more likely to demand a price that's too high, and thwart their own best interests in the process. Nonetheless, it can be hard to dissuade people from this. It's human nature to believe only what you want to believe.

Negotiation will affect final price.

Negotiation involves give and take. The viewpoints of buyer and seller always differ, so some amount of compromise is necessary to bring them together. After all, each side has different objectives, so they each assign a different value to the firm. The possibility of resolving those differences will depend upon the relative desire of each to make the deal.

Keep in mind that price isn't the only important consideration in a deal. There will be other terms and conditions wanted by each side, but those can all be translated into a monetary value, and each can be bartered-off for something else.

When people sell something, they tend to ask considerably more than they intend to get. Likewise, buyers usually start by offering less than they're really willing to pay. There is an unspoken assumption that they'll meet somewhere in the middle. As long as your opening number isn't completely unrealistic, you can take this approach. Add 10% or 15% to the price you really want - but don't get

carried away. Horse trading tactics don't take you far in acquisitions because, at some point early in the game, you'll have to explain the rationale behind your numbers. At that point, any ridiculous numbers will make you look foolish. And don't get comfortable with the higher number just because you get used to saying it.

Ego seems to have a big affect on these offers. For example, many buyers have a hangup about paying asked-price for anything. They need to think they cut themselves an awesome deal. And sellers are sometimes so emotionally tied to their company that they regard any offer lower than their target price as a insult and fail to even counter the bid. Those people should prepare the prospective buyer by warning them against low ball offers.

The best route for buyers is to avoid any discussion about price until you know something about the firm. Talk about your general pricing concept, but don't discuss particular numbers.

Chapter 20 treats the whole topic of price negotiation in a lot more detail, so refer to that before you start trying to make your deal.

Income taxes don't count:

Sellers aren't allowed to jack up their number in order to cover the income tax they'll have to pay on the sale proceeds. The figure you arrive at through valuation methods is a before-tax number. It isn't the buyer's responsibility to pay your taxes. The sale proceeds for a business can be large, so it definitely hurts to give away a third of that for taxes, but that's how it works. Besides, you wouldn't be paying a lot of tax if you weren't making a lot of money. Your gripe is with Congress, not the buyer. I know of no buyer who ever increased their offer to help cover a seller's tax. But you'd be shocked to know how often this affects the seller's perception of the price he should get.

Value the Company As It Stands Now

It 's sometimes said that valuation reflects the present worth of a future flow of earnings. This is true, but that prediction is always a continuation of the present. There's too much uncertainty in business to ever say for sure that the future will outperform the past. For that reason, it's inappropriate to base a valuation on higher sales than the company is producing now. It also isn't fair to base your price on the assumption that operating costs can be drastically reduced. Maybe they can, but you really don't know for sure.

You can use an income statement that has been adjusted to give a more accurate view of what's happening, but never base your valuation on a hypothetical proforma* income statement. If the future produces better results, that will occur at the buyer's risk and due to the buyer's efforts - not the seller's, so the seller can't expect to be paid for it. The seller only gets paid for what he has accomplished to date. If the seller foresees growth in the future and wants it reflected in his selling price, then he should retain ownership a bit longer in order to take advantage of it.

If you prepare a proforma or earnings forecast for others, make sure the client receives your disclaimers. They must realize that those figures only reflect opinion and speculation - that they're nothing to count on. In general, its better to let the principals do the forecasting. Many bad deals have resulted from overly optimistic sales forecasts. There are a million factors that can cause

actual results to differ from the forecast - unforeseen cost increases, unstable employee relations, new government regulations, a change in the tax laws, the general condition of the economy, international events, and so on.

Any buyer who is tempted act on the basis of a *seller's* projection should regard it as pure speculation,  and perhaps hold back part of the purchase price until those earnings actually appear. This is called an "earn out", and the sums that are paid later are contingent payments. For example, this might be used when a company has developed a new manufacturing process but hasn't had time to put it on-line. However, if future earnings rise, it might be impossible to determine whether it's due to the new process, or whether it resulted from other changes implemented by the new owner. In that situation, it's usually better to just go on faith rather than try to trace the source of earnings, because the latter just creates a big issue.

Divorce Situations:

If the company is being sold pursuant to a divorce settlement, and a spouse with indispensable knowledge or abilities is leaving the firm as a result, then the value of that business must be adjusted downward. Anytime you lose someone who is vital to the company's success, its value is negatively affected. Sometimes the business is completely worthless without them, at least as a going entity.

Even if there's no plan to actually sell the business to fund the settlement, the same rule applies. Business value is *always* based on market value - which, *without exception, necessarily implies that the thing being valued will be sold*, and if the spouse being sued is the major reason that firm produces income, then it is very safe to say that person won't be there after the sale (unless forced servitude is once again legalized). As a result, the firm's value will simply be the liquidation value of its fixed assets. That's it. There's no logical argument around it.

When most of the company's assets is inventory:

Buyers should make sure the seller does n't let inventory slip below normal levels between the time the contract is signed and the date of settlement. The contract should provide for a price adjustment, based on an inventory audit conducted the day before settlement. In addition, sellers should always adjust the price downward for obsolete or unusable stock.

Consultants who are paid a contingency fee based on the size of the deal can be hurt when the price is adjusted downward due to a depleted inventory. They should anticipate this possibility and take steps to preserve the integrity of their fee.

Have your accountant review your valuation before you rely on it!

Before you base any decisions on your valuation, have it reviewed by a competent professional. You've already pulled the data together and done the  basic calculations, so it shouldn't take long for the accountant to go through it. Make sure you take this precaution because there's a lot about valuation that can be overlooked or misunderstood. Make sure you provide the accountant with the details of your financial assumptions. Besides, there are tax conse-

quences to any transaction, and those laws change constantly, so the client will need up-to-date advice. Even professional appraisers should ask the client's CPA to get involved, at least to verify the raw data, assumptions, and calculations that have been used.

Deduct any liabilities that will be assumed by the buyer.

Have you discovered all of the liabilities (and potential liabilities) being assumed by the buyer? The purchase price must be adjusted to account for those. Since many of these are hidden, the buyer should have an attorney perform a legal review in order to uncover any tax obligations, contractual obligations, labor union contracts, potential litigation, and employee benefit plans.

Unfunded employee bonus plans, profit sharing plans, and pension plans can pass a HUGE liability on to the buyer. You can't just terminate those plans.

The employees are legally entitled to any benefits that have accrued to date. Besides, employee relations will go completely to hell if you try to yank those benefits. But problems arise if the plan is underfunded by the current employer. Defined benefit pension plans, particularly the multi-employer variety maintained through a parent corporation, are something buyers *and sellers* should always be wary of.

Anyone owning a company should be very careful about setting up benefit plans, because if the cost of providing those benefits should skyrocket later on, the employer really gets hammered. Another problem is that the pension plan may automatically terminate according to its own terms when the assets or stock of the company is sold. The plan is then frozen and the seller is held liable for all unfunded liabilities. That liability can actually exceed the proceeds of sale. Instead of retiring to Hawaii to go surfing, the seller ends up in the poor house. The government isn't very sympathetic if you claim you didn't know what you were getting into when you set up the plan. Always consult an attorney specializing in pension plans before you get involved with them. You really have to think ahead.

Have you included every asset?

Some valuable assets are easily overlooked. For example, the company might have a sizeable investment in research and development activities that have not yet resulted in a patent. It's just as important to uncover hidden assets as it is to discover hidden liabilities.

Can the business pay for itself at this price?

To most buyers, an acquisition doesn't make sense unless the business produces enough cash flow to make the payments on a conventional acquisition loan, with a reasonable safety margin to spare. That's the bottom line for most buyers, since they finance the purchase with borrowed funds. See Chapters 13 and 14 for more information on this.

When a buyer pays with its own stock:

Sometimes acquisitions are accomplished by trading the stock of one company for that of another. The seller ends up holding stock in the parent company, but how does he really know what it's worth? If the stock of the parent company isn't traded on a public exchange, then the seller will want to see a valuation of the parent company. That valuation should be based its worth *after* the acquisition. Sometimes the acquisition of a less-profitable company will dilute the earnings-per-share of the parent, which reduces the post-acquisition value of the parent's stock.

Investment banking firms often conduct valuations specifically for this purpose. Their job is to determine the fairness of the price offered to minority shareholders, so these are known as "fairness opinions".

Keep in mind that stock is a riskier mode of payment than cash. Cash usually means no risk. If you assess a risk factor of 20% to the stock of the parent company, that means you will want at least 20% more for the company if paid in stock than if paid in cash.

The chapter on "Selecting a Capitalization Rate" will give you some input on how to estimate the risk associated with the parent company's stock. Also keep in mind that more risk is added if you hold a "minority interest" in the parent company. See Chapter 21 for guidance on how much to add for that factor.

Many sellers have gotten very rich when the value of the stock they received went up, but my gut feeling is you are more likely to lose-out when you take stock as payment. Companies that buy this way are trying to fast-track their way to growth at a time when they have little cash or credit to do acquisitions. If they're on a such a shoestring budget, then the risk factor will be very high, especially when it's a service-type business because there aren't any fixed assets to have recourse against.

Squaring results from the different methods (Correlation of Results):

Once again, by this point you should have calculated the company's value according to several methods, and each will have produced a different figure - perhaps substantially so. What you have now is a *range* of possible values, and you should try to identify a figure within that range that makes the most sense.

First, narrow it down on the basis of how well each method actually fits your particular case, from a theoretical standpoint. Some methods will apply better than others, and those should be accorded more weight. If a certain method produces a very high or very low number, but the theory behind it doesn't really apply very well to your situation, then it's usually best to discard the figure from your results.

So start by assessing how well the methods you've used actually fit your case. For instance, if the company if profitable and will continue to operate as a going-concern, then the income-based methods are more appropriate than the asset-based methods, unless there are major assets that have greatly appreciated in value (such as real estate).

Some companies are asset-based holding companies, in which case the asset methods are most appropriate. Some businesses are composed mostly of liquid assets, such as wholesale companies and distribution companies that have most of their capital tied up in large amounts of inventory. These are more likely to trade on the basis of asset value. For a review on the theoretical applicability of each method, go back and look at Chapter 4, and read the first few paragraphs of each method.

Next, try to fine-tune your answer based on the other factors that influence sale price. Some of those are discussed below. For example, the contract terms of sale can affect the price so much that your final figure ends up completely outside of the original range.

So think of your range-of-value as a starting point, not as a set of absolute limits.

If your project doesn't involve the sale of a company, then there's a lot less to think about because many of the adjustments you make are based on actual terms of sale. However, even if the business isn't being sold, many of the factors listed below will still be relevant because valuation always refers to "market value", which assumes that a sale of the company will take place.

We acknowledge that it's hard to predict the impact of any given factor in dollars. You'll just have to use your best judgment. Going through this will help you appreciate how imprecise business valuation really is. Even people with years of experience have a hard time predicting the effect any given factor will have on price. That's why expensive professional appraisals still have limited value.

Valuation is not an exact science, but a matter of informed opinion. No two appraisers will have the same opinion, and no single number generated by an appraiser will be absolutely correct.

However, you should *try* to zero in on a particular value. Your final estimate should be based on a lot more than the calculated results of these methods. Start with the number from the method that it *theoretically most applicable*, then adjust it based on common sense, the anticipated effects of negotiation, the impact of probable contract terms, and market demand for a company of that type at that particular time.

By now you should realize that valuation only provides an approximation of value. Due to human nature, that estimate is usually skewed in the direction "hoped for" by the appraiser. You might be able to make a very intelligible argument from your own perspective, but someone else can probably make an equally meritorious case for a far different amount. Each represents one individual's point of view, based on a whole bunch of variables and judgement calls.

If you're both right, who wins? You run into this situation any time there are two parties with differing interests. If its a legal

battle that goes to trial, then the judge or jury may just split the difference between the two opinions. If it's a business deal, the final price will favor the side with the most bargaining power. The point is, whenever a party-in-interest performs a valuation, their conclusion is usually colored by a certain bias, rather than reflecting the fairest result.

For that reason, you would be wise to take your own conclusions with a grain of salt. Whether you realize it or not, it's probably too high or too low, depending on your stake in the matter.

Remember, the real value of a business is the price it can really be sold for, today, in its present market, to the buyers who actually exist, who have a reasonable yet not overwhelming desire to buy. It isn't worth more just because the seller wants more. It isn't worth less just because the buyer has little tolerance for risk.

If valuation is so imprecise, does that mean it's a waste of time? No, because going through the valuation process will let you know what the possibilities are, and what factors will come to determine the price that's finally negotiated. If you are a buyer or a seller, it will tell you what the company is worth to you. You have to start your negotiation somewhere, and this will provide you with a number that you have good reason to believe in. If it doesn't correspond well to the other side's point of view, then no deal will be made.

When you conduct an appraisal as a third-party, you are supposed to be impartial, but it may appear that you are siding more with the buyer's point of view, because if there's no willing buyer, then there's no sale. Your figure must reflect market value - the number at which buyers are really willing to buy.

Valuation can also give you a benchmark for comparing other companies valued by the same method. Periodic valuation of the same company, using the same method each time, provides a great measure of growth or decline, strength or weakness.

But valuation can't tell you exactly what the firm is worth, and don't believe anyone who says otherwise. It's too nebulous, too imprecise, too subjective. If the parties can agree in advance that a certain *method* of determining value shall be used in their case, then they can "assume" that the resulting number reflects true value for that purpose. But that's about as close as you can get to having "certainty". Even when you try to agree on a specific methodology, there is still a lot of subjectivity involved in applying it.

That last point is worthy of some elaboration. This book has attempted, to the greatest extent possible, to present you with a cookbook approach to valuation. You are provided  with the author's opinion of the best ingredients for each recipe, but many of the measurements are left up to your personal judgment. As a result, the dish will come out different for every cook. This is unavoidable, so it's important to document your financial assumptions and the reasoning behind them. At least others will have the opportunity improve upon your result if they disagree with what you did.

In the end, always ask whether your results are reasonable. Would a buyer really pay that much? From a practical perspective, would the owner be stupid to sell at the price you came up with? If the end result doesn't make sense, then you need to re-think it. In the final analysis, the market value of a business is limited to what someone will really willing to pay for it.

Other factors Affecting Purchase Price:

When valuing a business, always remember that you are predicting the price it would really, ultimately sell for today. In reality, that's impossible, because so many elements of the actual sale transaction will affect the final negotiated price. Nonetheless, here are some things to consider:

Will the transaction take the form of a purchase of assets or a purchase of stock?

An asset sale is usually preferred by buyers because they don't want to inherit the pre-existing liabilities of the company. An asset deal also gives the buyer a fresh depreciable tax basis for each asset, which increases cash flow and lowers income tax. (See Chapter 10, Step 3; and Chapter 13, Step 3b) It is also possible to get a stepped-up basis when the deal is carried out through a purchase of stock, using Section 338 of the Internal Revenue Code, but double-check this with your accountant because the tax laws change constantly.

If you buy the company through a purchase of stock, but don't qualify under Section 338, you inherit the company's old depreciable basis, which may be used up by that time. Usually, in a purchase of stock, all of the existing tax attributes of the corporation pass to the buyer since the company is not altered by the sale. It just changes hands. If an asset costing $50,000 has been completely written off except for $1000, then that's all the depreciation the new owner will ever get out of that asset.

On the other hand, in an asset deal, a new corporation is formed to acquire those assets. In that case, the company can depreciate their entire purchase price. You take the purchase price for the whole company and divvy it up among the individual assets, and that's how much you can depreciate for each one - just like when you buy new property.

However, an asset deal is not as favorable to the seller. Unless it qualifies as a partial or total liquidation under the Internal Revenue Code, the seller loses the ability to treat the proceeds of sale as capital gain.

Periodically, the government decides to tax capital gain at lower rates, and this distinction can sometimes amount to a big difference. If all of the gain is treated as ordinary income, then it's all taxed at the higher rates. The seller may also have to recapture some of the depreciation that was deducted in prior years. In other words, he is deemed to have received ordinary income that he never really got, and now he has to pay taxes on it. However, if most of the assets of the company are older and don't have much depreciation left in them, then the seller will have to offer an asset sale in order to interest buyers. Acquisitions usually don't work without the cash flow and tax deductions produced by *increased* depreciation. That's a given, so the seller usually isn't in a position to demand a higher purchase price in exchange for giving up a more favorable tax treatment. But if the current depreciation schedule will provide healthy deductions for a few more years, this might become a negotiable point.

In a stock sale, the buyer acquires all of the seller's unknown and undisclosed liabilities. It's usually worth something to the buyer to be able to avoid these liabilities by getting an asset deal, but in order to assess that, you really need to know what kind of risks actually exist. All else being equal, most buyers will pay a little more just for peace of mind on this issue, even when they aren't aware of any specific potential liabilities. On the other hand, if the company, or that particular industry, has a history of legal problems, the seller is usually forced to offer an asset deal (or some type of legal indemnification) before any buyer will be interested, and the seller can't expect more money for doing that.

In an asset sale, how will the purchase price be allocated? Price allocations that benefit one party a lot more than the other may justify an adjustment of the sales price. Both parties are committed to the same allocation. Usually, however, the allocation is a compromise and no adjustment is made to price.

For instance, if the company is deemed to have no goodwill value, yet the parties agree to allocate part of the purchase price to goodwill, the seller will receive a tax benefit that he otherwise wouldn't enjoy. This is because the profits that are attributed to the sale of goodwill are treated as capital gain rather than ordinary income. However, by agreeing to this, the buyer incurs a detriment, because the "goodwill" he acquires is not a depreciable asset under the tax laws. This would justify some price adjustment in favor of the buyer.

If it's a stock sale, is there a net operating loss that can carry-over to the buyer? This will happen if the company sustained losses in past years but didn't have enough taxable income against which to apply them. The losses carry-forward as a deduction available in the future. If you buy the stock of that company, you inherit the unused part of the loss deduction. Companies in this situation usually don't have high values to begin with. Usually, the assets of the firm are sold separately, and the proceeds of sale are distributed to the stockholders. Then, the empty corporate shell (which still owns the unused tax loss deductions) can be sold to a different party. The price for that is based on the discounted value of the tax benefit available to the buyer. However, before you enter into such a deal, consult your accountant because there are restrictions on the use of a tax loss "carryforward" by a different business. The law on this could be different by the time you read this.

Seller Financing - Where the seller offers the buyer an installment sale or a second mortgage, at better terms than the buyer can get from conventional sources, then the buyer should be willing to pay a little bit more in  exchange for that. It all depends on the loan terms. The fact that the seller offers to finance the deal usually isn't enough to warrant a higher price, because the seller also gains something in the arrangement. By receiving his sale proceeds in installments over a number of years, he will probably be taxed at lower incremental rates. In addition, he will recover the entire company if the seller defaults. Conversely, if he gets all of the proceeds in one big lump, they will probably land him in a higher tax bracket.

In other words, by financing the sale, the seller saves on taxes and gets a nice interest-bearing mortgage investment at the same time. But if the buyer is a poor credit-risk, or if loan terms do not allow recourse to other funds of the buyer, or if the company is weak or the industry is risky, then the seller would not be wise to finance the deal. Any substantial risk undertaken by the seller in financing the sale will warrant an increase in price.

Another case that may warrant an increase in price is when the seller loans part of the purchase price at better terms than are offered by commercial lenders. Some sellers will even finance the price on an unsecured

basis. If the seller's loan terms are only slightly better, then it's usually a wash. One side must incur a detriment in order to justify an adjustment from the other party.

In many cases, the seller must offer financing, in order to make up for other problems inherent in the company. Sometimes the seller has no choice because the company won't produce enough cash flow to make the payments on conventional financing. If he wants to sell the company, then he has to finance the price, and no increase is justified.

When the seller finances the deal with a small down payment from the buyer, it might warrant some increase in the sale price in order to compensate the seller for the added risk. The normal downpayment is 10% to 20%. (The tax code sometimes imposes a limit on how small the down payment can be and yet still qualify as an installment sale. Make sure you consult the code.) Conversely, if the financing seller demands a lot of loan security, that's not good for the buyer. Sellers shouldn't expect a lot of enthusiasm for the deal if their financing terms are too onerous.

The availability of buyers and acquisition financing will affect the company's value. Even if the company is being valued for purposes other than its sale, you must remember that valuation is always based on market value, so there must be a market demand for that company or it will have no value as a going entity.

Any very unique business can run into trouble for this reason. It might be very profitable for its present owner, but only because of the way he's willing to operate it. If nobody else would be willing to do what he does in order to turn a profit, then you have to appraise it at a lower value. This is more common than you think, particularly among very resourceful entrepreneurs. They might be working 70 hours a week to squeeze a tidy profit from a facility that's old and in constant need of repair. They carry little or no debt. Their assets, and even their business concept, may be on the verge of obsolescence, but the owner's energy, personal magic, and lack of debt makes it a cash cow for him. Anyone else, carrying a normal debt-load, working normal hours, and relying on ordinary management ability rather than unique vision, would be hard-pressed to turn a profit. To them, it might have no value except for the underlying assets. The net result is often that there aren't any buyers at a price that would interest the seller.

Similarly, if conventional sources aren't financing the acquisition of that kind of business, then its market value will nosedive. A good analogy is what happened to the value of shopping centers in the early 1990's. These facilities were overbuilt throughout the 1980's, and many lenders got burned as a result. As a consequence, by 1992, lenders wouldn't lend money to buy one. A center that would have sold like greased-lightning in 1986 at a cap rate of 8% on Net Operating Income, couldn't be sold at all in 1992, even  at a cap rate of 14%. The market value of that center was the price it could really sell for right then, within a reasonable period of time. Since the only buyers around were bargain hunters, many of these centers were worth little more than the value of their underlying land - and real estate portfolio managers were terrified at the prospect of having their properties re-appraised. The same thing happens with businesses. Anything that affects the availability of buyers affects value.

An exception might be a glamorous, high-profile company that attracts buyers who can purchase with their own cash (a pension company), or using a standing line of credit or a new stock offering (a huge corporation). Few businesses are this attractive. Their names are household words. They are mentioned regularly in the business magazines. If you think you own one, you're probably mistaken.

What do you do if you're in this situation? You can't use an old appraisal from an earlier date. An appraisal is only valid for the date on which it's performed. If the decline in value is due to changeable market conditions, you can keeping running the business and just wait for the upturn. Just try to stick it out, and hope that day arrives before other developments that affect the industry or market in a negative way. But the fact remains: its value is what it is today.

The owner of a very unique business doesn't really have that option. Once again, we're talking about the kind of firm that few others could squeeze the same kind of profit from, even during great market conditions. After concluding that they will never find a buyer at a price that interests them, those owners often take a different route: they reduce their overhead, loan interest, and other costs - and just run the business into the ground. They milk it for all the income it's worth until it's dead, then sell the assets for liquidation value.

Another alternative is to sell the company to a key employee, and gradually turn over the helm. The owner slowly steps aside, and gets paid over time in installments. Still another alternative is to gradually convert the business into assets that are more marketable. For instance, if the area surrounding your plant has developed commercially, then you might be able to slowly convert your facilities into high-quality, multi-use commercial space, rented under long-term leases. Maybe you can even have portions of the property re-zoned to a more valuable classification.

Available lending terms affect value.

In addition to the availability of conventional financing, the actual loan terms will also affect value. Interest rates are particularly influential. Obviously, when the cost of financing is less, the loan payments can support a larger debt, so the purchase price can be larger as well. Therefore, the market value of any company actually fluctuates as interest rates go up and down.

How old are the assets? Are they fully depreciated?

This was mentioned earlier. But another thing to watch out for is when profits are actually overstated because the depreciation deductions have been unusually low. In that case, you might adjust the income statement to show realistic post-acquisition depreciation charges. (See Chapter 13, Step 3; Chapter 10, Step 3; and Chapter 3)

How large is the asset base?

The assets of the company will be pledged as security (collateral) for any acquisition loan. The lender will only advance a portion of their value, so the higher the total asset value, the larger your loan will be. You will be very lucky if that asset base is valuable enough to cover the entire purchase price. To the extent it falls short, the buyer will have to put down more cash, or pledge personal assets as collateral. Due to the difference between asset value and the amount a lender will advance, the actual sale price must sometimes be lower than the calculated value of the company. If a buyer can't obtain a loan of minimum conventional size (70% to 90% of the proposed purchase price), then the company just can't be sold for that price, so it can't be considered market value.

> Sometimes, when hard assets are lacking, the lender will loan money on the strength of cash flow alone - the loan is said to be "secured by the cash flow". But that's rare.

The company must be very profitable, it must show a consistent upward trend in earnings and sales, and the future prospects for both the company and the industry as a whole must be very strong. There must be utterly no doubt. Otherwise, buyers will have to dig too deeply into their own pockets, or give away equity to outside investors in order to raise the extra cash, or take on unsecured financing at high interest rates. Nobody wants to do that, so you have to adjust the price downward to avoid it.

Are you appraising less than a majority interest?

The methods in this book assume that you are valuing a majority ownership interest in the company. If you own a smaller share of it, and can be outvoted on management issues, then the majority shareholders can take actions that are completely against your interests, and you will be powerless to do anything about it, short of bringing a lawsuit. For that reason,...

> Minority interests are worth less than their respective portion of the whole value. Refer to Chapter 21 for more information on this.

When the buyer pays with stock:

Buyers don't like to lay out cash for acquisitions, so they frequently offer a higher price if they can pay in stock. It might be stock in the buyer's existing company, or stock in a new firm set up by the buyer.

Sometimes the transaction is structured as a "tax-free exchange of stock", whereby the seller trades her stock for stock in the buying company. In that case, the seller doesn't have to recognize taxable gain on the sale right away. That gain is taxed later, when she resells the stock to someone else.

However, if no one wants to buy it, then she's stuck in this new "investment" with no financial liquidity. There's also a risk that the stock will decrease in value before she can sell it. This risk can be significant in a tax-free exchange because there are restrictions imposed by the U.S. Securities Exchange Commission on how soon that stock can be resold. If you don't adhere to those rules, the entire tax-free status is lost and the seller ends up with a hefty tax bill. Therefore,...

Sellers who agree to stock as payment should always demand a higher price from the seller.

Is that stock overvalued?

Market enthusiasm can drive up stock prices to a level that's well beyond what's justified by the company's earnings. That stock is "overpriced", or "priced above its earnings value", and its value usually drops

(suffers a "market adjustment") soon thereafter. If the seller receives overpriced public stock as his payment medium, then perhaps the purchase price should be inflated to the same extent.

Is part of the purchase price contingent?

Sometimes part of the purchase price is held back and paid later if certain events occur. One form of this is the "earn out", where additional payments are made to the seller if the company's post-acquisition earnings exceed a certain level. This happens when the seller says the company's adjusted income is greater than the buyer believes, or when the parties differ over capitalization rates (which should reflect profitability). By agreeing to this kind of arrangement, the seller is saying he's willing to put his money where his mouth is. This setup can make the deal happen, but it can also be a burden for the buyer, so there is usually some further reduction in the amount paid at settlement to offset the inconvenience of it.

As an example, let's say the stated earnings of a company justify a price of $1,000,000, based on a mutually agreed cap rate. But the seller insists that the adjusted earnings are higher and justify a price of $1,200,000 at the same cap rate. In order to make the deal, the buyer agrees to pay a total of $1,150,000, but only if the earnings claimed by the seller are actually met or exceeded.

The downside is that the buyer doesn't have a clean break with the seller at settlement. He has to allow inspection of his books, argue over fair accounting practices, and so forth. In addition, the additional payments will have to come from the company's cash flow, since they can't be borrowed up front with the rest of the purchase price. In that case, to reflect those disadvantages, this buyer might agree to pay $900,000 at settlement (not $1,000,000) plus

$25,000 after each year (for the next 10 years) the earnings meet or exceed the level claimed by the seller. In theory, the buyer shouldn't have to pay interest on these delayed payments because they're based on something that hasn't occurred yet. These earn-out arrangements are not recommended if they reflect speculation about the level of future performance. The buyer should never pay for unrealized future potential.

For example, the buyer could assess the company a hefty allocation of home-office expenses from the parent corporation, or raise salaries or bonuses, or just plow all earnings back to fuel future growth -any of which could leave nothing at the bottom line.

Can you structure part of the purchase price as an employment or consulting contract?

That can be treated as a tax deductible salary expense, and it defers part of the purchase price to the future. This arrangement usually allows the buyer to pay a slightly higher price. Often, the seller isn't really expected to put in a lot of time at the office, other than dealing with the normal post-acquisition transition to new management. This setup usually benefits the seller as well, since it spreads out receipt of the purchase price over several years, thus lowering the overall tax bite. This arrangement usually doesn't affect the price, since there's no net detriment to the buyer or seller.

Will the current managers remain after the sale?

Many buyers view this as a precondition to any deal, so it's hard for the seller to waive it around as a big advantage to the buyer. More often than not, the continued success of the business depends on the special talents, contacts, and abilities of the people who are currently employed there. That means the business is worth less if they leave, but not more if they stay. In most cases they have to stay for at least a minimum period of time in order to insure a smooth transition to new management.

On the other hand, if the buyer plans to assume an active role in managing the business, that will displace at least one manager. Plus, the buyer may have new people she wants to bring in. In that case, management's desire to stay is almost a detriment, and hard feelings will occur when they are eventually terminated, which can affect the business. However, most buyers will require current management to stay on for at least a brief period of time. After that, they play it by ear. Buyers sometimes condition their offer on success in getting employment contracts with each of the key employees, along with covenants not compete.

For a seller who believes that his continued presence will be needed, the best approach is to let the buyer bring up the issue, and just say that it's negotiable. Then try to defer any further discussion on it until the basic price has been agreed to. On the other hand, a buyer would be wise to resolve this issue right up front, and state that it's a precondition to any offer he makes.

As part of their due diligence, buyers should study the current management group. If certain people should be replaced, that will probably cost money, and those extra expenses should be included on the proforma income statement they use to predict post-acquisition performance of the company.

Keep in mind that most owner-managers do a disproportionate share of the work, so you might need to hire two people to handle that person's job. If the buyer's company has a particular management culture, current managers are often replaced with people who are already indoctrinated with that company's ways, rather than risk a damaging and stressful culture clash.

Will the seller give a "covenant not to compete"?

This is a standard item, but they can be onerous agreements. If a seller refuses to provide one, it might lower the price. Few buyers will consider any acquisition without a covenant not to compete, since that leaves the door open for the seller or key employees to start a competing business after the acquisition, using company knowledge.

Is there a labor union?

The presence of a union is seen as a disadvantage by most buyers. Any seller whose employees are represented by a union can expect a lower price for that company than would be obtained without one. Many buyers will not go near a company whose employees are represented by a union.

What's the outlook for that industry as a whole?

The company might have great market position and show great profitability, but its success will still rise and fall with its industry as a whole. Everything else being equal, a business in a growing industry is worth more than one in a declining industry.

Do your homework and get a good feel for this factor. Read the predictions that appear in business magazines. Talk to competitors and suppliers. Call the trade association. Consult with firms like Robert Morris Associates (Philadelphia). See what the analysts are saying in publications like Value Line, Standard & Poors, and Moody's. It's their job to evaluate the future of each industry. Take a look at the "U.S. Industrial Outlook" published by the U.S. Commerce Department each year. Try to sense the impact of technological changes that are in the air.

How healthy is the general economy?

Very few companies are immune from the influence of external economic factors. The performance of many industries is directly tied to cycles of recession, inflation, and fluctuating interest rates. It doesn't seem fair, but a company can be worth much less just because the economy is off, so try to time your deal with that in mind.

Investigate the vitality of the local markets in which this company operates.

The unique conditions, expenses, or competition in its own market can make a company worth less (or more) than one located elsewhere.

Will the buyer have to make huge capital expenditures, or spend large sums on research and development, in order to remain competitive?

In anticipation of a sale, owners often stop keeping their equipment and product technology up to date. If that's the case, buyers need to determine how much corrective action will be required. How about product development? You must adjust for these costs on the income statement, so if you completed your valuation without taking them into account, then reduce the final value accordingly. A common situation is when owners defer capital expenditures and normal maintenance in order to reduce their expenses and show artificially high income. That can really throw your valuation off. If the company has gotten itself so far behind the competition that it's just too late to catch up, the whole deal might be a waste of time.

Have you looked at the company's financial ratios?

Before crunching any valuation numbers, many buyers compare ratios from the past several years in order to detect trends and get an overall picture of the risk associated with that particular business, which you'll need in order to select a capitalization rate. If you've already worked through several valuation methods, these financial ratios will help you to zero-in on a particular value within your range of figures.

Has the seller disclosed everything about the company?

A buyer should never commit to a deal while the seller is still holding back information. Don't even talk about price until everything is out in the open. Even after your offer is made, you may discover problems during your due diligence study, and your agreement should provide a way out if surprises arise.

Have you assessed the competition?

Generally speaking, the more competitive the business, the less profitable it is. Even if there isn't much competition now, that situation can change fast - particularly if the entry cost is relatively low, or if the start-up period is short. Likewise, if profitability is high but the business doesn't entail a lot of training, government regulation, and potential liabilities, then you might be an easy target. Service businesses are particularly susceptible. On the other hand, if the business requires millions in initial capital outlay, or a professional degree, or three years to break-even, then the number of new entrants will probably remain limited.

Will the acquisition produce some special synergy or competitive advantage for a different business owned by the buyer?

If so, it will be worth more to that buyer than to someone else. Sellers should look for buyers whose existing operation will be enhanced when the subject company is integrated with it.

Is the product or service proprietary?

In other words, does it own the exclusive rights to its products or services (for example, by way of patent or copyright), or is it protected from competition by some other kind of agreement or regulation? Obviously, this helps with pricing and profitability, which, in turn, enhances value.

Is the buyer a publicly-held company?

If so, it usually won't pay a multiple of earnings (inverted cap rate) that's greater than the P/E ratio of its own stock. Unless the acquisition is very small, that deal would dilute the parent company's earnings-per-share, which is a very undesirable in the eyes of the investment community.

≈≈≈

These are only a few of the factors that can affect the final value you select. Contract terms, method of transfer, tax treatment, and market conditions - these all have a bottom line impact on the buyer and seller, so they affect the price. The list of considerations above will give you an idea of what to look for. It's important to consult an acquisitions attorney and an accountant early in the game so you can get their input as well.

≈≈≈

Finally: Buyers should determine whether the company's cash flow will service the acquisition loan at the proposed price. See Chapter 14.

The Pragmatist's Point of View

There's another point of view out there concerning the value of a business - a very pragmatic approach that rejects all of this fancy analysis. We're not saying we subscribe to this line of thinking, but we'll present it so that you can decide for yourself. It produces very conservative numbers, so it isn't favored by most sellers. However, since buyers are the dominant force in determining market value, you really can't ignore it. People involved in many acquisitions often to seem come around to this line of thinking, especially when they have to run the acquired business. So here you go...

ॐ

After it's all said and done - after you've spent days working up a formal valuation, and then try to actually negotiate an acquisition price - you may wonder why you even bothered with all the number crunching. This disillusionment will arise because, in all probability, the acquisition price will be determined by the buyer, on the basis of reasoning that completely ignores all these sophisticated valuation theories. Real prices are determined by way real buyers think, while these valuation methods seem to be off in a different, very unrealistic world.

The fact is, most professional valuators are detached from real deal-making. Perhaps we are trying to make a science out of something that's really more simple and subjective.

Why have we done that? Maybe people need a greater degree of comfort because there's so much money involved - and all this complex analysis suggests that plenty of careful thought has gone into setting the price. Business finance tends to be complicated anyway, since it's designed around a hopelessly elaborate tax code.

All of this complexity has been aided and abetted by thousands of people whose livings are derived from the practice of business valuation. The more complicated it seems, the more legitimate their career seems. How can appraisers justify decent fees if they concede to the public that simple rules-of-thumb [Chapters 15 and 16] are often just as good as anything else?

Perhaps many of these methods have evolved from efforts to rationalize the existence of non-existent value. Everyone involved in acquisitions has a stake in that. Owners want to think their companies are worth more than they are. Consultants working for owners want to make their clients happy. Dealmakers, who earn contingency fees based on the size of the deal, want each the deal to be as large as possible. The IRS wants to take in maximum taxes by asserting maximum value for every business interest transferred by will. Divorcing spouses and departing partners want to claim as large a settlement as possible by fashioning arguments for new heights of value. Ditto for owners, when they apply for bank financing on the basis of their net worth.

In other words, there's lots of support for any valuation method that tends to produce an inflated figure. The more complex the reasoning, and the more information that's waived around, the more believable the argument will seem. Give 'em a nice thick report, full of tables, and numbers, and graphs. By nature, people believe what they want to believe, and then fashion arguments to support it.

In addition, humans don't cope well with the realization that we don't fully understand something in linear terms. So we try to reduce everything to cut-and-dried rules, no matter how convoluted and complicated the resulting rationale might be.

Go out and find someone who has seen many formal valuations followed with real price negotiation. Not a professional business appraiser, but a knowledgeable dealmaking intermediary. In deals that actually get made, ask them how close the valuation number is was to the final negotiated price. Many will confirm that the results of these methods rarely correspond to market value.

You can believe your company is worth any amount you want, but if real buyers won't pay that price, then it's not market value. Unless we're missing something, that means it's the way *buyers* think that influences value the most, and any method that ignores this is worthless.

So, you want cut-and-dried terms? You want to know how buyers really arrive at a price? Here you go: The average business will sell for a price that is 3 to 4 times the annual net profit (after tax) the buyer believes that company will really produce over the next year. In other words, someone will buy the company if they can get their money back in 3 to 4 years. *That* is how buyers really think.

This 3-4 multiplier assumes that the business will require someone's full-time management attention (50-60 hours per week), and that the expenses will include his salary, and that the business entails average risk. If the business is riskier than average (profitable, but with lots of competition, or has constantly changing markets and products), then it will sell for about 2 to 3 times profit. If the company involves low risk and requires little management attention, then it will sell for about 5-7 times profit. Low-risk means it's in a very stable, non-cyclical industry, and has a secure position in its own markets, with little serious competition present or likely in the near future.

Keep in mind that "risk" is relative. We aren't talking about a passive investment in a large, well-backed, diversified public company managed by some of the most talented people

in the country. Small private companies are a lot more vulnerable. There's always a lot of risk lurking around. Many business brokers used to toss around the idea that a profitable business should sell for 8 to 10 times its after-tax profits, but deals almost never occur at those prices. A multiplier of ten corresponds to a cap rate of 10%, which implies virtually no risk and nothing to do. That scenario just doesn't exist with these companies. Remember: These aren't huge, blue-chip corporations or government savings bonds. The risk is there and it's significant.

You should also realize that most buyers won't put days of study into figuring out the company's annual net profit before tax. It's easier, faster, and safer to be skeptical. Most will just look at 5 years of financials, knock off any revenues that may not occur consistently in the future, and then beef up expenses to a safer level. Next, they'll try to get a gut feel for where that industry is headed and the outlook for the company's local markets - both of which will be interpreted with safe skepticism. If the predictions they receive contain any scary news, they'll question the continuity of the company's profitability. Maybe there are exceptions, but this is how it usually works.

It's easy to criticize the comparable sales method from a theoretical standpoint [Chapter 16]. In reality, it's probably the most reliable technique - but it's so difficult to implement that it's just not very practical.

With public companies, you're lucky. Their value is determined by the stock market. You can look at the price real buyers are currently paying for stock in that very same company. Very simple. No guess work. Control premiums can be surmised from widely available information concerning public-company takeovers occurring all the time.

So go ahead, knock yourself out. Fine tune your valuation according to thousands of factors. Stay up all night. Generate spreadsheets. Give me a report six inches thick. I don't care. The price is still probably going to be 3 to 4 times the after-tax profit, or the liquidation value of the assets, whichever is greater.

ℰᏦℂᏒ

Well that's the viewpoint you are likely to hear in certain circles. You'll have to decide for yourself whether it's really true. But no book about the value of private companies would be complete if it didn't let you know that it's out there.

Chapter 20

Negotiating Tips For Buyers and Sellers

This chapter supplements the more specific negotiating advice offered throughout the book.

Are you a negotiator?

Standout dealmakers seem to have hard-wired personality characteristics that enable them to come out ahead in most negotiating situations. It's just their natural way of dealing with people, and they've probably shown those traits since childhood. However, even if you don't fall into that category, you can still learn techniques that will help you cut a better deal.

Are you a "principal" in the deal?

Be advised that even the best negotiators find it much more difficult to deal *on their own behalf.* Most people don't think as clearly when their own money is involved. They lose objectivity, and emotion starts playing a role. Lawyers have an old saying, "The attorney who represents himself has a fool for a client". If you"re in that position, it's best to realize it up front and hire someone else to represent you.

The basics of negotiation

There are plenty of good books on this subject. But most of them repeat the same idealistic advice and assume that you are dealing with reasonable, predictable people. Here's a summary of the conventional wisdom:

- In the beginning, instead of trying to make deal-points, concentrate on developing *personal rapport* with the other party, as this will be conducive to open communication and trust.

- Listen more than you talk.

- Try to become aware of the real needs and expectations of the other side. The unspoken ones are often the most important.

- Set reasonable goals - both overall and for each individual meeting.

- Ask for the reasoning behind particular demands so that you'll have a basis for challenging their position.

- Go after several small, easy "yeses" before you bring up a big issue, after the other side has already developed a momentum of "yes" responses.

- Don't try to win all the chips.

- Always offer something in return for what you want. Always demand something in return for what you give.

The real world

The advice above reflects the so-called "win-win" approach to negotiation, and it works well if both sides think that way and have relatively even bargaining power. Unfortunately, we don't live in an ideal world, so while dealing that way might make you a nice person, you'll still probably get run-over by most seasoned negotiators because what makes them tick is that they really do want to come out ahead - win-win isn't good enough. They put a much different spin on these rules.

The truth is - they play hardball. Depending on where their conscience draws the line, they may take advantage of circumstances, or  even create them, in order to improve their price and terms. They're not out to make friends, and they really don't care what you think of them after it's all said-and-done, unless they still need you after the deal has settled. But they do offer reasonable-sounding justifications that seem to soften the one-sidedness of their demands.

Much of their advantage comes from the experience of having done similar deals before. They already know the best terms to shoot for, and they know what arguments you'll probably give in to.

But don't let this put you off. You don't have to become a master manipulator to avoid being taken to the cleaners. If you learn the most common tactics, you should be able to stay out of trouble and cut a yourself a respectable deal. We'll try to advise you on how to handle them. Beyond that, just try to get good outside advice before you commit yourself to anything concrete.

Sellers: Identify the buyer's motives

The most basic rule of negotiating is: "Know the other party's agenda". Sellers should always try to figure out what the buyer really wants to achieve through this acquisition. If you can put yourself in the buyer's shoes, you will be able to anticipate many of their demands, and that will give you a chance to prepare your responses in advance.

Most buyers have a shopping list of characteristics they are looking for in a potential acquisition, ranked in order of their relative priority. When you first meet a prospective buyer, don't be afraid to ask what these are. Try to become privy to that information at the beginning, before the real negotiating starts and their guard is up. Some buyers are more apt to disclose their motives in the beginning, as a way of introducing themselves to you. However, what they say is sometimes very different from the truth.

Bear in mind that what motivates one buyer is not necessarily what motivates another. There will be some conscious, practical goal setting - and there be subconscious motives as well.

Try to see the real issue:

It's not always what it seems to be. Like in personal disputes between two people, where they are arguing about one thing, but the real issue is something else. The other person is flogging some inane point to death, until it finally dawns on you that something completely different is bugging them. In acquisitions, a common example is the owner who's afraid to let go of the company because he's worried that he'll feel lost without it, so he squelches the deal through obstinance over other issues.

What is the buyer's style?

The ideal buyer. . .

- knows exactly what they want,
- is very well-qualified to undertake the deal,
- is professional and knowledgeable,
- offers empathy regarding the emotional difficulty of selling, and
- is responsible when it comes to getting their end of the deal done.

Not everyone is like that. Companies, like the people who run them, all have a business personality which gets disguised once job of impressing each other begins.

Some buyers are seat-of-the-pants entrepreneurs, making deals quickly and decisively - almost impulsively. This type usually relies on the seller or other support people to pull all the loose ends together. They often try to renegotiate the deal later because they didn't think it through clearly the first time. They tend to have so much going on at once that things rarely get done on time, so extensions are usually needed and settlement is delayed.

Some buyers are very cautious and take forever to decide on anything. They feel they have to turn over every stone before committing themselves. You can expect their agreements to be long and full of contingencies. They are unwilling to take reasonable risks, so they seek an unreasonably degree of certainty. Some are perennial tire kickers, never actually closing a deal. Large companies are guilty of this too, using their alleged interest in an acquisition to educate themselves about a certain kind of business and decide whether they want to get involved in it.

Some buyers are ambitious but short on wherewithal - wishful thinkers who tie up a company with a multi-contingent purchase contract, but don't really have the means to carry it out. This type of person is a promoter. Someone who is full of promises, and if everyone believes him, he just might pull off the project. Often it's a little guy trying to do a deal with OPM (other peoples money). Their offers tend to be "creative", and a lot of "ifs" must be satisfied before the deal can close. A high proportion of these people are young entrepreneurs trying to do a lot with

skimpy resources, and executives with early-retirement settlements who want to try their hand at being the boss. You have to admire them for trying, but they can drive you nuts.

Some people buy strictly as investors, looking only for companies that can stand alone and "run themselves" while providing a certain return on cash. They usually want the owner to stay on board, but sometimes they bring in a staff of professional managers to replace everyone.

Some buyers are liquidators - they look for companies whose parts are worth more than the whole. You have to decide for yourself how you feel about that. It's not always a bad idea.

> *Don't expect to find a buyer who will preserve the status quo for your employees, no matter how long they've been with you. That's an admirable concern for a seller, but it really doesn't wash.*

Most buyers have to make significant post-acquisition changes in order to create enough upside to justify the deal. Few believe in artificially supporting jobs that the market won't.

Minimize the right to extensions:

A common problem for the seller is a buyer who agrees to buy the company, but keeps taking advantage of contingencies in the contract to get more time extensions. Sellers want to sign with someone who has firmly decided to buy the company, but that's not what really happens. The buyer is seriously interested, and he intends to make a final decision sometime during the contract period, as he receives more information and has time to reach a personal comfort level.

However, the extensions can give the buyer a chance to renegotiate changes in the deal. Psychologically, the sellers have gotten  used to thinking of this party as their buyer, so they want to avoid conflict - particularly if they are worried about post-acquisition changes. As time passes, alternate buyers disappear, so they feel more vulnerable. Often some financial, competitive, or economic condition worsens to put the seller out on a limb. Or some defect is revealed during due diligence is magnified. Now the buyer has leverage to ask for better terms. Otherwise, he threatens to walk. The sellers are worn-out from the whole process, and they dread the thought of starting over from scratch again. Their enthusiasm for running the company has probably waned as well. As a result, the buyer often get his terms.

In defense of the buyer, a contract with due diligence contingencies is very reasonable. It is very costly to do a full investigation of a company, and you certainly are justified in demanding exclusive rights to the deal if you agree to undertake that. Besides, you do not want to give the seller the power to shop your offer around while you do your homework.

Advice for sellers:

- Try to negotiate with alternate buyers simultaneously, and don't sign a contract without having a back-up deal in your pocket.

- Make sure there are specific dates in the contract for the performance of everything the buyer needs to do, without automatic extension rights.

- Make him put down a large cash deposit, held in your own attorney's escrow account, which is yours as soon as he defaults on the contract.

- Don't fall for the argument that his cost to pursue the deal is so high that it alone should be adequate to demonstrate his good faith.

- Don't accept a deposit in the form of an unsecured promissory note, or leave it in the hands of a third-party who won't release it as long there's a dispute

- Don't let the standard for default depend on nebulous terms such as "reasonable". The contract should terminate automatically upon default and your written notice to the seller.

- The contract should state that it is not recordable in the public courthouse.

- Make sure you are provided with copies of all studies and due diligence reports obtained by the buyer - and get them by the resolution date for that contingency or else you may never see them. Should this buyer drop the deal, they can be provided to a replacement buyer to help facilitate the route to settlement.

This is an ideal scenario - your ability to get a contract this strong will depend on how attractive your company is, and how much the buyer wants it.

Make the contract terms specific from the start.

Items "to be agreed upon by the parties" at some point in the future always seem to cause nightmares. A provision that depends upon someone's subjective approval or discretion is also likely to become a headache. Stipulating that approval "must not be unreasonably withheld" still leaves you with an potential problem.

Another kind of clause to avoid is one that leaves the valuation of certain assets open until a later date. Unless you specify, in detail, the method for valuing those items, you are creating a dispute in advance. Instruct your attorney to write the contract in a way that does not create these subsidiary issues in advance.

Every contract will include some contingencies, but you should be most concerned with those labeled "buyer's conditions to settlement". Make sure each one includes a timeframe for its performance. You eliminate a big source of potential abuse if the buyer is obligated to start and complete each item by specific dates, and is required to use "continuous, best efforts" to satisfy them. You don't want an agreement with ten or twenty contingencies where the buyer has all sorts of leeway to determine when and how to pursue them, and whether the results are satisfactory to him. Any contingencies that turn the contract into an option should be scheduled for completion as soon as possible.

The contract should give the seller the option to remedy defects that would otherwise allow the buyer to terminate the deal. The buyer usually gives the seller notice of the defect, and the seller has a certain period of time within which to cure it, at his own expense and without an offset in the purchase price, or else the buyer can walk away from the deal and get his deposit back.

The transfer of real estate usually involves many additional contract conditions. At the very least, there will be contingencies for a land survey, a title report allowing only certain exceptions, and a commitment for a title policy.

In addition, the buyer will want to make sure he isn't buying into a hazardous material cleanup liability, so there will be conditions allowing for environmental studies. These can include leaking underground storage tanks, asbestos, lead paint, radon, chemicals dumped into the soil, buried waste, and so on. If the buyer plans to develop more of the property, then there may also be contingencies for a wetlands study, geotechnical testing, topographic survey, municipal zoning and land plan approvals, approval of a storm water management plan, extension of utility service lines, lack of a building moratorium, road improvement permits, estimate and approval of impact fees, and so on.

Sellers should not withhold information that will help the buyer determine whether a contingency can be satisfied. The buyer is probably going to discover all that (and more) by himself, so holding back just creates bad faith and delay.

However, it's usually a good idea to demand copies of any reports commissioned by the buyer in studying the company. If the deal doesn't go through, this is valuable information to help guide future decisions, or expedite sale to a different buyer.

It would be nice to avoid any contingencies in the deal, but that's impossible. The buyer is entitled to find out what he's getting. You might begin to wonder if there's any such thing as a firm deal, or whether you can only arrange an elaborate option. One way to keep it simple is to just give the buyer an outright option to purchase the company for a set period of time. That approach eliminates all the haggling over specific contingencies. The buyer can study whatever he wants, but by a certain date he must decide for sure whether to settle. During that time, he can also arrange financing and secure any outside approvals. Usually, a purchase contract is attached to the option agreement, and the only contingencies are to cover last minute details. If the buyer elects to go through with the purchase ("execute the option"), then settlement occurs quickly and without further uncertainties.

Raising the issue of price:

How should the seller bring up this subject? You want the buyer justify his offer, so the best approach is probably to ask what formula he intends to base it on. Don't press for a hard number prematurely because once some people mention a figure, their ego won't let them back off, even if they realize they were wrong. They feel they are losing face.

Before any prices are mentioned, sellers should ask how the buyer intends to pay. Certain modes of payment bring additional risk, and the price should be adjusted accordingly. For example, if the buyer asks the seller to carry part of the purchase price, that normally justifies a higher price. The down payment should be high and the interest rate should reflect the degree of risk associated with making the loan. The risk is increased greatly if the price is too high to begin with, because if the business can't provide the loan payments, the company will land right back in the seller's lap after a couple of years, much worse for wear.

Another method of payment that involves additional risk is where the seller receives stock in the buyer's company. See Chapter 19 on that.

Be firm in your decision to sell.

The decision to sell is an emotional one that seldom comes easily to the private owner. An unequivocal decision doesn't just arrive one day, with no second thoughts. Everyone needs a push.

Once the business is on the market, it's important arrange and carry out the sale expediently. It's usually a mistake to put a business up for sale by word of mouth, or to casually let it be known that you might be receptive to an offer. The impression you really make by doing that is different from the one you think you're making.

Instead, owners should be deliberate in their approach to selling. Once you have made a decision to sell, be firm about it and be realistic about its value. You are better off accepting a fair price than trying to hold out for more than it's worth.

Make sure you have a rational basis for your asking price. Just because you think you need $2 million to retire doesn't mean anyone is ever going to pay you that much. With that approach, you may go to your grave still tied to the business.

Timing the sale of your business:

Keep in mind that it usually takes 18 to 24 months to sell a business. It's rare to see a deal assembled and executed in less than a year.

Theoretically, the optimum time to sell a company is when . . .

- Sales and profits are a high point,
- There's been a consistent trend of growth over several years,
- Your plant and equipment are in good shape,
- You have assembled and trained a strong management team,
- The economy is robust in general,
- Interest rates are reasonable,
- The future outlook for your particular industry is very good.

But fulfilling all these conditions at once is very difficult. Some are extremely hard to predict. Realistically, you should balance your goal of ideal timing against the risk of letting a good opportunity pass you by. It's easy to be wrong in your timing.

There are also a lot of uncontrollable events that can occur to undermine all of your careful planning. Entire industries can become unstable in a matter of months. Unexpected events can blow you out of the water - like wars, riots, or natural disasters. Political events have severe effects on business. The financial markets can nosedive unexpectedly, taking your industry with them. All kinds of things can happen to really screw up your business, and you are virtually helpless to intervene. It happens all the time. So, bear in mind these timing considerations, but realize that trying to time the sale is always something of a gamble.

Many conditions affecting value are uncontrollable and unpredictable, but there is still plenty you can do to enhance the value of your business. Some of these involve long-range planning, and others can be put into effect in a matter of months. If you have a conscious understanding of the factors that contribute to value, you can intentionally create a more valuable entity.

Nonetheless, if a nice opportunity to sell arrives before the company is in optimum shape, don't snub the offer.

General tips for buyers:

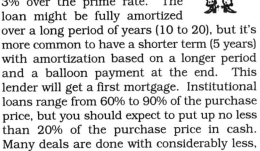

As soon as you think you are getting close to a deal, you should start talking to lenders to get some ideas about how to finance the acquisition. Interest rates usually range from 1% to 3% over the prime rate. The loan might be fully amortized over a long period of years (10 to 20), but it's more common to have a shorter term (5 years) with amortization based on a longer period and a balloon payment at the end. This lender will get a first mortgage. Institutional loans range from 60% to 90% of the purchase price, but you should expect to put up no less than 20% of the purchase price in cash. Many deals are done with considerably less, but don't count on it.

The cash part can come out of your own pocket, from co-investors, or from a venture capital firm. All major equity players will probably have to sign personal guarantees. If you can't come up with enough cash, you can ask the seller to finance the balance. That can take the form of a second-mortgage, an employment or consulting contract, or an earnout. Earnouts are discussed later in this chapter.

Dealing with the seller's emotional needs:

You may encounter a seller who wants you to make promises concerning the way the company will be run after settlement, but you should try to avoid tying your hands in any way. What makes all acquisitions difficult is that, once you pile a load of acquisition debt on top of the firm's normal business expenses, you have created a very vulnerable situation. The new owner must have the freedom to cut out the dead-wood and make any change possible to improve the bottom line.

For this reason, asking you to keep all the current personnel on board is an unreasonable demand. An employment contract might be in order for certain managers, but only if you consider them vital to your success, in which case getting them to sign a contract would be something you would require anyway. Keeping sellers on the payroll is often just a way to pay part of the purchase price on a deferred basis. If you need them to step out of the picture so you can institute changes, then that's the way it is, even if it means they collect a paycheck but don't come to work. That's why these payouts are usually structured as consulting contracts instead of employment deals. Their cost should be part of the purchase price, not an added expense.

Keep in mind that, while you may be looking at this acquisition in very pragmatic, dollar-and-cents terms, the seller of a private company probably has personal and emotional needs that must also be addressed during negotiation.

While he may not admit it, these may be even more important to him than the price and other technical aspects of the deal, so you should listen carefully to find out what they might be. After all, he is giving up control of something that has conferred a certain amount of prestige and power on him for years. He may be selling a business he has created from scratch and identifies with very closely. He is probably concerned that you don't understand his business. For the first time in years, he may not know what lies ahead, in terms of his career or purpose in life. If other family members are working in the business, he will be concerned about their future. Power issues may affect the way negotiations are conducted and information is exchanged, because of the owner's need to still feel in-control during all this. If he's compelled to sell the company for reasons he can't control, then you may notice a certain amount of hidden resentment leaking out. Try not to take it personally.

In other words, for the private seller, this isn't just a business deal. You will have to devote a certain amount of energy to smoothing the seller's easily-ruffled feathers. On the other hand, if you patronize him, you may be encouraging a lot of irrational nonsense, so don't overdo the empathy if it seems to be having that effect.

Checking out the details:

The buyer should make sure he and his advisors have a right of entry onto the premises during normal business hours, given reasonable notice and perhaps management accompaniment. You have to be able to conduct your due diligence unhindered. Your accountants should have full access to all financial records in order to verify the facts you're counting on.

The seller should make warranties and representations in the contract, but there's a limit to how far any seller will stick out his neck. It would be foolish to make representations that exceed your actual knowledge, so that always leaves the buyer with some risk he can't escape. Sellers usually won't make warranties that involve constructive knowledge or imputed knowledge, so if those issues come up later, it will be in the context of a dispute.

Buyers should hire an attorney to undertake a full investigation regarding potential claims and liabilities that could arise after the transfer of ownership, and the seller should be asked to make a warranty providing reimbursement or indemnification against any damages, claims, or costs arising out of those. If the investigation indicates that the seller has consciously withheld information, then it's reasonable to assume that were other misrepresentations as well. That's a signal to dig deeper.

It's possible that state or federal securities laws may restrict the transfer of stock in some way, so buyers should check this out and include a contingency to cover it if there's a problem.

A complete discussion of all acquisition contract terms is outside of the scope of this book, but you should realize that this is not a simple contract. There's a lot to cover. Since many terms confer a benefit on one party or the other, each provision may entail give-and-take negotiation.

Avoid unrealistic buyers and sellers

If the business is worthwhile, the seller will probably have a pretty good head on his shoulders, but that's not always the case.

For instance, you may spot a company with a nice facility and a good foothold an industry you want to enter, yet the owner is off in la-la land when it comes to price and terms. Maybe the business itself isn't worth a lot, but it's something you can build on, which would shorten your startup period. But if this owner's driveway doesn't go all the way to the house, the whole exercise may be a waste of time.

As for buyers - well, they aren't all Bill Gates, either. There are lots of people with entrepreneurial yearnings who don't have what it takes to pull-off an acquisition, and run a company successfully, even if they've had great jobs with large corporations in the past. Unfortunately, this isn't always obvious in the beginning, especially if their net worth and resume are impressive. There are lots of dreamers out there.

> When you first come into contact with a potential buyer or seller, trust your intuition to tell you whether the prospect is realistic and capable of making the deal. It can be very frustrating to spend weeks exploring a deal with someone and then walk away emptihanded because they weren't really a player.

Fortunately, intuition can tell you a lot about someone. For example, I involuntarily flinch whenever I hear someone spouting off idiomatic gems like "make a killing", "the wave of the future", or "everything he touches turns to gold". When people start spewing out their business wisdom in those terms, I think it's reasonable to assume that they probably aren't an astute player. On the other hand, stereotyping can cause you to unfairly underestimate someone. After all, another common stereotype is the uneducated, grammatically incorrect, small-town entrepreneur who, nonetheless, eats your deal for lunch.

Another personality you might run into is the owner who goes through all the motions of trying to sell, but can't bring himself to follow through. For instance, I heard a story about an owner who agreed to sell his company, and on settlement day two dozen professionals traveled across the country to consummate the deal in L.A.. In the middle of closing, the owner excused himself to go to the bathroom

and never returned. Everyone waited around in the conference room for hours, incredulous that he would do such a thing. This occurred after the buyers had invested months of effort and untold expense. That's an extreme example, but it is common to find sellers who bail out at some point for emotional reasons.

Some degree of seller ambivalence is normal, so most need a little push now and then. At least in the beginning, it's rare to find an entrepreneur who is totally firm on the decision to sell. Often they are leaning in that direction and exploring the possibilities, but it's up to the buyer and intermediary to help convince him. This type of seller vacillates for a variety of reasons, but he is counting on the negotiation process to help him make up his mind. He has to jump into the dealmaking and hope it tells him what he needs to know. However, the buyer should realize that this decision can go either way, so you undertake these deals at your own risk.

If several people have ownership interests in the company, it's important to confirm whether they are all committed to selling, not just the person you are talking to.

Some sellers are reluctant because they can't imagine what they'll do with all their free time after the business is sold. That person is probably looking at this as a door that's closing, not one that's opening. Everyone needs some sense of purpose in life, so it helps to get the seller thinking about his options in positive terms. Ask him what he'd do "if he could do it all over again". Ask about the opportunities he's passed by, and about the things he's never had time for. Many people suffer from fear of the unknown. If you can help get the seller excited about his future, it's more likely that a deal will happen.

Along with all this, try to discern his real reasons for selling. This is very material information. You may think you've done your homework, but is there something else you should know before plunging into this? How badly does the seller want out? What does he want the most? The best way to find these things out is to just keep your mouth shut during the first couple of meetings. You've heard it before: Smart negotiators do more listening than talking.

How and when to raise the issue of price:

Any time you consider a deal, the first thing to do is figure out whether the seller really has a sincere desire to sell. If an owner says "anything's for sale, if the price is right", it's usually a complete waste of time.

More often than not, sellers have an inflated opinion of the value of their company.

This is due to their understandable lack of objectivity. Private owners tend to have a very strong personal attachment to their business, especially if they created it from scratch. For them, selling becomes an emotional experience that can sometimes work against their own best interests. You stand a much better chance of agreeing on a fair price if both sides have taken the time to learn something about the subject of business valuation. You might consider giving everyone a copy of this book so that they can attempt a real valuation themselves. At least you'll all be talking on the same wavelength.

The subject of price is generally dealt with in one of two ways. If you are unlucky, one side or the other (usually the seller) will blurt out a figure right at the outset, with little or no justification for it. Since it's usually an unrealistic number, this places a huge and unnecessary hurdle in front of the deal - one that is fraught with sensitivity. Now there are delicate ego issues to overcome.

More typically, however, the issue of price sort-of hovers around in the air in an unspoken way, through the first two or three meetings, with everyone justifiably curious but careful to not say anything presumptuous. This is the right approach. Except to make sure the other side is on a realistic plane by talking about pricing methods generally, it's probably not a good idea to mention any numbers until you've gathered enough information to know exactly what the seller has to sell. Then you can engage in some informed analysis and come up with your price.

The parties may be able to circumvent a lot of nonsense by agreeing on a specific pricing formula up front. Spell it out, including underlying assumptions, and an appropriate cap rate formula.. Detail how adjustments will be made. Discuss the impact of common problems that might be discovered during due diligence. This puts both sides on notice that their price had better make sense.

Some parties respond to premature price inquiries by giving a broad range of possible prices, to be refined later. This usually isn't a good idea, because the seller will instantly gravitate toward the top end of the range, and the buyer really doesn't have enough information to justify any of it. It's better to side-step the issue entirely until you have all the data you need to do an informed analysis.

Another reason to respond by talking about valuation formulas is that it gives you a chance to educate the seller. Sellers always have a number in mind, and this allows you challenge their expectations without putting them on the spot or causing them to lose face. Hopefully, you can do that before he opens his mouth and commits his ego to a certain number. Go ahead and take this route even if the seller hasn't blurted out a price, because you want him to start thinking in terms of recognized, acceptable valuation methods. This is the most productive way to counter unrealistic expectations.

Sellers should see the advantage of this approach too. Chances arc, the buyer has a lot more experience at cutting these deals, but you don't want the price to be driven by negotiating tricks.

Remember that there's a difference between market value and what the company is really worth to you. Valuation may produce a certain number, but the ability to do something special with the company can sometimes justify paying more, and that's what it may take to cut the deal. Buyers should realize that the price it takes to make any deal is usually higher than the limit they have in mind at the outset. Everyone has to stretch a little to make a deal work. Just make sure you know the cost at which it stops making sense for you.

If your employer is the buyer, you'll find that much of the negotiating will take place within your own company, trying to sell other managers on the deal.

Many will harbor preconceptions about the target company or its industry, and they'll probably respond to your acquisition proposal with a knee-jerk reaction. This is complicated by their own agenda for personal advancement. Educating and selling them from the start will allow you to avoid hurdles they might otherwise put in your way. Your goal is to generate, in them, the same enthusiasm that you have for this acquisition.

Once a deal is made, move quickly toward settlement.

It's usually a mistake to let things drag on. Get to settlement as soon as possible. Once the seller has decided to sell, he isn't going to pay as much attention to how well he runs the company. That opens the door for deterioration, and vulnerability to attacks on market share from the competition. He may also develop "seller's remorse" and do something to undermine the deal. Of course, expediency is counterbalanced by your need to conduct careful due diligence before closing the deal.

Keep in mind that the value of a company can change from month to month, based on dozens of factors that are constantly in flux. These variables include financial performance, the security of large accounts, emerging liabilities, market conditions for that industry, interest rates, the condition of the economy as a whole, and uncontrollable cost increases. For that reason, you should close the deal quickly once the price and essential terms have been agreed upon.

Some changes may occur prior to settlement, but in most deals the parties agree in advance that variations (in sales, inventory level, etc.) affecting value prior to settlement will be regarded as immaterial if they are within a certain tolerance (say, five percent). That way, the parties share the risk and can avoid renegotiation.

After the contract is signed, keep the meetings and communications flowing at a steady pace. Try to develop and maintain a certain momentum in moving toward settlement. Once that rhythm is interrupted, the whole process is much more likely to break down. All it takes is someone who isn't prepared for the next step. Downtime represents an opening for doubt to slip in and make the other side question their own judgment. Your job is to keep things happening.

Hardball tactics:

Some buyers let the negotiations proceed until they are very close to a contract, then they call up the seller to announce that the deal is off. They have exuded all kinds of optimism and purposely allowed a great deal of time to pass without actually committing themselves on paper. Meanwhile, the seller has let his other options cool. Once that happens, the buyer has lots of leverage to suddenly ask for better terms. They say that new developments or recent information forces them to conclude that the deal just won't work as structured.  They say they are sorry, but can't do anything about it, and it's nothing personal. The response they are hoping for is: "I'm disappointed, but I understand. What can we do to make the deal work at this point?" By this time, the seller is weary of the process, and doesn't want to go through it all again with another buyer. Often, he'll just bite the bullet and change his terms to make the deal.

Sellers also need to be cautious *after* the contract is signed. Don't reveal a financial vulnerability that could be taken advantage of by the seller. Once they know you are over a barrel, they may threaten to pull out of the deal if you don't renegotiate.

Tips for both sides:

When you first meet with someone to discuss the possibility of a deal, start by dealing with the most non-controversial issues first. This will help you to develop enthusiasm and a momentum of agreement before you move on to the more difficult items.

This gets the other side thinking positively and accustomed to saying yes. Be aware, however, that sometimes the euphoria of a deal can obscure real problems, so keep your wits about you.

Honestly - don't get too hung up on price - it's not the only thing. This book focuses on that issue, but sometimes other terms of the deal are more important.

Sit down and think about all the things you are trying to achieve by this transaction, and get the relative priority of those items straight in your mind. If the deal is worth doing - if it accomplishes other good things - then a price that differs from your expectations by only a few percent shouldn't matter.

When negotiating, you should have a drop-dead price in mind that represents your highest (or lowest) figure, beyond which you will walk away from the deal because it doesn't make sense anymore. But don't mention that bottom line figure unless you reach an impasse in negotiation. Reserved it for your final play - a "take it or leave it" position - but don't bluff. If you say you'll walk, then mean it.

Avoid coming up with a nice round figure - like $3.0 million. Be more specific - a figure like $3.02 million - conveys the impression that you have prepared your offer thoughtfully and based it on intelligent, detailed reasoning. Just be ready to back up your figure with real calculations.

Targeting companies for acquisition:

Many prospective buyers put together a wish-list when they look for potential acquisitions. The companies they locate all fall short of that ideal, but they are definitely closer for having defined their goal in advance. This is a good approach, so take some time to figure out what it is you're looking for. Here are some things to keep in mind:

- Never enter completely unfamiliar territory. Stick to what you know. Many subscribe to the rule-of-thumb that says you should have experience with at least two out of the three "P's":
  - the particular *product* or service
  - the *people* involved (past dealings with that company and its management)
  - the *place* (their market)

- If nothing else, at least stick to industries you understand so that you're aware of the risks and challenges involved in your investment. Besides, this will enable you know whether it's a business you will actually enjoy.

- Many finance-people focus too exclusively on the numbers. Net income can distract you from other important considerations. Check out the quality of the assets, management, and the technology they employ. Understand the company's competitive position - market share, proprietary products, and so on.

- Do your own projections. Find out where the industry is headed as a whole, and gain an understanding of this company's niche in it. A great past doesn't insure a rosy future. The seller may be bailing-out just in time to avoid a major fallout. Or the company might be in a bind where expensive new retooling will soon be needed in order to remain competitive.

- Don't assume you can rapidly integrate the target company with another one. Each company has its own culture, and most people are uncomfortable with change of any type. You can expect a lot of grousing and subtle resistance over anything you want to do differently.

- On the other hand, it's usually wise to announce and carry out all the big personnel decisions quickly. It's important to be decisive on this because whenever a company is purchased there's a lot of anxiety in the air over who is going to get canned, and it really interferes with productivity. Employees become more concerned with trying to insure their own survival than they are with doing their jobs. If you plan on making big changes, get it over with quickly so the surviving employees don't have to work in an atmosphere of fearful anticipation over the next wave of firings. If that tension is allowed to persist for long, your most valuable and marketable people may leave just to escape the stress. Besides, waving an axe over everyone's head is a lousy management tactic, and only the losers will put up with it for long.

How to approach a target company:

Unfortunately, by the time you contact a target company, the waters have often already been muddied by amateurish, cold-calling brokers and want-to-be's on fishing expeditions. That means you'll have to find a way to quickly establish your credibility from the start. You'll have about 5 seconds before the door gets slammed. It helps if you are a "principal" - owners like to talk to owners. But most owners are reluctant to tell anyone they want to sell, even if they do.

The best way is to network your way to company owners through some other involvement. Trade associations, club memberships, and the like. Otherwise, try to get an introduction through a mutual advisor. Besides, it stands to reason that the company's attorney or accountant would be the first to know that it's susceptible to purchase. However, these advisors usually won't do anything to *encourage* a sale of the business because they'll probably lose a major client as a result.

Some employ the approach used by many job hunters - interviewing for information. The job seeker calls the prospective employer, but instead of putting him on the spot by asking for a job, he asks for advice on whether and how to pursue employment in that field. That way the prospective employer isn't on the defensive. If, during the course of their meeting, it looks like there's a fit between the company and the individual, that fact will become apparent to both parties and the conversation will naturally steer in that direction. Otherwise, the job seeker receives some good advice and perhaps some referrals to other companies. Anyway, people seeking acquisitions often take the same approach.

Trying to talk an owner into selling can easily turn counterproductive. You can explain the advantages, and how they will lose out if they let this opportunity pass them by, but it usually doesn't help. Instead, it's just a sales pitch that they want to escape. They have to their own reasons for themselves in their own time. When the seed does get planted, its usually not by a prospective buyer.

> *Finding acquisitions is a long-term endeavor that requires a lot of patience. Don't try to make it all you do, because you'll probably be waiting a long time for that next deal to appear.*

Spotting a sick company:

This section gives you an overview of what bankruptcy experts look for when they review the financial statements of a public company for signs of trouble. Doing turnarounds is risky business. What looks like a bargain might really be a nightmare in disguise. It takes a special magic to pull these off.

1. The most obvious sign is a decline in *earnings or cash flow*. Make sure you look at financial statements from several years so that you can spot trends.

2. Borrowing at high interest rates can erode profit margins even though total earnings appear healthy, so look closely at the company's *loan terms*. If you can refinance those obligations at better rates, you will strengthen the company. Otherwise those old loans may continue to drag it down.

3. Compare *profit margins* over the past several years. For each year, divide the net income by total sales revenue. That's your "margin". If it's declining, you better find out why. Don't buy unless you are sure you can do something about it.

4. Have *cash reserves* been dropping? Again, look for a trend over several years. The ratio of "current assets" to "current liabilities" is a good indicator. Some people also use the "quick ratio", which is a more stringent test because it doesn't include inventory. It only includes receivables, cash, and short-term investments that can be turned into cash readily. If cash reserve has been decreasing, then there's a problem somewhere that needs to be addressed.

5. Watch for a continuing decline in *net worth (assets minus liabilities)*. The same applies to the reserve for bad debts.

6. Look for an *abnormal increase in certain expenses*. For several years, pick out items that constitute major expenses and compare them to total sales. (Cost of goods sold, selling and administrative expenses, interest, etc.) Then compare that percentage to what it was in previous years. This will tell you something.

7. Insist on *audited financial statements* from a CPA accounting firm. You want to see an "unqualified opinion". Read the footnotes to the report carefully. If the accountants have reservations about certain figures, investigate thoroughly and don't accept casual assurances from the seller.

8. Watch out for a *change in accounting methods*, since that can have a significant effect on earnings and mislead you in your trend watching. Make sure you are comparing apples to apples.

9. Compare the company's financial ratios *to the industry averages*. Ratios for the average company in that same industry are compiled and published in resources available through your accountant or the reference section of your library.

Sellers: Do you really have something to sell yet?

While there are plenty of stories floating around about business owners who received huge prices when they sold, it seems ridiculous to have to remind someone that their business may not necessarily be worth a lot. But somehow there are always people who manage to defy common sense.

Owners can accumulate a lot of wealth in a business but it requires conscious planning. Making a fortune when you sell is not the inevitable conclusion. You must understand what contributes to value in the eyes of a buyer, and then set about building those characteristics in your company. That is the key. Don't leave it to chance.

If others have received high prices, it was because they knew how to create real value. For example, your company might have millions in annual revenues, but if it has out-of-date assets and unstable earnings, it will probably only sell for its fixed asset value.

One common situation is the high profile business whose owner has maintained an expensive lifestyle in the face of increasing competition and declining earnings - running the company into the ground by siphoning off working capital and using debt to replace it. The business seems impressive, but after paying off all the debt, the owners will be lucky to have anything left.

My point is that sellers need to get busy about creating value. Having dealt with hundreds of businesses over the years, I would guess that most owners think their company is worth 30% to 50% more than it actually is. If you skipped to this chapter without actually performing a valuation, you better go back and do it now.

Option to buy vs. pre-emptive bid:

After a seller has been approached by a number of potential buyers, one may come forward and ask for an exclusive look at the company. They don't want to go to a lot of effort and expense only to see the company sold to someone else. Nor do they want to make an offer and then have the seller shop it around to other interested buyers.

How should a seller respond a request for an exclusive look? If you are tempted to grant this, you might ask for a "pre-emptive bid" - an informal offer that's high enough to justify shutting out other prospects for 60 to 90 days while this buyer studies the acquisition. Assuming they find everything in order, you will be expecting them to produce an acquisition agreement at that price by the end of that period - hopefully one that you both can live with. This is similar to an option, because the buyer doesn't have to sign an agreement of sale if he doesn't like what he sees during the inspection period. But since the buyer isn't paying anything for this exclusive opportunity, he may not actually have any enforceable rights. It's really a good faith arrangement. On the other hand, since the seller isn't bound, there probably isn't much harm in granting a free look. But what often really happens is that the buyer will use the problems he finds during the inspection period to renegotiate the deal. On the other hand, if the buyer decides that it's a bargain at the pre-emptive bid price, and the owner tries to back out, then that buyer might have a promissory estoppel argument that will enable him to get specific performance, so make sure this interim agreement is exactly what you think it is before you sign it.

Buyers sometimes go in too optimistically, and later find that the company is worth much less. That means that even if you have exclusive rights to the deal, you'll lose them when you go back and offer less than the original bid amount.

Remember that these are legal matters resulting in rights, duties, and liabilities - so don't just rely on these comments. Make sure you consult an attorney.

Due diligence:

Due diligence refers to the process of verifying your assumptions about the company and the representations of the seller. This investigation is to find out whether you're getting what you think you are getting. The buyer usually learns as much as possible before making an offer and entering into a contract. Then, after the contract is signed, the buyer has a period of time to dig into the details. The agreement will have a lot of conditions in it, making settlement contingent upon the results of various studies.

Discoveries made during due diligence may lead to renegotiation of the price and terms of sale. Most sellers seem to prefer this route because they figure the changes probably won't be as severe if the basics are already in writing, but I'm not sure it really works out that way.

Some sellers feel they are better off not volunteering any due diligence information. Instead, they wait for the buyer to specifically ask for something. However, withholding material information or hiding skeletons in the closet can sometimes lead to liabilities. Fraud indictments can even result if it amounts to intentional misrepresentation. The voluntary disclosure of sensitive items goes a long way toward establishing an atmosphere of trust. Trying to sell the business "as is" usually won't enable you to get around this.

Some buyers are very picky when it comes to due diligence, but the seller doesn't have much choice but to cooperate. However, you might be able to justify withholding info that would be damaging if leaked to a competitor. You might be able to hold that back until certain conditions are met or the contract is strengthened. This approach is sometimes referred to as a "staged release of information". If you are sharing company secrets, don't feel shy about asking for a written confidentiality agreement as well.

Should decision-makers be at the bargaining table?

When you get to the point where you really want to wrap things up, it's a good idea to bring all essential decision makers to the bargaining table. Prior to that, however, you may want to leave an essential party behind, so that you can't be pressured to commit on the spot to issues you haven't had a chance to fully examine.

Similarly, the absence of a key party is sometimes used as an excuse to avoid changing some provision - or even discussing it. Negotiators frequently claim they can't compromise on some issue because of the intractable position of a key decision maker who isn't present. Someone who isn't there can't be pressured to cave in. The negotiator holds firm and rolls right on to the next item,

Psychological ploys:

Watch out for is the "good guy/bad guy" act. People really do try this. It's similar to what you've seen on the police shows, where they're sweating some guy in the interrogation room. One member of the other team comes on strong with a ridiculous position on some issue, or blows up in response to some proposal you've made. Then, after you are sufficiently intimidated by all the ranting and raving, someone on his side pulls him off, gets him to leave the room, and then apologizes for his unreason-ableness. It looks like he's taken your side and come to your rescue. In doing so, he's hoping you'll see him as the good guy, and thereby gain your trust and cooperation. That creates a false rapport that tends to give him an edge in persuading you.

Try to keep the number and power of the players on each side even. If two people show up to negotiate against six, they can easily become overpowered and intimidated. In a threatened state, negotiators can cave in, shut down, or let their tempers flare.

Stay on an even physical posture with your opponent as well. If the other side is standing, then you should stand. If the seats they provide for you are lower than theirs, then don't use them. This stuff really happens.

It's a good idea to try to have crucial meetings at some neutral place - rather than the office of one of the principals - to avoid the psychological "home game" advantage. Believe it or not, some companies even place microphones to eavesdrop on your private conversations in the conference room, in the reception area, or in the elevator.

Are these games really necessary?

Most dealmakers will say that, regrettably, it's not feasible to be totally straightforward in these discussions. We all expect the other side to hold back, and really it's only a turnoff when people are dishonest or try to be too cute. That creates resentment, even if the deal ultimately gets made.

Aside from that, it's hard to deny that deals are a lot more rewarding when you have gained the maximum advantage. The tactics mentioned in this chapter are definitely used by many people, but some are things that most of us would never feel comfortable doing. I guess each person ultimately decides for themselves where to draw the line.

Attorneys and Accountants:

You should have good legal advice throughout your dealings, but meeting at a lawyer's office may not be a good idea. When you take lawyers along, everything tends to become very "legal". On the other hand, a lawyer can provide on-the-spot justification for a position you need to take, since deferring to your lawyer's advice is something that most of us can relate to.

Lawyers and investment bankers relish opportunities to pull off a big grandstand play, but those efforts often destroy the deal instead. That's why lawyers are often referred to as "dealbreakers", since they will often try to re-make a deal that the buyer and seller have already struck.

If someone is trying to justify their fee or be a hero at their client's expense, you should remind them that it's not their job to make the deal, just to put it into writing. You are the businessperson, and they are the technician. Keep the lawyer away from the issue of price and other central terms, and restrict his input to writing the contract, taking care of the details, and checking for hidden trouble. Listen to their advice, but make the final decisions yourself.

Sometimes attorneys and accountants put a lot of effort into fighting over small issues. Lawyers sometimes try to achieve an unrealistic degree of certainty for their client. Similarly, some accountants look for an unrealistic degree of accuracy. Both are meticulous by nature. Nonetheless, make it clear to them that you aren't going to wage battle over every dollar. Their concern is admirable, but sometimes it's overdone, so keep an eye on what they are really fighting over. Sometimes, it's just to cover their own butts. My philosophy is that there's a certain amount of risk inherent in all business, which you have to accept if you want to get anything done. Acquisitions are no exception - they require some leaps of faith in order to happen. As long as you are aware of those risks, you should be able to decide whether or not they are acceptable.

Keep it confidential!

Don't let word of your deal go beyond the most essential parties. Every potential buyer should sign a confidentiality agreement including a promise not to inform others that the company might be for sale. Business brokers or acquisition intermediaries can be a problem because they often want to bring in back-up buyers. It's a good idea, but it must be carefully orchestrated.

Another reason to keep it quiet is that there are always parties who don't want the company to be sold, and they might start running interference. For instance, a spouse may get nervous about losing a comfortable lifestyle, and try to discourage the deal. Professional advisors, worried about losing a big client, sometimes do the same thing.

Deadlocks:

Deals are frequently threatened by stalemates that are avoidable. First of all, hold negotiations to a reasonable pace. If you raise too many details too quickly, the parties can overload. When people get tired or tense, small issues can turn into major disputes, so just save it. Deal with one major issue at a time.

It also helps to string minor issues together and roll them out when the other side is already in an agreeable frame of mind. If you become deadlocked on a particular issue, try putting it aside for a while. Introduce it again later, during a period of agreement.

One way to keep disputed items in perspective is to translate them into dollars and compare that amount (as a percentage) to the total dollar value of the deal. In other words, if the item in dispute translates into $100,000 and it's part of a $5 million deal, ask yourself if 2% is worth screwing up the whole thing over.

Keep the lid on your emotions and never let it get personal. Someone who "loses it" at a meeting is thereafter at a great psychological disadvantage. If there's tension in the air, take a break for a couple of days. During that time, try to view the dispute as a puzzle you need to solve, and ask the parties work on it from a creative, problem-solving angle.

Don't worry about "the principle of the thing". Be pragmatic, because if you try to claim the high-road, real-world practicality will always knocks you off your horse.

Seller warranties:

Many sellers get hung up on this. You should expect to make warranties, particularly concerning the company's financial condition and the presence of known or suspected liabilities. There's no way around it.

You can't offer a company "as is". You have to make material representations about the business in order to give the buyer a reason to be interested.

Letters of intent:

 The letter of intent is a short memorandum, often in the form of correspondence and framed in non-binding language, that expresses the general intent of the buyer and seller to transact a deal. In most cases the parties are careful to avoid creating a contract, but it does have some psychological binding power. Some people say it's a statement of good faith, but that might be stretching it. The real reason is to put what the parties have verbally expressed into writing so that they can get any big misunderstandings out in the open before they go any further.

Always have your attorney review a letter of intent, not to question the terms of the deal, but to make sure that it *isn't* a binding contract. It should state outright that no obligation is intended by it.

At contract time, get everything in writing!

Make sure that absolutely everything that's important to you is embodied clearly in the contract. A major source of hard feelings is the unfulfilled representations of the other side. The contract usually states that it embodies the complete agreement of the parties as of that date, and that all previous agreements and discussions to the contrary don't count. Usually the parties overlook this enforceable clause as mere boilerplate when they really are counting on the fulfillment of additional understandings discussed prior to making the contract.

Often the party making representations hangs them out there as an inducement but regards them as a big maybe. This frequently happens with subsidiary agreements, such as employment contracts. You might challenge the buyer successfully in court, but as soon as you have to litigate, you lose anyway.

My advice is to get everything in writing at the same time as the original contract. Leave nothing out. Don't agree to discretionary payments, or let a promise hinge on issues of interpretation or variations in bookkeeping methods.

For sellers anxious about letting go:

Selling a business that has occupied your attention for many years can be emotionally wrenching. One way to overcome your hesitation is to hang on to one part, retaining ownership of a small division, a single product line, or a piece of real estate that you lease back to the company.

Negotiating the form of payment:

Know what the buyer's money is worth. A cash offer gives you little to worry about. $10 million in cash is worth $10 million. But if the buyer offers promissory notes or stock in lieu of cash, then you are taking some risk. Practically speaking, you might be receiving somewhat less than the face amount, so you should always get a price premium to compensate the additional risk.

If you accept notes, invest in credit reports on the buyer. Call their bank references as well, and tap any other contacts who might have the inside scoop on them. If they are a public company and they offer you stock as payment, then you should contact a securities analyst who monitors that industry to get an opinion on its real value. Many stocks are overpriced at their traded value.

Cash is not necessarily the best payment medium. If you receive a large lump sum of cash, you'll pay the maximum amount of taxes, and you'll have to figure out how to invest it. If you are selling to a blue-chip buyer whose debt securities carry relatively little risk, then their notes might be almost as good as cash. Ask your accountant to rate the risk associated with the company whose name is on the notes. Just remember that there will be some risk involved, and the interest you receive should be appropriate to compensate you not only for the use of your money, but for the additional risk. In other words, the interest rate you get should be a "risk-free rate of return", plus a premium for the amount of risk you assume by loaning your money to that particular party. It's something of a gamble, but if you have doubts about the stability of the company, you can demand that the notes be secured by specific property or by the stock of either company.

But what if you do this, the buyer defaults, and you get the company back, only to discover that it has been ruined or looted? At worst, only an empty corporate shell might remain. You can try to protect yourself by including covenants in the agreement of sale, surviving settlement, that prohibit the buyer from liquidating any assets of the company without the seller's consent, plus a promise that they will operate the business to the best of their ability and with adequate working capital.

Sellers can also ask for negotiable notes, which can be re-sold later to someone else. Buyers, on the other hand, should insist on giving non-negotiable notes, so that if the seller defaults on some post-settlement promise or if seller's guarantees are not fulfilled, the buyer can withhold payment. Sellers who do receive negotiable notes should assume that those notes can only be sold at a discount, unless the borrower is a large public company whose securities are actively traded and highly rated.

Sometimes, however, a seller can unwittingly increase the chance of default, simply by driving too hard a bargain, since an overpriced and over-leveraged acquisition has a much greater chance of failing. Similarly, if you drag out your negotiations too long, your competitors will have a chance to steal market share while your attention is focused elsewhere.

When should a seller accept stock?

The decision to accept stock is an investment decision, so you should scrutinize the company issuing those securities just like any other stock investment. Buying stock is always something of a gamble, so do your homework.

- Is the stocked overpriced? You want stock that is priced at or below its earning value. Earnings value is equal to the company's net earnings per share, divided by the appropriate cap rate. That cap rate should be equal to the annual return (a percentage) you would expect from an investment in that company, once you understand the amount of risk associated with it. A rough measure might be the average total return from publicly-traded stocks in the same risk category, over a long period of years. If the company issuing the stock is privately-held instead of public, then you should add a premium for additional risk. (See Chapter 5 for more guidance on selecting a cap rate.)

- What is the future outlook for this company, for its industry as a whole, and for the stock market as a whole? Pay particular attention if your ability to re-sell the stock is restricted for a period of time.

- Chart the history of this stock's price. How volatile has it been? Have unusual events, or manipulation by majority shareholders, accounted for some of those price increases? How have price movements compared to those of the market average?

- If this is a private company, keep in mind that its performance will be harder to track, and the stock will be harder to resell. Can you stay reliably informed on how well the company is doing?

Much depends on what kind of stock you receive. The "common stock" of a publicly-traded company is valued according to its daily traded price on the stock exchange. "Preferred stock" is different. You can negotiate its value and its dividend, but it won't grow in value like common stock. However, preferred stock is considered safer because if the company fails and has to be liquidated, preferred stockholders have priority over common stockholders in the distribution of any assets remaining after the company's debts are paid. Preferred stock can also be "convertible", meaning it can be converted to common stock under certain conditions.

If the stock is not registered with the SEC (Securities Exchange Commission), then there will be restrictions on how soon you can resell or trade it. These rules are complicated, but basics are (1) that you can't resell the stock for a certain period of time (currently 2 years), (2) you have to notify the SEC when you do resell it, and (3) you can only sell a small amount every so often (currently every three months). Check the current rules.

If you decide to accept unregistered stock, the deal should include additional shares or provide higher dividends in order to compensate for all this inconvenience. Also keep in mind that if you continue to work for the company, or if you sit on the Board of Directors, or if you receive a sufficiently large portion of the buyer's stock, you may be considered an "insider", and thus subjected to additional restrictions.

What about the fact that the stock price may change prior to closing? You might stipulate that you will use the market price on a certain day, whatever it may be, or you can use the average market price over a period of days. You can also take your chances by using the stock price on the date the contract is signed, or the day settlement occurs. If you stipulate that today's price will be used in calculating the number of shares you receive, but the price goes up before settlement, you will receive more for the company. However, that can work the other way, too. If the purchase price is a fixed number of shares, to be based on the stock's price on settlement day, the seller is certain to receive that set value.

Net proceeds after tax:

Buyers worry too much about the income tax on their proceeds of sale. If you make money, you pay taxes - that's the way it works. You should be happy you've made the money, so don't whine about getting a higher price so you can offset the taxes and still have the same amount let over. Consult a tax accountant or tax attorney before the deal is put together to see if the transaction can be structured in a way that reduces your tax liability, but don't walk away from selling because of the tax bite.

Bargaining over the accounting method to be used:

The buyer's acquisition accounting method can affect the seller's purchase price. If the buyer uses the "pooling of interests" method, that can increase the price for the seller. This is a complicated distinction. If used, the effect of the pooling method is that the financial statements of the two companies are combined ("pooled") and merged into a single company. Goodwill is kept off the books. The pooling method is often used when an acquisition is accomplished by swapping stock between two companies. Buyers tend to prefer it, but it isn't available unless lots of conditions are satisfied that have to do with how business was conducted prior to the sale.

In all other cases, the buyer will use the "purchase" method of accounting. This is an "acquisition" of one company by another, as opposed to the "merger" of two companies into a new entity. The key feature is that, if the buyer pays more than book value for the assets, the excess will show up on the buyer's books as goodwill. Goodwill is not a desirable asset because it can not be depreciated. This means more taxes for the buyer and lower earnings. Since this a disadvantage to the buyer, he will usually insist on paying a lower price in order to offset it.

Earnouts:

If you are deadlocked over price, consider an earnout. The seller gets additional future payments, but only if the company attains a certain level of performance. The timeframe for earnouts is usually three to five years. The earnout formula can be whatever you want it to be, but it should be based on a simple, objective, easily-ascertained measure of performance. If it's affected by the discretion, interpretations, or changeable accounting methods of the buyer, then you are creating a dispute in advance.

If the seller agrees to an earnout, then it may be in his best interest to hang around and help manage the company after the sale to make sure those earnings appear. It's one way buyers can help influence the seller to continue lending his or her expertise to the company after settlement. It also defers taxation on some of his sale proceeds, which can lower the overall tax bite.

Sellers should view the amount they receive from an earn out as icing on the cake. The amount they receive at settlement should be their real, rock-bottom price.

That amount might correspond to the low end of your range of calculated values.

If the buyer can't borrow enough money from traditional sources to finance the acquisition, then an earnout can be used to bridge the gap and serve as a form of seller financing. It's a flexible way for the seller to get paid, assuming he has faith in the company's ability to produce the minimum earnings. This places some of the risk after the sale on the seller. Since these are delayed payments of purchase price, their amount should reflect a certain amount of interest.

The parties should also specify whether the earnout payments will be made in cash or stock. If it's stock, remember that stock value fluctuates, so you must specify a method and a reference date for valuing it.

The earnout payment is usually a percentage of annual net earnings exceeding a minimum threshold amount. Sometimes you have to exceed the earnings of the previous year to get an earnout payment for the following year. Sometimes the earnout is paid as a lump sum after several years - as a percentage of the combined earnings from those years, assuming each year exceeds a certain minimum. Sometimes the earnout is only paid if the buyer achieves a minimum annual return on its acquisition investment (net earnings for each year must exceed a set percentage of the total amount invested in the company). If actual earnings exceed that minimum return, then the buyer shares a portion of that excess with the seller.

Sometimes the parties agree to a minimum earn out payment, regardless of sales or earnings. Sometimes they impose a maximum on the payment, but the seller should argue against this if the earn out is used as seller financing, since he wants to be compensated for the risk of not getting paid at all.

> *The parties can base these payments on anything they want, but they should have their accountants define precisely how that base number is calculated.*

If the payments are based on net earnings, then you should specify exactly which expenses are included and excluded in the calculation. Your definition should also deal with allocated expenses of the parent company, and it should specify the accounting method to be used in calculating each expense item. If you don't nail down all these details in advance, the buyer can pad the expenses to cut down the earnout payments.

If the net earnings approach is used, the books of the acquired business will have to be kept completely separate from those of the parent company. In other words, you can't allocate income and expenses back and forth between the parent company and the new one.

> *Obviously, it would be simpler to base the earn out payments on sales volume, but that's riskier for the buyer, because higher sales don't necessarily translate into higher earnings. The first couple of years after settlement are very touchy, and there will be unforeseen additional expenses. You should able to charge those against the income of the business without being penalized.*

Adjustments in price:

Sometimes the purchase price is made up of a number of different components, particularly where the deal is structured as a sale of assets. The value of some components may fluctuate between the contract date and the date of settlement, so the actual sale price will vary accordingly. In such cases, you should define how value will be determined for those fluctuating items, and the date upon which their value will be fixed (which is usually the day before settlement). Items falling into this category usually include the current assets and any "off the balance sheet liabilities" such as funds owed to retirement plans. Inventory is usually counted in a last minute rush.

Part of the purchase price can be escrowed for a period of time after settlement, in order to provide assurance to the buyer concerning any hidden liabilities. Money can also be held-back to cover any seller indemnifications (promises to reimburse the buyer for any breach of the seller's warranties) Since the seller usually wants all his money with no strings attached, the warranties, representations, and indemnities in the purchase contract are hotly negotiated items.

Chapter 21

Valuing a Part Interest in a company

Part-owners in a business are usually surprised to learn that their share is worth much less than they thought. If you own one-third of a business, it's logical to assume that you are entitled to one-third of its total value, but that's not necessarily the case.

Lack of control and lack of marketability are two different concepts, but their combined result is that the minority interest may be worth as much as 90% less than the value per-share of the majority interest. Never assume that a minority interest carries a pro-rata share of the total value of the company.

If you own less than half of the business, you have what's called a "minority interest". Common stock ownership usually has voting rights attached to it - one vote per share. Therefore, if others have more shares than you, they can simply out-vote you on all issues affecting the company - including return to the stockholders. This is called a "lack of control", and it causes the stock to be worth substantially less per share than a controlling interest.

There's another problem as well. Since it carries almost no voting power, a smaller share in a business is harder to re-sell to someone else, so you also experience what is called a "lack of marketability".

This discounting applies only to private companies valued according to the methods in this book. Stock in a public company is already discounted for minority interest. The price it trades for on the stock exchange reflects the assumption that its owner will hold only a tiny percentage of that company's stock. If you were actually able to buy enough to give you voting control, that block of shares would carry a premium of 30% to 35% *over* the stock exchange price.

This discounting also applies to an unincorporated partnership if you can be outvoted by another partner, or if you are historically outvoted by several who combine their voting power to promote interests that are contrary to yours. Your voting rights are spelled out in the partnership agreement, so read it.

Lack of control

- The degree of control held by any particular owner varies greatly. It depends not only on the percentage of ownership, but also how those rights are spelled out in the documents that created the partnership or stock. Most states have statutes that define the voting rights when the creating documents fail to. This varies from state-to-state, but the law may automatically create certain rights for the stockholder unless specifically denied to him in the creating documents. In fact, the law may confer those rights even if the creating documents purport to deny them. Therefore, a 10% interest in a company might be worth a lot more in one state than in another.

Some stock, such as "non-voting preferred stock", has absolutely no voting rights. It confers only a financial interest. However, preferred stockholders do have the advantage of getting first priority when it comes to dividend payments, so if there are profits to distribute, the preferred stockholders get paid before anyone else gets anything. They also get priority on the distribution of assets if the company is shut-down and liquidated. However, they usually have no control over the way the business is conducted.

The advantages of voting control:

You need to understand why a lack of control diminishes the value of a minority interest. Whoever has controlling interest in a company usually has the following powers:
- the power appoint directors and officers (and pay them salaries)
- the power to declare or withhold dividends
- the power to appoint managers and determine their salaries and bonuses;
- the power to change the articles of incorporation;

- the authority to make acquisitions, liquidate assets, sell or recapitalize the company;
- and the authority to set company policy.

The point is that these rights can be exercised in such a way that all of the financial benefits of the business flow to the majority owners, and none to the minority owner, which can make that minority interest practically worthless. Many of these decisions can be made only by the "board of directors", but the majority stockholders have the votes to elect whomever they want to the board, and those people, in turn, are going to act in accordance with the wishes of the person who put them there.

Less than 50% isn't necessarily a minority share.

You have to consider the overall ownership scheme. If there are three 33% stockholders, then each would normally own one-third of the total value of the company. However, if one party owned two of those 1/3 interests, they would have control, so your share would be worth *less* than one-third of the total value of the company. Likewise, if two of the owners always join together to outvote you, that "ownership group" has control, so you would be deemed to have a minority interest.

On the other hand, someone owning 51% usually has control no matter what. In that case, the remaining 49% is not worth 49% of the whole.

Where voting interests are spread out among a lot of owners, a 30% or 40% interest might give you control if the other shareholders are not united on most issues. They dilute their power by casting their votes in different directions, so they can never actually outvote the 30% owner. However, if the corporation is really huge, the small stockholders usually have no clue on how to vote their shares - they just follow the recommendation of the existing board. That, in itself, can keep the 30% owner in the minority boat.

Lack of Marketability - Considering these disadvantages, it's usually hard to sell a minority interest to someone else. In fact, if the majority owners don't have to listen to you, and if they have the ability to award most of the profits and benefits to themselves, then someone could buy their interest from them and never even bother to buy you out because, unless they plan to liquidate, there's no advantage to owning your shares. For this reason, we usually add an additional discount for "lack of marketability", top of the discount for lack of control.

As mentioned earlier, the stock market prices for publicly-listed companies are already discounted for lack of control, because it's assumed that an individual investor can't usually buy enough shares through the stock market to gain control. To achieve that, they usually have to make a formal "tender offer" to all voting shareholders, according to regulations promulgated by the SEC. So if you are trying to base the value of a minority interest on the daily stock price of publicly-traded companies in similar lines of business, don't discount those market prices for lack of control, only for lack of marketability.

How much do you discount?

It depends on what control rights you do have, if any. It depends on how the minority shareholder has been treated in the past. It depends on the past history of dividend distributions to minority shareholders. If the record on these items has been good, the discount will be less.

On the other hand, imagine a situation where the majority shareholders appoint themselves as managers, authorize large salaries and bonuses that put all of the profits in their own pockets, and refuse to declare any dividends for the shareholders. On top of that, let's say they approve all sorts of favorable dealings for themselves. They lease their own building to the company at high rental rates. They lend funds to the company at high interest rates, and borrow from it at low rates. They cause the company to donate money to charities of their own choice. That's a pretty bad deal for the other owners, so there's no way a minority share can be worth much in a situation like that. Even if the company is dissolved, the minority shareholder might get a proportionate share of the liquidation proceeds, but by then it may not amount to much.

In fact, if the company is acquired by someone else, that buyer might buy only the majority interest, and leave the minority shareholder sitting there, holding onto the same bad deal as before. However, the laws in some states prohibit this. Those laws are usually in the form of "appraisal right statutes". They give the minority shareholders the right to sell their stock to the buyer or the majority shareholder for cash at its appraised value. However, those statutory rights are usually only triggered by certain actions, such as the breach of an implied fiduciary responsibility by the majority stockholders to manage the company in a way that is fair to all of the shareholders, or bad faith on the part of the buyer. Procedural rules spelled out in the statute must be followed precisely by those seeking to rely on them. But that still doesn't mean that an appraisal shouldn't discount the minority share for lack of control.

Not surprisingly, it is very difficult to determine the amount of the discount. It's an issue that often leads to great controversy and there is no precise method for figuring it out. Unfortunately, it's a matter of opinion, and often your only guidance will come from looking at the discounts used in other cases.

Even that is difficult because the information isn't readily available. Some appraisers and appraisal societies try to collect the data, but it still tends to be sketchy.

With regard to the discount for lack of marketability, the only thing we can tell you is that it is said to average between 35% and 50% in well-reasoned, professional valuations.

We know that's not much help. All you can really do is use your best judgement and provide plausible reasoning to justify the discount you think should apply. Obviously, the most convincing evidence will be information on discounts accepted in the past for the stock of similar companies, but when that data isn't available, some intelligent guessing is all you can do.

If you are trying to determine the value of a *privately-held* company by referring to the stock prices of *publicly-held* companies that seem to be similar, you have to discount heavily for lack of marketability because these publicly-traded stocks are considered very marketable to begin with. Privately-held stock is always more difficult to sell, even if a controlling interest is involved.

How about the discount for lack of control? Well, that's another guessing game. Many appraisers say that the discount averages between 30% and 35%.

Try to find info on any "takeovers" of publicly-held companies in a similar line of business. Check out the price of its stock about two weeks before announcement of the takeover attempt, and then compare that to the price of the stock after the announcement, or to the price of any successful "tender offer" made to the shareholders, whichever is higher. Why two weeks before the announcement? Because news of a possible takeover attempt usually leaks out well in advance of the formal announcement. Anyway, the difference between the before-vs-after prices will give you the implied discount for lack of control. People who follow takeovers say that the discounts for lack of control averaged about 30% during the 1980's.

However, don't just assume that your discount falls into that range. Legal cases show combined discounts ranging from less than 10% to over 90%. The discount is more likely to be on the high side than on the low side. If you are dealing with a minority interest that might carry disadvantages pertaining to lack of control *and* lack of marketability, you might use the average control discount of 35%, and the average marketability discount of 40% - for a total discount of 75%.

How to avoid this problem in advance:

Anyone buying a minority partnership interest should make sure they also negotiate a buy-sell agreement that includes a pre-determined method for calculating the value of that interest, including any minority discounts. This will avoid surprises later on. If you can, you should also try to include provisions that will help protect you from unfair or biased actions by the majority partners during your ownership. Bear in mind, however, that it's usually a bad idea to pay pro-rata value for a minority interest because you may never get it all back again.

If you are investing in a corporation, there are different precautions to take. The documents that create the stock you receive will define the rights attached to it. These are usually in the form of amendments to the Articles of Incorporation. Before you buy, try to negotiate your voting rights, as well as the right to approve certain management decisions, so that your interests are adequately protected.

For example, as a condition to investing, you can insist that the Articles of Incorporation be amended to require more than a 51% majority vote for approval of certain actions. You can also try to get a separate contract between yourself and the corporation (or the majority stockholders) which requires them to buy you out under certain conditions, at a price determined by a preset formula. The minority shareholder can also be given the right to buy out the majority shareholder upon the occurrence of certain events, such as the death or disability of certain persons. Also, several minority shareholders may be given the authority to combine their voting rights into a "voting trust" whereby they agree to vote as a block and thereby achieve a majority.

Legal remedies for unfair abuses:

We have already mentioned that states sometimes enact laws that confer protective rights upon minority shareholders. In addition to these, the courts have often ruled that majority shareholders have a responsibility to operate the company in ways that do not unreasonably compromise the interests of the minority shareholders. Like the statutes, the case law varies from state to state.

The IRS View:

The IRS has always disliked minority discounting because, when an ownership share is transferred by gift or estate, they look forward to a hefty tax on its value. If that value is discounted, the government gets less tax. In fact, in 1981, the IRS issued Revenue Ruling 81-253, which disallowed minority interest discounting on shares of stock transferred between family members when the same family controls the rest of the company. However, beginning with a case called Estate of Bright vs. the United States, the courts have repeatedly rejected that IRS position. Nonetheless, the tax laws change frequently, so it would be wise to get a current update on the status of this issue if it affects you.

Valuation for ESOP purposes:

The courts have also upheld the use of minority discounts when valuing the interests of individuals in an Employee Stock Ownership Plan, even if the ESOP plan as a whole has proportional voting control over the company. In this case, however, the discounting is much more modest, because an ESOP is unlikely to call for the liquidation of underlying company assets (since that would end the employment of its beneficiaries).

In fact, the ESOP is unlikely to ratify any corporate action that is contrary to the interests of the smaller shareholder. So, while the individual employee-beneficiaries of the plan are regarded as having a minority interest when it comes to voting control, they are not vulnerable to the disadvantages that would justify a large amount of discounting. For example, in a well-known case involving an ESOP for employees of U.S. News & World Report, the discount was merely 10%.

Chapter 22

How to Increase Value Quickly

First of all, go back and read the intro chapter for an overview. Then review the valuation methods presented in this book in order to gain an understanding of the various elements that contribute to business value. Your goal is to deliberately cultivate those factors in your company over time. Most of these are long-term endeavors. If you have several years to work with, you can really make a significant difference.

However, there are also things you can do during your last few months of ownership to pump up the value of the company. This chapter reviews a few of those.

Timing the sale:

Most experts agree that there is an optimum time to sell a business. The main thing is to be profitable and show a steady trend of growth over several consecutive years. However, there are also short-term timing considerations. The general economy should be healthy, interest rates should be reasonable, lenders should be making acquisition loans available, predictions for that particular industry should be rosy, and the company's own local markets should be healthy.

That's your best-case scenario, but all those things probably won't happen at once. Nevertheless, it's a good idea to time the sale to coincide with as many attractive indicators as possible. On the other hand, you might be taking a gamble if you wait for better conditions that may not arrive. If you plan to sell when you reach a certain age, say 8 years

from now, but your projections indicate that a very good time to sell will be within the next 2 years, then reconsider your plan. Staying in longer may actually cost you money.

It's probably true that most owners sell too late rather than too early. One problem is that they can't break their emotional attachment to the company before things start sliding downhill. In addition, when things are really going well, owners start questioning their plans to sell. The exhilaration of success blinds them to the fact that all businesses have down-cycles as well as up-cycles, and that things are eventually going to slow down or move the other way. Lots of cash flow can make for shortsighted decision making.

Owners should try to get some objective input on where their industry is headed. Ignore the unbridled optimism that may typify the articles in your trade magazines. Many of these publications are promotional boosters for the industry, regardless of its real state of health, so we suggest you find more objective sources of information. You should also be wary of the projections published by the commerce department, because a lot of that data ultimately comes from the same sources. What you want are critical assessments from objective analysts, and you want very current information. Using old projections is a mistake. Any industry can get turned on its ear overnight. For example, the healthcare industry was traditionally seen as invincible - that is, until the prospect of healthcare reform. Then everyone went into a panic, and all those rosy ten-year projections went straight out the window. Within five years, it turned the other way.

Another thing to remember is that competition can multiply in no time, splitting the pie into smaller and smaller pieces. You can't relax when it comes to protecting your market share. There is always the possibility of a new, well-funded player coming onto the scene with a very attractive program. In addition, your geographic market area can fall upon hard times, and sales will plummet for reasons that have nothing to do with how you operate the business.

Each new day will bring new challenges. There's a lot that can go wrong, so if you plan to hang on to the company, then put everything you have into making it grow the entire time, or value may just move in the other direction.

If there are a limited number of buyers for your business, and yet someone is interested right now, then think twice about waiting. Not only do owners tend to overestimate the value of their company, but they also err in thinking that there will always be someone around to buy it. The truth is, there usually aren't a whole lot of *real* potential buyers out there for a particular company. You probably already know most of the logical buyers for your firm.

And don't become overly confident about finding a buyer in the future just because several have asked you to notify them "if you ever decide to sell". In my experience, it's extremely rare for any of those to forward with a serious offer. Real interest combined with the ability to actually make a deal is a very transient thing. If you only consider your *own* state of readiness, then when the time comes, your best prospects may not be in a position to do a deal.

Be prepared to add more systems and management as sales volume hits higher thresholds.

This is inescapable. As much as you may want to keep it simple, things are going to have to change upstairs. You'll need more than just more production employees. You'll need more managers, new policies, more controls, more recordkeeping, more everything. It all adds complexity and increases your operating expenses. The culture of the company will change, the work atmosphere will change, and the owner's jobs will change. Levels of responsibility and stress will increase. Because of the higher fixed overhead, there will be more pressure for everyone to perform, and heads will have to roll if they don't. Costs will increase every year, resulting in constant pressure to keep on growing or die. Any growing business eventually becomes very different from what it started out to be - from what you originally had in mind.

So, if you find growth exciting, just remember that it comes at a cost. Take that into consideration when planning your exit. Someone who has created and sold a half-dozen big companies offered his opinion recently that creating a company from scratch can be a very rewarding and pleasant experience, until you hit about 10 million dollars in sales - at which point, in his mind, the trade-offs start outweighing the advantages. That was his scheduled point of departure for each new endeavor.

The point here isn't to talk owners into selling early - just that many of the nice things about a small company disappear as it grows beyond a certain point. Some of the most brilliant entrepreneurs of the 1980's tried very hard to retain a "small company culture" as their businesses grew, and most of them eventually conceded that it isn't really possible. One reason is that our economy is based on growth, so very few businesses are able to stand still without getting run-over. Another reason is that our government wants to be involved in everything, and its regulatory systems increase their demands on a business as it becomes larger.

Fixed-Costs vs. Variable Costs:

In doing your projections, keep in mind that the changes necessitated by growth cost money, so profit margins will also change as sales increase. You can't keep projecting the same percentage of net profit at higher sales levels. Remember that if you continue to grow, you will soon need new systems and more management, and those are going to eat into your current margin quite a bit. Not all expenses are proportional to sales revenue. Many improvements will involve a fixed-cost that takes a big bite out of your margin at the outset, but does not keep increasing proportionally along with subsequent increases in sales. Take that into account when you make your projections.

Assuming you are ready to sell, there's a lot you can do to enhance the value of your company while you stage your exit.

---

1. Clear up any loans made by the company to stockholders, and any loans made by stockholders to the company. At least make sure they are repaid on schedule.

2. Keep as much of the balance sheet in current assets* as you can. It's a lot harder to retrieve dollars that are invested in fixed assets*. Buyers and lenders will dispute the value you assign to a piece of equipment, but inventory and cash are harder to argue with.

   (Over the *long* haul, your goal would be to improve the quality of your *fixed* assets.)

3. Avoid writing off personal expenses and unreasonable perks through the company. And resist the urge to inflate costs on your financial statements and tax returns in order to reduce the taxable bottom line. Even if they are totally legitimate expenses, they detract from the appearance of profitability. If you have to explain these items, then you've lost ground. Don't assume they'll be added back to the bottom line on the adjusted statement. Since there is no way to prove that they were optional expenses, there's a good chance you won't get credit for them. Besides, if your buyer is a public company, it's accustomed to being judged by its official bottom line. So do what you can to reduce unnecessary write-offs and increase your own bottom line profit.

4. A company is more valuable if it has a special market niche because that makes it less vulnerable to competitive attack. Less risk justifies a higher price. So, if you have time, consider repositioning your company so that you aren't just going head-to-head with every other competitor in your industry. (That's more of a long-term strategy.)

5. Trim down excessive salaries - gear them to what public companies pay their managers with similar responsibilities. Remember - even if a buyer adjusts an expense item on your financial statement when doing their valuation, you probably won't get credit for the improvement unless you've actually carried it out yourself.

6. Owners should gradually start transferring their own responsibilities to other employees. Buyers may question whether anyone else can really fill the owner's shoes, and this quells those doubts in advance. Plan ahead by delegating key functions to qualified people who will remain after the sale. This might mean grooming various levels of management to succeed you. Give those

people titles and spell out their control and responsibility. Hire people who are smarter than you for that job.

7. Consider deferring unnecessary bonuses if it helps you demonstrate a trend of increasing earnings. Nothing makes a company look more valuable than a consistent pattern of growth over time.

8. Don't be afraid to leave cash in the company as retained earnings. You may pay a little more tax as a result, but the business will look like a better risk to both buyers and lenders because those reserves put the company on better footing to withstand adverse market conditions in the future. It also increases future borrowing capacity since the company won't be as highly leveraged. If you plan wisely, you should be able to recoup the additional taxes many times over, but get your accountant's opinion on the matter first.

9. Try to reduce fixed overhead expenses as much as possible without creating problems with inadequate management, deferred maintenance and tooling. Buyers get nervous when they see a company with high fixed costs. They especially dislike expensive long-term obligations like expensive leases and high salary obligations - things they are stuck with beyond the date of settlement.

10. Make sure that all of the income shows up on the company ledgers. If it doesn't, you probably won't get credit for it. Don't skim.

11. Consider longer depreciation options. As a private company, your goal has probably been to hold down stated profits by using faster write-offs. Your buyer, on the other hand, will assign more value to the company if the bottom line is greater.

12. Polish your image. Spend some money to improve your offices, and at least the appearance of your communications.. Make sure your information systems are sophisticated. Have slick promotional material for your company and its products. If you sell services, you should have this anyway because it puts something in the customer's hand that seems concrete.

13. Recruit a Board of Directors that includes some distinguished individuals. Not only will you benefit from their wisdom, but they will enhance your company's image by lending their name it. Drop family members and friends from the board if they don't really add anything special.

14. Consult your accountant for "tax-advantaged exit strategies". These are arrangements that reduce the amount of assets being held by the company or the amount of taxable current income that might otherwise pile up beyond a conservative safety cushion. "Planned giving" is one popular example. There, you transfer income or assets each year, up to certain deductible limits per donee, to family members or some organization that is underfunded and needs your help, such as the Humane Society of the United States. That way, you can avoid the heavy estate taxes and also do some good during your life. Another route might be to set up a private foundation under the tax laws, which you administer yourself or through an independent trustee. Again, the assets and income can go in tax-free as long as they are administered for good of the designated charitable beneficiary or cause (which includes things like the environment).

15. Get adequate insurance to ease the concern buyers might have over potential liabilities that may carry over to them after the sale.

16. If there's real estate involved, remove any underground tanks and clean up any environmental contamination (including asbestos) in advance. Be able to provide clean environmental test results.

17. Hire a locally prestigious accounting firm to prepare audited financial statements that include their "unqualified opinion". These should cover the past 3 to 5 years. The financials of a private company's are always viewed with suspicion, so this provides a much-needed stamp of legitimacy.

18. Develop a 5-year strategic business plan. Even if you don't plan to own the company that much longer, the plan will give buyers a picture of your company's history, its strengths, and its future potential. You can suggest ways to build sales, benefit from improving demographics, enter new markets, develop new products, and so on. Besides, doing the projections will help you to double-check your timing. However, don't get so wrapped up in optimism that you defer your exit plan past the date when you should. Remember that business plans are rarely carried out in the way they are written. Their value is that they give the company direction, goals, and visions to strive for. You have to believe in your plan, but at the same time realize that things probably won't pan-out exactly that way.

Why do these things now?

Many seller's wonder why they have to make changes to get their best price - why they can't just tell the potential buyer what kind of improvements can be made, and what financial effects will result, without actually carrying them out. It's true - the buyer could look ahead and adjust your financial statement for many potential improvements that haven't taken place. But then it's additional value that he or she creates, not value that already exists. Buyers adjust for their *own* benefit - not yours.

Nevertheless, keep in mind that it's a good idea to leave something on the table for the buyer. Very few buyers want to acquire a company whose value is already maximized. If all they want is an pre-set investment return, there are safer and simpler ways to produce that without buying and running a company. They need to see some unrealized upside potential - specific ways to create more value later.

The buyer's point of view:

Prospective buyers should realize that some sellers fiddle with their expenses in ways that are misleading. It's not uncommon to see owners puff up the bottom line by drawing unrealistically low salaries, paying business expenses out of their personal fund, deferring important property maintenance, using very lengthy depreciation periods, or capitalizing items that could be written off in one year. These practices understate the business expenses, and can sometimes cause problems later on.

Chapter 23

How Developments in the Tax Law Can Affect Your Deal

The influence of court decisions:

We have already pointed out that valuation methods are greatly influenced by the tax law. (Make sure you have reviewed Chapter 12 for the basic IRS approach to valuation.) *Realize that the courts are constantly interpreting and modifying the rules* through their case decisions. These establish precedent that will be followed in most later rulings on the same issue.

If you are involved in a tax dispute involving valuation, you should ask your accountant or tax attorney to look into any court decisions that deal with the same issues. The following are regarded as some of the more influential decisions involving valuation. They are only paraphrased here, so make sure you read the entire case if you believe they may affect you.

The Northern Trust Company et al vs. Commissioner

(87 TC 349; 87 TC No.2, Dec. 43, 261).

This case was decided before the Federal Tax Court in August 1986. The IRS claimed that minority stockholders in a privately-held company had undervalued the stock of their company and, as a result, underpaid their taxes when it was transferred. The case is considered influential, and, while each court decision is dependent upon the specific facts involved, this decision appears to make several points clear:

1. Income-based valuation methods are clearly preferred by the Tax Court over comparable sales methods. In this case, the court rejected the use of "comparables"* because the companies selected were not sufficiently similar to the subject company, their capital structures were different, and their sales growth was different. The court flatly rejected the use of companies from different industries as comparables, even though they had financial characteristics similar to the subject company. It was further indicated that the comparable sales approach can be rejected if it doesn't consider a large-enough number of companies.

2. In particular, the court upheld the use of the Discounted Cash Flow method because it takes into consideration all of the factors listed as important in Revenue Ruling #59-60: general economic outlook, outlook for the subject industry, financial condition of the company, the percentage of stock being valued, and the dividend-producing capacity (net profit) of the company. Revenue Ruling 59-60 is widely accepted as an approach for valuing the stock of a closely held company for gift and estate purposes. The IRS argued that income projections amount to mere speculation, but the Court said that they are acceptable predictions of future earnings as long as the basis for them is actual past performance. The Court said that "prior earnings records usually are the most reliable guide as to future expectancy".

3. Selecting A Capitalization Rate - The court supported the use of the CAPM (Capital Asset Pricing Model) method of determining the capitalization* rate in present value* calculations. This method tends to produce higher capitalization (discount) rates than other approaches and, hence, lower valuations. The Capital Asset Pricing Method usually yields capitalization rates of 20-30% for small private businesses. Since this Tax Court decision came out, the method has become popular in setting the capitalization rates. used in all the income-based valuations. It is explained in Chapter 5.

4. The court upheld the use of a discount to reduce the value of stock where the transfer involves only a minority interest in the company, because there is no voting control and the stock has limited marketability. (Privately-held stock is usually difficult to sell and is often coupled with a low dividend paying history.) However, the Court warned against using too high a discount where the company is financially strong, has good management, and has an upward earnings trend. In this particular case, the Court allowed a 25% discount for lack of voting control and a 20% discount for lack of marketability - for a total of 55%. The discount in any individual case will depend on its specific facts. Chapter 21 gives some guidance on how to determine these discounts, but there is a lot of subjectivity involved.

The result of this case will probably be a reduction in the use of comparable sales methods of valuation, along with some support for the use of more conservative (higher) capitalization rates and the use of discounts for minority stock interests.

As you can see, the Tax Court can be quite influential in shaping the techniques of valuation.

Here are some other important cases:

Central Trust Co. vs. the United States
(305 F.2d 393, 1962). The court's opinion stated:

1. For a manufacturing company, capitalized earnings are the most important factor in valuation. The income statements on which they are based should be adjusted for unusual or nonrecurring items, and earnings trends should be noted.

2. Revenue Ruling 59-60 states that dividend paying capacity should be given weight, but in the case of a private or closely-held company, it can be scaled back to reflect the company's need to retain some funds to finance future growth.

3. The court said that book value should be given some consideration, but in the final analysis, it wasn't given much weight here.

4. Prior sales of the subject company's stock are relevant, but only if those sales were conducted at arm's length and only if the company's financial condition hasn't changed substantially since then.

5. You can base value on the sale prices of comparable companies, but that analysis should include as many similar companies as possible.

6. With a privately-held firm, you can discount the value due to lack of marketability of its stock.

Buffalo Tool and Die Mnfg. Co. vs. Commissioner (74 TC 441, 1980).

Here, the court decided that where experts differ on the value of the business, the courts should not "split the difference" between those opinions, but should decide which value is most appropriate, based on the relative merits of the valuation methods used.

Estate of Bright vs. the United States (81-USTC Paragraph 13, 436, 5th Circuit 1981).

This decision was the first in a long line of cases rejecting Revenue Ruling 81-253, which sought to eliminate minority discounts for the stock of closely-held companies. The decision also said that just because members of the same family can combine their voting rights to control the company, that doesn't mean that the minority discount doesn't apply to the valuation of a particular family member's stock.

Charles S. Foltz et al. vs. U.S. News & World Report, Inc., Davis Richardson, et al. vs. U.S. News & World Report (U.S. District Court, District of Columbia, Civil Action 84-0447 and 85-2195, 1987).

The court's decision stated:

1. Where a valuation is performed for ESOP* purposes, and the ESOP plan holds numerical control of the company, that doesn't mean the shares of any one employee should be accorded a control premium. A discount for a minority interest still applies.

2. Since the individual shareholder in an ESOP plan holds a minority interest, earnings should be the primary factor in determining the value of that stock, even if the company's underlying assets have greater value, because the minority shareholder lacks any power or authority to direct the company to liquidate its assets and distribute the proceeds to shareholders. In this case, that conclusion was reinforced by the fact that no such plan of action existed among the majority.

Estate of Joyce C. Hall vs. Commissioner (92TC 19, 1989).

The court decided that you can't refer to only one company when using a comparable sales approach, even if it's the only other one in that same line of business. However, the court weakened the validity of this method by saying that "comparable" means "similar", but not necessarily the same.

Research the tax law for decisions that apply to your own case!

Obviously, the courts play a major role in interpreting how the tax code is applied. Before you undertake any transaction, you should consult a tax specialist (CPA or attorney) to see if your deal is set up in a way that entitles you to the most advantageous tax treatment. The rules aren't always clear-cut, and many taxpayers feel its worthwhile to argue their point with the IRS, even if it takes them into court.

For example, when a company buys another business, it acquires its customer base. In the case of a service-type business, that's the main thing being purchased. However, the IRS has long-held that a client base is a non-depreciable intangible asset. Many companies have disagreed, because such lists have both an ascertainable value and a limited useful life -just like a tangible asset. In fact, so many have disagreed that, in 1991, $23.5 Billion worth of intangible assets were in dispute between taxpayers and the IRS. The issue recently went all the way to the Supreme Court, which finally held that the value of an acquired customer base is depreciable. The difference is enough to make or break an acquisition, but most buyers will never know that this depreciation is available to them unless they hire someone to search for the case decisions that pertain to the acquisition they are planning.

Does the tax-bite affect the valuation?

Most of the methods in this book are heavily influenced by the concepts of taxation. However, keep in mind that, according to accepted valuation theory, while annual income taxation of net income certainly is taken into consideration, the value of a company is not affected by taxation of the sale proceeds. A company is valued without regard to the transaction costs.

However, value and negotiated sale price are not the same thing. Sometimes the impact of the tax laws is great enough to affect the price. Normally, the buyer can't be expected to pay more for a business than it's worth just because the seller will lose some of his proceeds to taxes. Therefore, most terms of sale having tax implications will not affect the price.

For example, in a purchase of assets, the purchase price must be allocated among the acquired assets according to certain guidelines in the tax laws. This affects the depreciation allowed to the buyer, as well as the taxation of proceeds to the seller. While it's something the parties have to agree on,

it's usually resolved by compromise after the price has already been agreed on, so it doesn't affect the price. On the other hand, if one of the parties wants something entirely optional included in the contract that will bring him a definite tax advantage, he may have to bend on the purchase price to get it, especially if it represents a disadvantage to the other party.

Get the latest info!

The tax rules change periodically, so it would be wise to look up the *latest* information before you assume anything. Most CPA firms receive tax updates on a weekly basis, so your accountant can probably tell you if you are relying on the most recent information. These rules are complex, and unless you're a finance professional you probably don't want to spend your time boning up on them. Besides, it's very easy to miss something important, so we suggest that you seek the advice of a good tax accountant before undertaking any transaction.

For those who are inclined to dig into the gory details themselves, a good source of up-to-date technical information on the tax laws is the C.C.H. (Commerce Clearing House) tax service, which includes the weekly updates. Refer to the Topical Index of the C.C.H. Standard Federal Tax Reporter for the current year. This will direct you to specific sections of the service. They also publish a Transactions Library that contains hundreds of individual portfolios on tax subjects such as reorganization, Subchapter-S corporations, the transfer of business interests between family members, capitalization*, liquidation* of a business, and so on. These books are usually found at county libraries, law libraries, and university libraries.

There are thousands of rules in the tax code, with different treatments for every situation. While general concepts of taxation are discussed in this book, it is essential to get up-to-date tax information and consult with an accountant.

GLOSSARY
of Financial Terms

Most of the concepts in this book are probably familiar to you, but just in case they aren't, many of them have been defined for you here in this chapter. The definitions have been separated from the main text so you won't be slowed down if you already know their meaning. Many are marked with an asterisk (*) when they first occur in a chapter.

We have defined these concepts only as they relate to valuation. These are not necessarily the most complete or technically correct definitions.

ഇൽ

Accounts Payable: The current debts of a business. Generally includes any amount owed to others for goods and services received on credit - i.e., all of the normal, unpaid bills of a business. These are often referred to as "trade payables", or simply "payables".

Accounts Receivable: The opposite of accounts payable - these are sums owed to the company for goods and services sold to customers on credit. Also called "receivables" for short.

In an acquisition, receivables can be purchased - that is, the right to receive the money is transferred to the new owner, and they take over as the creditor. However, receivables are often sold at a discount from their face value (book value*) because there are always some that may not be paid. These would include invoices to any customers who have not paid reliably in the past, and any accounts that are past due. Sometimes, even the current (on time) accounts are discounted because of the cost of collecting them. They may also be discounted in order to give their purchaser a reasonable return on his investment in them. A good analogy is a savings bond, which is purchased at a cost lower than its face value, so that the buyer has a built-in return on the investment.

Agings: Information that tells how much time has passed since accounts receivable* were billed. Agings show the total amount of receivables that aren't yet due, and the total amount that are past due, broken down into 30 day increments. For example, the following might be the receivables agings for a company that gives its customers "30 day terms" (bills sent out are due in 30 days):

$600,000 - 15 days or less [have elapsed since the bills were sent out]
$500,000 - 16 to 30 days old
$ 50,000 - 31 to 60 days old (past due)
$ 5,000 - 61 to 90 days old (past due)
$ 500 - over 90 days old (past due)

The farther past-due they are, the less likely it is that they will ever be paid. Lenders accept receivables as security for a loan, but will not usually give value for any that are past due, unless personally guaranteed by the seller or some other party.

A schedule of agings is meaningless without some explanation of the company's normal credit terms. It should indicate any customers who are granted special payment terms, sothat you don't mistake those for past due accounts. Customers are often given a discount if they pay early. (That's usually the only reason bills are ever paid before 15 days.) If the company offers a two percent discount on bills paid by the 15th day that are normally due in 30 days, the invoice will say "2% 15, net 30".

Allocation of Purchase Price: This subject comes up whenever an acquisition takes the form of a sale of assets (an "asset deal"). It refers to the process of divvying up the company's purchase price among the various assets purchased, to indicate how much each one supposedly cost the purchaser. The allocation may be hotly negotiated between buyer and seller since both must use the same allocation for tax purposes. It matters to the buyer because it determines how much depreciation* can be taken on those assets in subsequent years. It matters to the seller because it determines the amount of taxable gain on the sale of those assets. Therefore, the allocation is usually agreed upon in advance and included in the acquisition agreement.

The allocation determines the amount of taxable profit (or deductible loss) realized by the seller on each asset involved in the sale. The profit or loss on the sale of an asset is generally equal to:

The allocated price

minus its "tax basis", which is:
    its original cost,
    plus amounts spent to improve it,
    minus tax depreciation taken on it

minus any "recapture*" of accelerated depreciation or investment tax credits, if applicable.

Naturally, the seller wants an allocation that results in the smallest amount of taxable profit. The seller also wants the maximum amount attributed to "capital assets", so that any gain on them is considered "capital gain" instead of ordinary income, and thereby taxed at a lower capital gain rate. (Check the newest tax law.)

The allocation determines the buyer's initial tax basis for each asset. This is the amount that can be depreciated for tax purposes. Some kinds of assets can be depreciated faster than others, and some can not be depreciated at all, so buyers always want an allocation that gives them the most advantageous depreciation schedule. Of course, they want to avoid the allocation of purchase price to non-depreciable assets such as goodwill*.

The tax authorities, however, want the allocation to be based on the true market value of the assets, with any left-over amount going to goodwill. They discourage allocations that depart from economic reality and that are devised only to reduce the taxes paid by the parties. If the purchase price is less than the total market value of the assets, the allocation should be pro rata. In other words, it should be distributed in the same proportions that the real market value of each asset bears to the total market value of all of the assets. So, if inventory has a market value of $1,000,000, and the total market value of all assets purchased is $3,000,000, then one-third of the actual purchase price should be allocated to inventory.

See Chapter 10 for more on this subject.

Amortization:
1. The repayment of a loan in periodic installments rather than a lump sum. "Term-loans" are amortized by monthly payments for a definite term, at the end of which the entire indebtedness has been repaid.
2. A synonym for depreciation* of intangible assets*.

Assets: Everything of monetary value owned by the company. This includes cash, accounts receivable*, raw materials inventory, finished product inventory, supplies, equipment, buildings, and land. It may also include *intangible* things, such as rights granted under a patent or copyright. (See "intangible assets", below.)

The balance sheet generally categorizes assets into current assets, long-term investments (stocks, bonds, promissory notes for amounts owed to the company, etc.), plant & equipment (known as "fixed assets"), and intangible assets.

Current Assets are items that will be converted into cash, sold, or consumed within one year. They include cash itself, accounts receivable and notes receivable that will be collected within one year, bank deposits, merchandise or inventory that is expected to be sold within one year, prepaid insurance, supplies and the like (things that will be consumed within a year).

Prepaid insurance, office supplies, and prepaid taxes are included in a sub-category known as *pre-paid expenses.* They are purchased for use in the business and will be consumed within a relatively short period of time. At that point they become "expenses", but until then they are classified as current assets. They are seldom a major item on the balance sheet.

Quick Assets are assets that can be turned into cash quickly. They generally include cash, accounts receivable, and marketable securities. This is not a category that normally appears on the balance sheet because it can include both current assets and long-term investments.

Fixed Assets include land, building, plant and machinery, vehicles, furnishings and fixtures. These are long-lasting assets held for use in the production or sale of products and services. Fixed assets, with the exception of land, have a definite value which diminishes gradually over a period of time as they wear out. Since they are consumed over a period which is longer than one year, the IRS does not generally allow you to write-off their entire cost in the year of purchase. Any asset with a useful life of more than one year is usually classified as a fixed asset and is depreciated (cost is written-off over several years), rather than categorized as an "expense" and "expensed" (entire cost deducted in the year of purchase). The value listed on the balance sheet for a fixed asset is its original cost, minus any "depreciation" deducted on it to date. The resulting figure is known as its book value. If a fixed asset is repaired, reconditioned, or improved, the cost of doing so is added to its current book value (its "tax basis") and then depreciated along with the rest of its remaining value. The amount is not expensed in the year of repair. The resulting book value is called its "adjusted basis": its original cost, plus the cost of improvements, minus any depreciation taken to date.

Intangible Assets are assets having no physical nature. They have no intrinsic value. Instead, their value lies in the rights, savings, or increased income they represent to their owner. They include such things as goodwill*, patents, copyrights, leasehold improvements, leaseholds, and trademarks. See Chapter 6 for a discussion of intangibles and their value. Even intangible assets have a limited useful life, so their balance sheet cost is usually depreciated over a period of time. Depreciation of intangibles is often referred to as "amortization". Improvements to leased property are treated as intangibles and are amortized, since they benefit the tenant who put them there, but they become part of the property and revert to the landlord at the end of the lease. Notes and accounts receivable are also intangible in nature, but these show up on the balance sheet as current assets. Rights granted under a lease (a "leasehold") are not listed as an asset - unless the lease requires payment of rent for a year or more in advance, in which case the rent payment might be listed as a leasehold asset instead of as a prepaid expense. Normally, rent is paid on a monthly basis and written off as a current expense.

Securable Assets are the assets that lenders will accept as collateral for a loan. Normally, they are limited to accounts receivable, inventory, land & building, and machinery & equipment. This is not a category appearing on the balance sheet, just a way of referring to loan collateral.

Book Value:

1. Usually refers to the value of the company's assets, as listed on the balance sheet. It's the original cost of the asset, minus accumulated depreciation. Book value is usually less than actual market value.

2. The term also sometimes refers to the Net Worth of the company. "Net Worth" is equal to Total Assets minus Total Liabilities, using the figures from the company's balance sheet. See Chapter 7 for a full explanation.

Capitalization:

1. The total amount of cash and borrowed money (equity and debt) used to create a business. The total investment of the owners in a business.

2. The process of recording an expenditure as a long-term asset, which is then depreciated*, instead of listing it as an "expense", which is written off entirely in one year. Such an expenditure is said to be "capitalized".

3. "Capitalization of Earnings" - Calculating the present value of the projected earnings of a business. See "Discount Rate" for a detailed explanation.

Capital Expenditures:

Generally refers to the company's yearly investment in new equipment, machinery, real estate, and other assets of a permanent or fixed nature.

Capital Improvements:

Basically the same as Capital Expenditures, but refers to money spent to improve a fixed asset that is already owned, such as real estate.

Cash Flow (Net Cash Flow):

Not the same as "net income" on the company's income statement. Cash flow refers to the actual net inflow and outflow of cash. The net income figure on an income statement has certain fictional "expenses" deducted from it that haven't actually been paid during that year (such as depreciation) so it's less than the true amount of cash the company had available.

A cash flow statement shows the cash balance remaining from the previous year, plus the amounts and sources of incoming cash during the current year, minus the outgo of cash during the year. The result is the year-end cash balance. Some use this short-cut: just add the depreciation expense back to "net income after tax". The resulting figure provides an estimate of the cash available for further capital expenditures, dividend payments, debt payments, and so on.

Closely-Held:

Refers to a corporation whose stock is owned or controlled by a very small group of shareholders. The term can include a corporation whose stock is registered publicly with government securities agencies so that it can be publicly traded. However, if all of the stock is held by a very small number of individuals who rarely sell any of it, then the company is more like a privately-held corporation than a large public company. When the stock of a publicly registered company is widely held and actively traded, its value is subject to market influences that don't affect a private company's stock. For this reason, closely- held public companies are often valued by the same methods as privately-held companies.

Common Stock - (See "Preferred Stock" for the distinction between different classes of stock.)

Correlation (of valuation results): Comparing the results obtained by different valuation methods, according more weight to some than to others, and thereby arriving at a final estimate of value. See Chapter 19.

Current Assets - (See "Assets")

Current Liabilities: Current liabilities are debts or obligations that must be repaid within a short period of time, usually one year, and which will be paid out of current assets*. Includes accounts payable*, notes payable*, wages payable, taxes payable, interest payable, and so on. Also includes "unearned revenues", which are amounts received as prepayment for goods or services that have not been shipped yet. Those are liabilities because they represent an obligation to deliver something at a future date. Any obligation not classified as a current liability is grouped with **long-term debts:** The latter is any debt or liability whose balance is not due for a relatively long period of time (over one year) - including mortgages and notes payable more than a year after the balance sheet date.

Debt Service: The total amount of loan payments made during the year for liabilities that are being paid off in installments (amortized*). Includes both the principal and the interest part of the payments. May include other loan fees, insurance, points, and other charges required by the lender.

Depreciation: The annual reduction in the value of an asset due to use, wear, and tear. Depreciation reflects the gradual decline in value of the company's assets. It is accounted for in two ways:

(1) An annual amount of depreciation is *deducted from the value of the asset listed on the balance sheet.* This value ("Book Value') is usually the same as its adjusted basis, which used to determine whether there is taxable gain when the asset is later sold.

(2) When an asset is purchased, you pay for it in that year, but you aren't usually allowed to deduct its entire cost at once. You only get to deduct a portion of that cost each year, as the asset gradually loses value. The annual amount of "depreciation" is considered to be a cash expense for that year, so it is *deducted from current income* when you determine net taxable income. The idea is that "capital assets" are gradually consumed, and the annual amount of that consumption is one of the costs of doing business in that year. That way, the purchase cost is spread out over several years, rather than expensed* completely in the year of purchase. The tax code defines the kinds of assets that must be depreciated instead of expensed, and the period of time allowed for their depreciation. In general, they include any asset that is expect to last more than 12 months. IRS reasons that since they last more than a year, they are not fully consumed in that first year, so to that extent it is not yet an "expense" to the business. Most businesses, however, given the option, would probably rather deduct their entire cost in the year of purchase, and the tax code sometimes provides that option under

specified conditions. The disadvantage of depreciation is that you shell out the purchase price in today's dollars, but you are only allowed to deduct that cost in a mixture of less-valuable future dollars.

Depreciation is considered a "non-cash expense". That is, it's a real annual expense, in the sense that the asset suffers a legitimate decline in value each yea, but no additional funds are paid out after its initial purchase. Note that the depreciation listed on tax returns is sometimes different than the amount listed on financial statements.

Depreciation, for financial statement purposes, requires an estimate of the useful life of the asset, and an estimate of its salvage (scrap) value at end of that period. The difference between its cost and its salvage value is divided by the number of years in its useful life, and the resulting amount is allowed as a depreciation deduction each year. This is called the "straight line method".

There are also "accelerated" methods of depreciation. These use various formulas to allow a faster write-off. They usually allow greater deduction in the earlier years of the useful life than in the later years.

It should be noted that obsolescence is different from depreciation. *Obsolescence* is when an asset is no longer useable, because it is out of style or technologically outmoded. When an asset becomes obsolete before the expiration of its projected useful life, the amount of remaining undepreciated value is usually written off in that year. In cases where rapid obsolescence is foreseeable (such as with computers), or where there is high risk of obsolescence, the asset is often depreciated over a shorter period of time.

Not all assets used in a business or held for the production of income are depreciable under the tax code. Traditionally, depreciation has not been allowed for land and goodwill, at least for tax purposes.

See Chapter 10 for more on this subject.

Discount Rate: This term commonly refers to the interest rate charged by the Federal Reserve in loans made to its member banks. However, in valuation, the term refers to an interest rate that is used to calculate the present value* of a sum of money to be received in the future. That "discount rate" can take one of two forms, each having a different application:

1. *Capitalization Rate:* This is a single percentage rate used to convert a *series* of payments or earnings into a *single* present value in one step. A discount rate is called a "capitalization rate" when it is used in this way. Accordingly, "capitalization of earnings" is the process of estimating the economic worth of a company by computing the present value of the average annual net income it will probably produce in the future. First you try to predict the company's average annual net income by making a lot of assumptions about its performance in the future. More often that not, you will simply use the income from the last full fiscal year, assuming income is stable or growing. Then you *divide* this figure by the appropriate percentage rate (the capitalization rate).

For example, let's say you are trying to find the present value of an investment that is expected to produce an annual return of $15,000. The risk involved in this investment, as near as you can figure, is about the same as for other investments that produce annual returns averaging 10%. This information allows you to estimate the present value of the stream of income to be received from your investment. You divided the projected average annual income of $15,000 by 10 percent, giving you a present value of $150,000. Here the income of $15,000 has been "capitalized" at a capitalization rate of 10%.

Two practical difficulties are encountered when trying to use the Capitalization of Earnings technique. First is the problem of reliably estimating the future net income on an average annual basis. The other problem is determining the correct interest rate to use for capitalization. The rate of return from an investment is always commensurate with the degree of risk involved, so that risk must be accurately assessed. The rate selected must reflect a number of considerations. One is the reliability of the earnings estimate. Another is the rate of return generally expected on investments involving comparable risk. There is a lot of subjectivity involved in assessing the risk rate for a private company, so this is one area where your valuation will be subject to differences of opinion. However, there must be some sensible rationale behind the rate you choose, and to employ that you need to learn a lot about the particular business, its markets, and its industry as a whole.

To review - a capitalization rate is a form of discount rate which is used to convert a series of annual incomes, to be received *indefinitely* into the future, into a single present value. This is done by dividing the average expected annual income by the capitalization rate.

2. *Discount factor:* A "discount factor" is a form of discount rate which is used to determine the present value* of a right to receive a *single* payment at a *specified* time in the future. Present value is determined by simply *multiplying* the amount to be received by that discount factor (not dividing it).

The discount factor is the reciprocal of one, plus the discount rate, or $(1 + i)^{-n}$. Here, "i" equals the estimated rate of interest that would otherwise be earned on the money during the period before its actual receipt, and "n" refers to the number of periods until the expected receipt. For example, if the discount rate is 10 percent per period, the discount factor for three periods is $(1.10)^{-3} = 0.75131$. If the amount to be received in three years is $10,000, then the right to receive that amount has a value today of $10,000 X 0.75131 = $7,513.10. In this form, the discount rate represents the alternative return that is sacrificed by the investor when he commits his funds to the investment being valued.

You don't have to calculate the discount factor yourself by using this formula, since tables showing the discount factors at various rates are readily available (see the Appendix), and since most financial calculators also perform this function with ease.

Also see "present value".

Earnings: The following terms are often used synonymously:
- profit
- net operating profit
- net operating income
- net income
- net profit
- earnings

They all refer to income from the sale of goods or services, minus the cost of producing that income. However, to accountants, these terms may have slightly different technical meanings. Compare the following:

Gross Profit: Total sales revenue, minus the "cost of goods sold". The cost of goods sold is the cost to produce new inventory - raw materials, direct labor, freight, and factory overhead costs, including depreciation.

Operating Income or Operating Profit: Gross Profit, minus "operating expenses" Operating expenses are selling expenses, delivery expenses, administrative expenses, and other general expenses (office salaries, office supplies, office expense, bad debt expense, depreciation on office equipment, and so on).

Net Income or Net Profit: Operating Profit, minus taxes, interest paid on mortgage loans, and any other remaining financial expenses.

"Earnings" generally refers to Net Income (also known as Net Profit). For an illustration of these terms, see the definition for "Income Statement".

Expense (to Expense - used as a verb): Refers to the practice of deducting the entire cost of something in the same year it's paid, rather than depreciating it (spreading the deduction out over several years). The item is thus said to be "expensed". Sometimes a business can elect to write off an expense in one year, even though it might normally be depreciated. See "Assets", under the subsection for Fixed Assets.

Financial Ratios: These are ratios that supposedly gauge the relative financial health of the company. The idea is to calculate the ratio for your subject company and then compare that to the average ratio for other companies in the same industry. These ratios are published by several different sources, including Robert Morris Associates, and are commonly available in the reference section of libraries. The ratios fall into five basic categories:

1. Liquidity - Does the company have enough of its assets in a form that can be converted quickly into cash if an immediate need arises?

2. Debt Coverage - Are the earnings adequate to cover all of the company's debt payments with large margin for safety?

3. Leverage - Is the company carrying a dangerous amount of debt, compared to its fixed assets?

4. Operating Results - Is the company producing an adequate return on its assets?

5. Ratio of Expenses-to-Sales - Are the company's profit margins adequate? (Is it worth staying in business?)

This information will give you an idea of how the company measures up to its competition, and to other types of businesses.

Several financial ratios are described in Chapter 10.

Goodwill: The value of a business, to the extent that it exceeds the value of its assets. Results from being a profitable, ongoing business. There are various methods for calculating the value of goodwill. Most of them boil it down to this:

> the capitalized* value . . .

> of the amount of earnings produced by the business . . .

> that are in excess of the cost of financing the purchase of that business.

Business buyers don't want to attribute value to goodwill because it's hard to finance and they can't depreciate it like other assets. Sellers, on the other hand, tend to over-estimate the goodwill.

Just because a collection of assets is assembled into a business, that doesn't mean there's goodwill value. Just about every business, even a poorly operated one, has some customer accounts, ongoing patronage, and a business reputation, but that's not enough to give it goodwill value. In valuation, the definition is very conservative - goodwill exists only where the earnings of that business are greater than normal for its industry. Goodwill can be thought of as a special competitive edge held by that firm that sets it apart from the others, and which can reasonably be expected to continue in the future. For examples of how goodwill is valued, see Chapter 6, Chapter 11, and Chapter 12.

Income Statement: (Also known as a "Profit and Loss Statement", or "P&L") A statement of annual revenue and expenses, showing whether the company earned a profit ("net income"). Below is a format for the Income statement of a manufacturing company. Following that, certain items on the Income Statement are broken down into more detail.

Form for Income Statement

Gross Sales
    Less: Returns and allowances
    Less: Cash discounts

= Net Sales
    Less: Cost of Goods Sold[1] (detailed breakdown below)

= Gross Profit
    Less: Operating Expenses[3] (see detailed breakdown below)

= Net Operating Income (or Operating Profit)
    Plus: Non-operating income*
    Less: Interest, Depreciation* and other financial expenses

= Total Net Income before Taxes
    Less: Income Taxes

= Total Net Income After-tax

[1] Cost of Goods Sold:

Finished Goods Inventory at Beginning of Year
+ Cost of Goods Manufactured[2] (detailed breakdown below)
- Finished Goods Inventory at End of Year

= Cost of Goods Sold

[2] Cost of Goods Manufactured:

Raw Materials used during year
    (Beginning Inventory, plus purchases, minus Ending Inventory)
+ Direct Manufacturing Labor Costs
    (includes Wages, Workman's Compensation, and Payroll Expenses)
+ Factory Overhead Costs:
    Supervision
    Power
    Repairs and maintenance
    Factory supplies
    Factory insurance
    Depreciation on machinery & equipment
    Depreciation on building used for manufacturing
    Taxes on property used for mnfg.
    Other misc. labor ("indirect labor")
+ Beginning "Work-in-Process" Inventory
- End of Year "Work-in-Process" Inventory

= Cost of Goods Manufactured

[3] Operating Expenses:

Selling Expenses:
    Sales salaries and commissions
    Advertising and promotion expense
    Travel and entertainment expense
    Delivery expenses (not previously deducted)
    Sales supplies and shipping supplies
    Insurance or Delivery expense
    Bad debts expense
    Credit and collection
    Depreciation expense for delivery equipment

+ Administrative Expenses:
    Salaries & wages -executive & clerical
    Travel and entertainment
    Telephone
    Postage, stationary, supplies
    Dues and publications
    Depreciation on office equipment
    Rental expense for office equipment
    Miscellaneous Administrative expenses (Continued...)

+ General Expenses:
   Group insurance and other employee
      benefits
   General insurance
   Legal and accounting expense
   Payroll taxes (for non-manufacturing
      employees)
   Other real estate taxes
   Workmans Compensation expense
      (for non-manufacturing per-
      sonnel)
   Liability insurance
   Miscellaneous General Expense
   Other Financial expenses (including
      depreciation and interest)*

= Total Operating Expense

Note: Depreciation is sometimes included in the Operating Expenses or Administrative Expenses, but many feel that it not a cost of doing business. Instead, they move it down into to Financial Expenses.

Note: The expenses on this Income Statement include certain "non-cash expenses" (amounts for which no cash has actually been paid out in the current year - such as depreciation). For this reason Net Income is not the same as Net Cash Flow*. See the separate definition for "Cash Flow".

Intangible Assets - (See "Assets")

Leasehold Improvements: Physical improvements of a permanent nature made to a leased property by its tenant. The cost of these improvements is generally depreciated* by the tenant over the term of the lease, or over the life of the improvements, whichever is shorter. Ownership of the improvements reverts to the landlord at the end of the lease term, even thought they have been paid for by the tenant. May include "fixtures" - which are items of property attached to the property in a permanent fashion. Even if you can un-

screw and remove them, the lease generally stipulates that, once attached, they stay with the property.

Leverage: The degree to which a purchase is financed with borrowed money. The phrase "highly leveraged" usually means that the buyers paid for the deal by taking out a higher proportion of loans than would normally be expected.

Leveraged Buyout: Refers to an acquisition that is financed mostly with borrowed money, so the buyers put very little of their own cash into the deal ("equity"). In more-conventional deals, the buyer comes up with 20% to 30% of the purchase price in cash. In an "LBO", however, the cash investment might be cut back to 10% or less. These deals are considered much more risky because the principals don't have much personally at stake, and because the ratio of fixed loan payments to available cash flow will be relatively high. Lenders usually won't finance such deals unless:

1. The company has lots of securable assets available as collateral for the loan.

2. The company has a stable history of cash flow* which is adequate to make the loan payments along with a large margin for safety.

A reasonable purchase price is important in these deals because if it's too high, that means the acquisition loan (and thus the loan payments) will be dangerously high, compared to the limited amount of cash flow available to make those payments. The lender wants to see 30% to 50% more cash flow than is necessary to make the payments, just in case there are unforeseen problems or fluctuations in business.

It is difficult to get a loan for more than the secured loan value of the collateral assets. (See Chapter 18.) However, given the right purchase price, a large base of securable assets, and good cash flow, buyers with very little cash have been able to pull off some very large acquisitions.

LIFO Inventory Accounting Method:

("Last in, first out"). This is a method of inventory accounting where you assume that the last inventory you've purchased is the first inventory sold (or used in producing goods sold) during that fiscal year. You deduct the cost of that inventory from gross sales to determine your income during that year.

The theory behind LIFO is that every sale depletes inventory and necessitates the replacement of those goods, so replacement costs should be matched with the sales that caused them. This method allows you to use the higher cost of your most recent inventory purchases to offset sales income, so your taxable net profit will be less than if you used the lower inventory cost associated with your oldest remaining inventory. This doesn't mean that you actually use the new stuff first, because then you would have a lot of obsolete materials lying around. It just means that the inventory value carried on your books is skewed toward the lower cost values of the past. This is an attractive tax break for most businesses when inventory costs are rising. Old inventory purchased at lower prices in the past will remain on the books at those prices, even though its real value may be significantly higher, or even though it may really be used up. This means that the book value of inventory on your balance sheet may be considerably understated if you use the LIFO method.

Other inventory accounting methods include:

FIFO (First In, First Out) - Here, you

assume that the oldest inventory is used up or sold first. This matches old, lower costs with few sales.

Weighted Average - Smooths out inventory cost fluctuations by using a weighted average of past inventory costs.

Specific Invoice Price - When it is

possible to track and match each item sold with a specific inventory purchase, this method lets you assign those specific costs to the goods sold. It exactly matches costs and revenues. Most businesses cannot use this method.

Liquidation Value: Refers to the amount

of money a seller is likely to receive if the business is terminated and its assets are sold individually, under hasty or forced circumstances, at an auction. In this situation, the price is likely to be less than market value*. The liquidation value of an entire company is the total of the liquidation values of all of its saleable assets, minus the company's liabilities, minus the costs of liquidating those assets (brokerage fees, auction commissions, sales taxes, transfer taxes, accounting fees, attorneys fees, appraisal fees, and so on). See Chapter 6 for a complete explanation.

Liquidation is often initiated by the company's creditors due to financial insolvency. Lenders and investors are interested in knowing a company's liquidation value because it tells them whether they can get their money back quickly and easily if the business fails and they have to foreclose. They don't want to fool around with trying to get top dollar through normal sales channels for those assets. They want to be repaid through the fastest and most convenient means possible: a quick auction sale. Even then, going through the foreclosure and liquidation is a procedural nightmare they would rather do without.

Buyers like to know the liquidation value because it tells them whether there will be anything left for them after the other creditors get paid. It tells them whether their cash investment is at risk. They also want to make sure that the other creditors are repaid in full so that they won't be held liable for the shortfall through their personal loan guarantees.

Sellers are interested in liquidation value because that figure usually represents the minimum possible value of their company - the rock bottom price they can get.

Liquidity: The relative speed and ease with which any particular asset can be sold - i.e., converted to cash.

Market Value (or "Fair Market Value") - Refers to the probable sales price of an asset resulting from arm's length negotiation between a willing buyer and a willing seller, neither being under any particular compulsion to act, and both having reasonable knowledge of material facts. It does not refer to the best price that could be obtained in the current market. The value is always estimated as of a specific date.

Multiplier or "gross income multiplier": The amount of sales or income from a certain period is multiplied by this figure to produce a rough estimate of value for the business. The multiplier generally corresponds to a capitalization rate* - the annual rate of return that would normally be expected by an investor in that deal, given the level of risk involved. For example, a 12% capitalization rate is the same as a multiplier of 8.3 (1 divided by 12%). In other words, when you "capitalize" a figure by 12%, you divide that figure by 12% - and that's the same as multiplying it by 1 divided by .12 .

For more on the use of multipliers in valuation, see Chapter 16 (on Price/Earnings Ratio and Rule-of-Thumb methods) plus the first part of Chapter 8.

Net Profit - (See "Earnings" and "Income Statement")

Net Sales: The total revenues taken in by a business from the sale of goods or services ("gross sales"), minus returns and allowances, and minus any cash discounts given to customers. (See "Income Statement")

Non-Amortizing - (See "Amortize")

Non-operating income: Income derived from sources other than the ordinary business of that company. It is not considered when valuing a business. Might include loan interest on money lent to others, rent received on excess space that is leased out, dividends or interest from excess earnings that were invested, a judgment in a law suit, payment from an insurance claim, or anything else outside of the firm's normal realm of business activity.

Notes Payable: Promissory notes, executed by the company, which evidence a debt owed to another. On the balance sheet, they are usually classified either as Long-Term Liabilities (not due and payable for more than a year) or Current Liabilities (if payable within one year).

Notes Receivable: Loans made by the company to someone else. On the balance sheet, these may be classified either as Long-Term Notes Receivable (if repaid over a period of several years) or Current Assets (if they you expect them to be repaid within 12 months).

Notes receivable should be valued the same way as accounts receivable*: discount them from face value to the extent that you expect defaults, and also discounted them further in order to give the buyer a reasonable return on his investment in them, and to compensate him for the cost of maintaining the accounts and collecting them. (See "Accounts Receivable")

Note that long-term notes receivable from the owners of the company may be carried on the books without any intention that they will ever be repaid. If that's the case, these should be assigned no value. Some owners do this to take money out of the business tax-free, and the obligation is later written off as a bad debt.

Operating Profit: (See "Income Statement", and "Earnings")

Percentage Operating Profit: On an income statement, income and expenses are often expressed as a *percentage of net sales*. In other words, if Operating Income is $600,000, and Net Sales are $4,000,000, then Percentage Operating Income is 600,000/4,000,000 = 15%. If you assume that same level of profitability will carry on into the next year, and next year's net sales are predicted to be $5,500,000, then the projected operating profit for that year will be $5,500,000 X .15 = $825,000, assuming this same "percentage operating profit" will continue in the future.

Perks or Perquisites: Refers to incidental benefits that flow to an employee, over and above their regular salary. These can take the form of unusual favors, meals, clothing allowances, the privilege to enjoy certain amenities, and other "fringe benefits".

When you adjust an income statement, you add the owner's perks back if they would not normally be provided to an employee-manager. This reflects a more normal state of affairs. Many are personal expenses of the owner which are paid for by the company and then recorded as business expenses. They might include such things as automobiles, large travel and entertainment allowances, country club dues, vacation homes, life insurance, or higher than normal salaries.

Points: Additional interest charged by a lender up front when the loan is made, instead of waiting to receive it over time. If the originating lender plans to resell the loan to another investor in the secondary loan market, this might be their fee for originating the loan. On the other hand, most commercial loans are retained in the originator's own loan portfolio, so it's just a cheap way of extracting unearned interest out of the borrower. There certainly are costs involved in processing a new loan, but when the borrower also pays a separate loan origination fee, then squeezing more points out him seems unconscionable. A "point" is one-percent of the loan amount.

Preferred Stock: (As opposed to Common Stock) A separate class of corporate stock that has priority when it comes to the payment of dividends. If the company is shut down and its assets are sold (liquidated), preferred stockholders also have priority on the distribution of those proceeds. The specific rights attached to preferred stock are spelled out in the articles of incorporation (charter) or by-laws, and these can be customized to fit the objectives of the company and the investors.

Generally, holders of preferred stock receive a fixed dividend amount, which is paid from the company's surplus earnings. Usually, the dividend doesn't exceed the amount stated on the stock certificate, but it must be paid before dividends are paid on the common stock. This fixed dividend may be "cumulative" or "non-cumulative". If it's cumulative, that means any dividends the company fails to pay will carry forward as a charge against earnings in succeeding years, and they have to be paid in full before any other dividends get paid. If the dividends are non-cumulative, they don't accumulate from year to year and the right to receive a dividend for a particular year is lost if the company fails to earn or formally declare the dividend that year.

A corporation can issue different kinds of preferred stock, each carrying different rights, as defined in the charter or by-laws. Preferred stockholders usually don't get to vote at stockholder meetings, except when their dividends have been in arrears beyond a certain period of time. Preferred stock obviously has some characteristics of debt, but it doesn't have a fixed maturity date. Instead, the corporation can buy it back (redeem it or call it) through action of the board of directors.

Common Stock is different. It doesn't have a face value, per se. It's value changes along with the value of company as a whole. Dividends are declared at the discretion of the board of directors, and only to the extent that surplus net earnings are available to pay them. Alternatively, the board may decide to retain those earnings, or invest them in some other assets. There is no preference or priority among common stockholders. If assets of the company are liquidated, common stockholders share evenly in a division of the proceeds, after any preferred stockholders have been paid.

It is important to note that dividends are paid from the *after*-tax income of the corporation, and they are not a deductible expense on the company's tax return. On the other hand, the income paid to the holder of a debt-type obligation is "interest", which is a deductible expense that is paid from *before-tax* earnings. Obviously, the company would rather invest its surplus income in new growth than pay non-deductible dividends. If you finance a company with debt instead of stock, the investor can be paid the same return but the cost to the company is less. Plus, putting out

additional stock dilutes the ownership interest of the existing stockholders. The downside of debt is that you must make the loan payments on schedule; you can't withhold payments at your own discretion.

Pre-Paid Expenses - (See "Assets", under the paragraph on "Current Assets")

Present Value: The value *today* of something that will be received in the future. Present value calculation is based on the premise that a dollar received today is worth more than a dollar received tomorrow. Aside from the effects of inflation, this is because you lose out on any investment income from it in the meantime. Therefore, if you make an investment today that will give you a return of $1 a year from now, that $1 has a "present value" that is somewhat less than $1. *How much* less depends upon how much you expect to earn on your other investments of equal risk. For example, if you think you would probably earn a 10% annual return on your money somewhere else, then the expectation of receiving $1 a year from now has a present value of $0.909. $0.909 invested today at 10% annual interest will accumulate to a total value of $1 in one year. In this situation, the present value of one dollar is $0.909.

See "Discount Rate" for more information on the subject of present value. There are also present value tables in the Appendix that will give you the present value of a sum to be received in the future.

We rely on the present value concept a lot in valuation because, when you buy a company, you are purchasing future earnings. Those earnings have to be discounted in order to arrive at the present value of the business.

Investors always demand a rate of return that compensates them for the particular amount of risk involved - the risk of losing their investment principal. To find out if an investment will earn the required return, you predict the amount of income you expect to receive in each year. Then you discount each to present value, and add those figures up to see if it gives the total expected return. For example, let's say you have a chance to invest $20,000 in a project, the risk of which justifies a 12% compound annual return. The investment will return an estimated $10,000 at the end of the first year, $9,000 at the end of the second year, $8,000 at the end of the third year, and nothing thereafter. Will this project return the original investment, plus the 12% demanded? The following calculations show that it will, plus something extra.

Year	Expected Return	Present Value of $1 at 12% Discount factor	Present Value of Expected Returns
1	$10,000	0.893	$8,930
2	$ 9,000	0.797	$7,173
3	$ 8,000	0.712	$5,696

Total Present Value of the returns	21,799
Minus: Original investment	20,000
Excess return beyond 12%	$1,799

If the actual total return, when discounted to present value at the anticipated rate of return, is at least as much as the amount that was originally invested, then the required return has been earned.

Privately-Held: Refers to any corporation that doesn't offer its stock for sale to the general public, and hasn't registered it to be traded on a public exchange. These companies are usually owned by the people who started them or a small group of private investors.

Stock traded on a *public* stock exchange, or offered for sale to the general public, must be registered with the U.S. Securities Exchange Commission. The offering must conform to certain rules, and includes all sorts of disclosures.   The company has to give shareholders notice of matters affecting the value of the stock, the dates of shareholder meetings, the election of board members, and provide financial reports periodically. By law, those running a public company have a fiduciary duty to place the interests of the shareholders above their own interests. Privately-held companies are exempt from much of that.

In addition, when a public company is acquired, special procedures must be followed, and these are pretty complicated. Every shareholder must receive a formal "tender offer" to purchase their stock, which must satisfy a some very explicit requirements. The company's board of directors usually tells the shareholders know what they think of the offer, and this endorsement often determines the success of the acquisition. The offer usually includes the condition that a minimum percentage of shareholders must accept it or else it's void.

Private companies aren't subject to these rules.

NOTE: The value of a publicly-held company is affected by all kinds of factors that cause stock market prices to bounce up and down everyday. These often have little to do with the financial performance of the specific firm. Some companies might be registered with the SEC for public trading, but if the stock is actually owned by a very small number of people and rarely traded, then the company can usually be valued like a privately-held firm. Consult your accountant or investment banker in these cases.

Profit - (See "Earnings")

Pro Forma: This term generally refers to a prediction of the company's financial performance in a future year. Usually, it assumes certain changes will occur that have not yet taken place. Pro forma predictions depend on the occurrence of a lot of "ifs", so they are entirely speculative and should not be the basis for a valuation. Sellers get paid for what they have actually done, not for what a new owner "might" be able to do.

An *"adjusted financial statement"*, on the other hand, is based on actual results. It just provides a different way of interpreting current performance. It recasts the statement using different accounting methods, and eliminates expenses that are obviously excessive, and adds costs that are clearly warranted. The changes should be conservative. It does not show increased sales revenues or speculative cost cutting.

Publicly-Held - (See "Privately-Held")

Recapture: When an asset is sold, the amount of gain declared on your tax return is sometimes increased by the amount of any investment tax credits or accelerated depreciation you have taken in the past. Consult your accountant for tax advice whenever you sell business assets. The term "recapture" means that the excess amount of depreciation declared on past returns is viewed as having come back to you as taxable income.

Receivables - (See "Accounts Receivable")

Secured Debt: Any loan for which collateral is posted. The lender gets a conditional interest in *specific* property of the borrower, so that, if the borrower defaults on the loan, the lender can seize the property pledged as security, or have it sold by the sheriff to obtain repayment of the debt. On the other hand, if someone defaults on an unsecured loan, the lender has to go to court and obtain a judgment against the borrower for the amount of the debt. Then he has to take further legal action to levy upon the general assets of the borrower in order to obtain repayment. This is a cumbersome process, with no certainty as to whether the assets that exist will be sufficient to cover the loan balance.

If a borrower defaults on secured and unsecured loans at the same time, the lender holding a security interest in specific property will have priority regarding the proceeds from sale of that property. Unsecured creditors get what's left over after the secured creditors been repaid. If more than one creditor has a security interest in the same property, then (generally speaking) priority is assigned according to the date upon which the security agreements were recorded.

Chapter 18 tells how to determine the Secured Loan Value of a company's assets (how much money you can borrow against them).

(Sub-Chapter) S Corporations: A type of corporation that is taxed like a partnership instead of like a regular (C-type) corporation. *Consult your accountant* when dealing with S corporations.

According to the rules in effect at the time of this writing, shareholders must unanimously agree to the S Corporation status. The company doesn't pay corporate tax on its income, but the shareholders pay tax on their distributive share of that income, even if it hasn't actually been distributed to them. Sub-S status is often chosen if the investors think that large net losses will be sustained.

In valuation, you disregard the Sub-S status and recast the statements as if the company was a normal corporation.

Subordinated Debt (or "Junior Debt"): A type of debt wherein the lender agrees to subordinate the priority of his claim against the borrower's assets to the claims of other creditors. If the debtor defaults, those other creditors get first dibs. Senior lenders are those who stand first in line with regard to the priority of their claims. The loan agreements may give them security in specific assets of the borrower, or the terms and timing of their loan agreement may simply give them first claim against the borrower's assets in general. Normally, the priority of claims is determined by the terms contained in the loan agreements, and by the order in which those agreements are recorded.

The subordinated lender usually demands a higher rate of interest in order to compensate him for the increased risk of not getting repaid. He may also demand an "equity sweetener" in the form of common stock, or the right to convert his debt to common stock, or a warrant to buy stock at a certain low price later on.

Tangible Assets - (See "Assets")

Turnaround: Refers to the process of turning a poorly performing business into a successful one. Often refers to a plan to purchase and refinance an unprofitable company, along with a radical restructuring of the way it does business. Turnarounds are viewed as risky and speculative ventures.

Weighted Average: If the performance of a company has fluctuated a lot from year to year, then we normally according more weight to the most recent years. This is accomplished mathmatically by a procedure known as "weighted averaging". It gives progressively more importance to the figures from the most recent years. To calculate a weighted average for five years, take the figure (sales, income, etc.) from the most recent year and multiply it by five. Then multiply the figure from the *previous* year by four. Then take the figure from the year before that, and multiply it by three. Multiply the figure from the year before that by two, and the figure from the year before that by one. Then add them all up and divide the total by 15. The result if your weighted average.

Working Capital: This refers to the money a company uses to carry on its business. You can have a building and a collection of equipment, but nothing will happen until you add some cash to produce and sell the product or service. This is the working capital. The cash isn't just consumed, it changes form. It's transformed into raw materials and labor, and then into products, and then into accounts receivable, and then back into cash (hopefully *more* cash than it cost to get to this point - that's your profit). Accountants often define working capital as the amount by which a company's current assets* exceeds its current liabilities*:

Current Assets* - such as Cash, Accounts Receivable*, Inventory, etc. (see your balance sheet for other current assets listed)

MINUS

Current Liabilities* - such as Accounts Payable*.

If you don't have an adequate amount of working capital, you won't carry sufficient inventories, or meet your current debts, or be able to take advantage of cash discounts, or extend favorable terms to customers. Deficient working capital puts you in a poor competitive position and lowers your chances of survival.

Step 10 of Chapter 10 gives specific instructions on how to estimate future working capital requirements. This can be a crucial factor in the success of a business, so always consult your accountant when trying to plan these needs.

Valuation Example

To illustrate the methods described in this book, we have prepared a case example - a fictional mid-sized company, called Hammerhead, Inc.. Hammerhead is a progressive manufacturer of mountain bicycles, road bicycles, bike accessories and sportswear. The name, people, and details are entirely fictitious, so any similarities to actual companies or persons are purely coincidental. Since we made the whole thing up, some parts of the story may not jive with reality. For instance, the numbers are unrealistic for a company in this particular industry, and our cap rate may be off as well. We also used a few shortcuts here and there - mainly in the form of averaging, just to keep the details from getting too cumbersome. But the example should get the key points across.

The methods used here certainly apply to companies much smaller than this one, but there are some differences to keep in mind:

- The risk is generally greater with a smaller business, so the capitalization or discount rates will be higher.

- The impact of one particularly valuable asset - such as real estate - may be disproportionately large, compared to the total value of the business. In that case you should remove that asset from the calculations, and instead substitute a reasonable amount of rent for it in the operating expenses, as if the item was being leased. You can then treat the sale of that asset as a separate matter.

- For many businesses, there are rule-of-thumb valuation formulas that are so widely accepted that you may have to defer to them instead.

- It's harder to borrow money for a small business acquisition, so there's a good chance the seller will have to finance at least part of it by being paid in installments. That adds more risk for the seller. The buyer might ruin the business and then just default, leaving a mess back in the sellers lap. For that reason, sellers often find it worthwhile to discount their price in order to get an all-cash deal.

On to the story. . .

Hammerhead is owned by Catherine LePlant, a young entrepreneur who started the business after a career in advertising. An avid biker with a racing background, she has focused on one particular segment of the market - relatively affluent people who want to be part of the sport, and do so by acquiring what they perceive to be the best equipment. This group is attracted to image and the high price tags that suggest exclusivity. They are pushovers for hand finished bike frames and fancy paint jobs. They read the biking magazines and catalogs cover-to-cover and regurgitate details on command in order to give the impression of being serious riders. They salivate over items that are in limited production, and are often willing to pay an additional premium to have what everyone else doesn't own. Catherine suspected that if she could key-into this market niche, she could enjoy very nice profit margins.

While her target market amounts to less than 5% of all bicycle buyers, they account for 50% of the high end product sales, and 25% of all dollars spent in bicycle shops and catalogs. To entice them, her products must keep changing and always exude that leading-edge impression.

At the time she started this company, she was "involved" with a young engineer (Phil) who happened to be skilled in bike frame metallurgy, and he was able to produce her first prototypes. Phil also fashioned some interesting gimmicks to incorporate into the frames, which added little or nothing to their performance but were just the kind of thing a yuppy rider cues-in on. He was rather relaxed in his work habits, but he did a nice job on the frames. After adding creative paint jobs, Catherine was able to get the bikes into the hands of certain equipment reviewers at the bicycling magazines who were known to identify with her target market. She was gambling a lot on their support, because she didn't have the money to induce big-name racers to ride her bikes, nor have groundbreaking technical innovations to attract attention.

The gamble worked, and after a few complimentary articles, she was off to a blazing start. A tidal wave of direct orders and dealer inquiries rolled in, and soon there was a long waiting list.

Now she needed production capacity. Catherine was pouring all of her profits back into working capital and still coming up short. Her business was not well-enough established to secure a large line of credit, but she wasn't willing to ransom her equity to outside investors, so she ignored the warnings of her lawyer and accountant and used the cash from pre-paid orders to rent more space, buy needed inventory, and hire more experienced technicians. It was a very risky way to start. If Hammerhead ate up the money but was unable to deliver the product, she'd be in trouble. Somehow she pulled it off, and the company was profitable within months.

In time, the working capital squeeze ended, manufacturing space and equipment were purchased, and Phil split for Oregon. In a way, his departure was a relief, because Catherine was afraid that he would soon expect a stake in the business, and she didn't want to jeopardize her control by giving away equity.

In the meantime, Catherine hired an air brush artist named Mervin, who produced the bright designs Catherine needed for her products. Something of an anomaly, Mervin had actually grown up Amish, in Ohio. He was a free spirit by nature, so the subdued atmosphere of his upbringing must have seemed extremely confining to him, and may have been the driving force behind his wild creative talents. Nonetheless, Amish kids are imbued with a solid work-ethic at an early age, so by the time he was a teen, Mervin had enough of his own cash squirreled away to buy a car, which he hid in a rented garage two miles from his family's farm, along with a civilian wardrobe from the local mall. As soon as he dared, he bolted for the coast. His radical artistic imagination produced a constant outpouring of novel extremes in color and graphic contrast, which delighted Hammerhead's customers. At the same time, Mervin displayed the serious and resourceful business nature of his Amish heritage, so Hammerhead provided him with a profitable way to mainstream his talents.

Now five years old, Hammerhead has an established name and plenty of upside potential. New products are constantly in the pipeline, and there are still parts of the country where dealerships have not yet been granted. Meanwhile, the size of the biking market continues to increase. With all this growth, the entire culture of the company has changed. Size brought a need for more structure and more sophisticated operating systems. Catherine has groomed a staff of managers, designers, and technical people who can largely carry on the business without her - and she has hit a point where she places more value other aspects of her life. She yearns for balance, and a smaller, simpler business. Rumors have it that the company is "in-play" (can be purchased), and you decide to take a run at it.

After a few confidential meetings, you think you understand the business and its market position. You know you want to make an offer, and the seller has let you know that she would expect a price no lower than $10.6 million. Although wary at first, she is now convinced of your good faith, and after asking you and your advisors to sign confidentiality agreements, she agrees to release income statements and balance sheets for the last 5 years so that you can figure out if the company is worth her asking price.

Hammerhead's adjusted balance sheet and existing loans:

ASSETS

Current Assets
Cash	1,256,524
Accounts Receivable	2,246,428

Inventory:
Raw materials 1,066,660	
Work in progress 380,000	
Finished goods 1,347,520	
	2,794,180
Pre-paid (rent) expense	149,761

Non-Current Assets
Fixed Assets:
Real Estate	6,000,000
Equipment & Mach.	1,330,200
Intangibles	450,287

Other non-current:
Leasehold improvements	335,810
Notes from employees	413,000
	14,976,190

LIABILITIES

Current Liabilities:
Line of credit	3,500,000
Trade Payables	1,797,142
Taxes Payable	148,000

Long-Term Liabilities:
Equipment Loan	898,571
Realty Mortgage	876,000

Loan from Owner	1,048,333
Deferred Liability	118,184
Other Non-Current Liability	300,000
Net Worth (Owner's Equity)	6,289,900
Total	14,976,190

LOANS AND TERMS

- Line of credit: Interest only at 9.5%
- Real estate mortgage: 9.25% on original principal of $1,110,000 for 15 years. Purchased for $1.6MM. Now 5 years into the loan.
- Equipment loan: 10% on original principal of $959,000 for 15 years. Now 5 years into the loan.
- Note to owner: Interest only at 9%
- Other note: $300,000 at 10.5% for 10 years.

Adjusting the Income Statement:

In any valuation, the first thing you do is adjust the income statement. Here are the original figures from the statement:

Gross Sales	$20,505,051	100.0%
Net Sales	$20,300,000	99.0%
Net Income	$ 1,567,000	7.6%

After questioning the company controller thoroughly about their expenses, you decide that some adjustments are in order. The owner is the driving force behind the company, yet she only pays herself an $80,000 salary. It would cost at least another $50,000/year to replace her with a competent executive. In addition, as a bike designer, she contributes a lot to product development. You know a talented engineer who could fill that role through a combination of technical knowledge and market awareness, at a salary of $70,000. You also suspect that marketing is underfunded, and you estimate another $100,000 for that. When these items are added to the operating expenses, Net Income is reduced to $1,347,000.

Hammerhead leases an expensive car for its owner at $900 a month, which you feel is extravagant. The company would save $6,000 by providing the new executive with a less fancy model. You also think you can eliminate $8,000 in travel and entertainment expenses without detriment. The company also leases a warehouse from the owner at $60,000 per year over market rental rates. These items reduce the expenses and bring the Net Income up to $1,421,000. This is 7% of net sales.

Selecting a Capitalization Rate for Hammerhead:

You exhaustively research the long-term and short-term prospects for the bicycle industry. You decide that bicycling in the middle of a hot growth phase, and you're comfortable with predictions of steady long-term growth for the next 5 years, plus more moderate increases during the following 5 years. Publicly-held sports equipment companies are producing shareholder returns that range from 3% to 15%. However, the smaller, more progressive bicycle companies like Hammerhead can produce higher margins.

On the negative side, you realize that smaller companies usually involve a higher risk factor. In addition, this segment of the sports equipment industry is characterized by constant change and innovation. The number of aggressive competitors has produced an atmosphere where any successful idea is subject to multiple knock-offs within months.

Nonetheless, some factors moderate this risk for Hammerhead. Even though it's a private company, it would be hard to characterize Hammerhead as small. It generates considerable sales volume from a broad, diversified product line that includes bicycles, accessories, and sportswear. That provides a certain resilience. The company has demonstrated a consistent pattern of growth and profitability over its 5 year history. In addition, its carefully nurtured image seems to insulate it from much of the competitive fray in this industry. Furthermore, the company has lots of fixed assets, which will help with financing.

At the present time, the prime interest rate is very low - averaging 6%. The risk-free rate is also very low - hovering around 4.5%. As a result, you feel that you can justify an argument for a relatively low capitalization rate. A review of current returns from investments of equivalent risk shows that a cap rate of 16.5% is appropriate. While not as high as the cap rates used in the past for many private companies, you are convinced that Hammerhead is a very strong firm that justifies the more conservative rate, at least during the projection period.

Example of Ability to Pay Method:

You decide to undertake this method first because you know you will have to borrow most of the purchase price, and you want to find out early if the company can provide the payments for that acquisition loan. There's no sense in spending your time on the other methods unless you know the deal is feasible on your terms.

The first step is to project Hammerhead's net sales for the next ten years and find the average. Assume that Net Sales in the first year after the acquisition ("year one") will be the same as the current year ($20,300,000). Starting there, you want to project sales for each future year, but you don't want to give the Seller credit for growth that has not yet occurred, so you limit the increase in sales for each successive year to a conservative percentage rate that reflects the normal rate of inflation for consumer goods. (We have decided to use 4.5% per year.)

year 1	20,300,000
year 2	21,213,500
year 3	22,168,108
year 4	23,165,672
year 5	24,208,127
year 6	25,297,493
year 7	26,345,880
year 8	27,625,495
year 9	28,868,642
year 10	30,167,731

Average net sales = $24,936,065

What percentage of net sales is the net profit? On Hammerhead's adjusted statement, it's 7%. So for this period you assume the Average Net Profit is also going to be 7% of Average Net Sales - or $1,745,524.

In this method we have to "assume" an approximate purchase price in order to come up with figures for interest and debt service, which are used in the formula. You make the assumption that the Seller has set her asking price ($10.6MM) about 10% higher than she expects to get. Since the buyer must also pay off the seller's loan to the company of $1,048,333, you also hope that she can be convinced to include that in the price. You decide to assume a purchase price of $8,500,000, plus the loan, bringing the total cost up to $9,548,333. For now, you assume that this can be your best-case scenario in terms of price. (The owner is actually asking $10.6 million, plus the loan.) Your objective here is to see if the company's cash flow will support the assumed price, and if not, what price it will support. If you are off-base on your assumptions, you can go back and interpolate.

You first need to calculate the Average Taxable Net Income. To do that, take the Average Net Income of $1,745,524, and then make the following adjustments:

+ $ 533,617 (adding back the current annual interest expense)
- $1,402,294 (subtract future interest expense - including line of credit, realty mortgage, equipment loan, other non-current debt, an acquisition loan of $7,638,666, plus preferred stock dividends of $238,708 to cash investors)
+ $ 748,081 (adding back current annual depreciation)
- $ 997,442 (subtracting depreciation expected in future (calculated according to the directions in Step 3b)
= $ 627,486 Average Taxable Net Income

Then,

- $ 175,696 (subtract income taxes - assume 28%)

= $ 451,789 Average Net Income After Tax

+ $ 997,442 add back Average Depreciation expected

+ $1,402,294 add Average Interest expense expected

= $2,851,525 Average Net Cash Flow After Tax

- $ 200,000 subtract Average Future Capital Expenditures

= $2,651,525 Average Net Cash Flow Before Debt Service

- $ 928,033 subtract 35% cash flow "safety cushion"

= $1,723,492 Average Net Cash Flow Available for Debt Service

From this, we subtract the anticipated future debt service. A reasonable post-acquisition scenario for Hammerhead might involve the following loan payments:

- a line of credit - starting at $2.5MM and increasing by 4.5% each year (@ 9.5% interest) for an average interest cost of $295,968 per year
- amortization of the non-current liability at $39,794 per year
- assumption of the equipment loan at $122,508/year
- assumption of real estate mortgage at $135,852/year

Total = $594,122

Trade payables and remaining current liabilities will be paid as part of the normal expenses. That leaves an average of $1,129,370 available per year for acquisition debt payments.

Now, there are two ways to back-into a price that is justified by this figure, depending on whether the buyer has any cash to put into the deal. Banks won't typically lend more than 80% of the acquisition price, because they want the buyers to have a good bit of their own cash on the line. So the normal scenario is to assume that you can borrow 80% of the assumed purchase price, and then back-into your actual price by determining what size loan can be supported by the cash flow available for loan payments.

The other way to set up the financing is to assume that you can use "OPM" (other people's money) for the whole price. That means you raise the 20% cash from outside investors, paying them a nice rate of interest. This is added to the loan payments on the 80% acquisition loan.

In our calculations above, we took the more conservative route and figured that passive investors will put $1,909,667 cash into the deal. We assume they have been promised a return of 16.5% on their investment, which comes to $238,708 per year. In exchange for their money, the buyer would probably give them preferred stock, so that interest would be paid as a Preferred Dividend. That reduces your "cash flow available for acquisition loan payments" to $890,662. Let's assume there will be a single acquisition loan at 10.5% interest for a 10 year term, with 25 year amortization. On that basis, these payments will support a loan amount of $7.86 million. When added to the $1.909 million from the investors, you get a total price of $9.769 million for the company. From that, you subtract the company's debt to the owner of $1,048,333 - so it looks like you can afford to offer about $8.720 million for the company.

But this approach cheats a little because you are assuming an unrealistically slick deal. Normally you should assume that the buyer will put down 20% in cash, and then consider the 35% cash flow "safety cushion" as its annual investment return, without figuring in an additional preferred dividend. That means you can use the entire $1,129,370 for acquisition loan payments, and that supports a loan amount of $9.967 million. Since we normally assume that the acquisition loan is 80% of the purchase price, this would suggest a total purchase price of $12,459,753 ($9.967 divided by .80). If you subtract the $1,048,333 used to repay the seller's loan to the company, that means you can afford to pay the seller $11.411 million.

In other words, you can afford to pay more than the asking price of $10.6 million. Knowing this, you now feel confident about proceeding with the full valuation.

In this scenario, note the amount of *return on your cash investment*. That "return" is the $917,129 (average) cash reserve we "set aside" in our calculations above. That gives you a whopping 48% return on your cash! In the event that you really do have to bring in outside investors to provide the $1.909MM in cash, you could comfortably pay them off over 3 to 4 years using that cash reserve. After that, the company would spin off bottom line profits averaging $917,129 per year, while you actually have no cash of your own tied up in the deal!

We are looking at this from the perspective of a buyer, but if you were the seller of this company, this same analysis might be used to justify an asking price of $11.4 million.

Example of Economic Value of Assets Method

There's always a chance that the company's assets will be worth more than it's value as a going concern. Since Hammerhead is a very profitable company, we will refer to "market value" instead of liquidation value wherever possible. When we can't refer to market value, we will use "cost" or book value, not liquidation value. This is because a profitable company is likely to be sold in one package as a going entity, rather than broken up in a liquidation sale. At the very least, the seller will probably recoup the cost or book value of those assets. We will deal with each class of assets separately:

Inventory is carried at the following adjusted values:

Raw materials: $ 1,066,660 (at cost)

Work in process: $ 380,000 (at cost, including labor)

Finished product: $ 2,560,288 (60% at wholesale market value, and 40% at cost)

Total = $ 4,006,948

We value 60% of the finished product inventory at wholesale market value because that portion of it is normally pre-sold for this company. The rest is valued at cost. (Nor-mally you would value everything at cost, since you still have to spend money to sell it. Full market value isn't realized until it's sold.)

We haven't discounted the raw materials or work-in-process because of strong product demand that tells us that it will probably be carried through to finished product and sold. (You would only do this for a very strong company.) None of the inventory is unusable or obsolete, so we haven't discounted for obsolescence.

There are some other current assets whose values we won't adjust:

Cash	$ 1,256,524
Leasehold Improvements	$ 335,810
Prepaid Expenses (rent)	$ 149,761

In an "asset purchase" the owner would keep the cash, and the rest would be transferred to the new owner. But, if ownership is transferred by means of a purchase of stock, the buyer will get the cash reserve as well.

Hammerhead also has trade receivables of $2,246,428. Historically, bad debt has been less than 1%, due to careful selection of dealers. We decide to value these at $2,224,000.

The fixed assets include real estate (the manufacturing plant and offices), machinery, vehicles, and fixtures. The plant is a large, one-level masonry building located in a clean industrial zone with good highway access. There is excess land, some of which fronts along a busy road. It has recently been rezoned to "commercial". In consultation with commercial realty brokers, you decide that 28 acres of the property can be sold off as a shopping center site for a net of $4.2 million. The remaining property has a market value of $1.8 million, even though the owner invested more than that to outfit it for her company's use. The company also leases a warehouse on an adjacent property, which is owned by the Seller personally.

The owner shows you an equipment appraisal of $2,562,500 which was received last year, but you notice that it was done for insurance purposes and is based on replacement value, which you can't use. Book value is $1,330,200 - reflecting original cost minus accumulated depreciation, so that isn't a reliable figure either. After talking to the appraiser, you decide to adjust replacement value downward by 60% as an estimate of market value. That gives you a figure of $1,537,500 for the equipment, fixtures, vehicles and machinery.

In addition, there are some non-current assets. The company has $413,000 in notes from loans to key employees. You discount these 20%, which you feel would be the maximum possible uncollectible amount. Their total value is then $330,400. In addition, there is an unamortized balance of $335,810 for leasehold improvements to the warehouse that is rented by the company from the owner. This figure reflects original cost, times the percentage of the lease term remaining, so it requires no adjustment.

Intangibles - There are $450,287 in intangibles on the books. That figure reflects the cost of developing products and securing patents, minus depreciation. However, it doesn't really reflect the market value of those patented designs, so you decide to re-value them using a profit contribution approach.

To start with, you decide that the Hammerhead brand name is an intangible with an ascertainable value. Some of that is based on income from sales of logo sportswear and decals. Those bring in gross sales of $900,000, which in turn produces gross profit of $780,000 per year.

You also estimate that the Hammerhead brand name alone allows them to charge about $85 more per bicycle. In addition, you figure they get an additional $160 per bike for their patented design features. Hammerhead sells about 7500 of these bikes per year.

$85 + $160 = $245 X 7500 = $1,837,500 in profit contribution from those intangibles.

Their other bike accessories carry a pricing advantage that is attributed to both brand name and design, and the total gross profit from those is $2,239,000. Without that brand name or those features, you estimate that revenues would be about 40% of that, so you attribute 60% of the gross profit on accessories to these intangibles (that's $895,600).

So, total gross profit contribution from these intangibles is $3,512,500. Net operating income is about 17% of gross profit, so you assume that these intangibles produce NOI of $599,695 per year. This is an industry where constant innovation makes the continuing success of any one company no sure thing, so you assume that these intangibles will continue to provide their full competitive advantage for only about 2 years, dropping to 50% in the third year, and to 20% in the fourth year, and to 0% in the fifth year. (Note that we are dealing only with intangibles held by the company today, not new ones that might be developed in the future.)

Year	Adjusted NOI From Intangibles	Present Value
1st	$ 599,695	$ 599,695
2nd	$ 599,695	$ 555,273
3rd	$ 299,847	$ 257,070
4th	$ 119,939	$ 95,211
5th	$ 000	$ 000

Total value of intangible assets = $1,507,249

The total economic value of all these assets is $17,684,002.

Liabilities - The balance sheet shows the following liabilities, which would be assumed by the buyer:

Current Liabilities:
Line of credit	3,500,000
Trade Payables	1,797,142
Taxes Payable	148,000

Long-Term Liabilities:
Equipment Loan	898,571
Long-Term Debt (Mortgage)	876,000
Loan from Owner	1,048,333
Deferred Taxes	118,184
Other Non-Current Liability	300,000
Total	8,686,290
Net Worth (Owner's Equity)	6,289,900
Total	$14,976,190

Since the company is very successful, it will probably be purchased as an existing business, with most of its liabilities assumed in the process. If Current Liabilities are not assumed, they will be paid off by the Seller at or before settlement, using the company's Cash, which is derived mostly from payment of the Receivables. In effect, the current assets will be reduced by that amount, and the seller will receive that much less. Therefore, just leave the Receivables as they are on the statement and assume the buyer will take them over.

In practice, when a contract to sell a business is signed, the amount of current assets and current liabilities are recorded on that date, and then they are recounted on the day before settlement. The purchase price is then adjusted to reflect the difference. In any event, since Hammerhead is a successful, thriving business, all of the credit accounts will probably be taken over and carried on by the Buyer. Therefore, the total liabilities to be assumed by the buyer will be $8,686,290.

When you subtract the total liabilities from the total asset value you get:
$17,684,002 - $8,686,290 = $8,997,712

Recall that the company's liabilities include a $1,048,333 loan from the seller, and we assume that the buyer will pay it off at settlement, so the owner will receive a total of $10,046,045.

Note: If Hammerhead was not a successful business, we would approach this differently, depending on (1) the form the transaction is likely to take, and (2) who is doing the valuation - buyer or seller.

These variables affect the measure of value we use and whether we would deduct the liabilities. If the transaction takes the form of a purchase of stock, then you subtract the liabilities because they are assumed by the buyer. (Transferring the company's stock automatically transfers both the assets and the liabilities.) But when a company is performing poorly, the transaction will almost always take the form of a purchase of assets. That's mostly because the buyer's bargaining position is stronger than the seller's, and buyers generally prefer a purchase of assets. In that case, the buyer wouldn't assume the liabilities unless there's some special advantage to doing so. For instance, if the buyer wants to operate the company as a going concern, it might be advantageous to maintain accounts with existing suppliers rather than try to negotiate new ones. That means the buyer would probably assume all of the accounts payable. But in that case, the seller might be able to demand that the buyer also purchase the accounts receivable, thereby saving the seller the hassle of collecting them.

You can see that an asset sale will involve lots of negotiation over the specific assets and liabilities to be transferred. If you know exactly what the buyer is buying, then you can base your valuation on those alone. But if you don't, or if your valuation is for a seller, you should go ahead and subtract the total liabilities from the total asset value, since, one way or another, they will net-out against each other. Either the seller will pay them off with the sale proceeds, or the buyer will assume them and reduce the price by that amount. At that point the only remaining question is whether you should use market value or liquidation value, and the answer to that depends on the health of the company and how saleable or collectable the individual assets are.

Simplified Example of Discounted Cash Flow Method

The first nine steps of this method are very similar to the Ability To Pay Method (above). To simplify this example, we'll use the results from that, and then pick up at Step 10.

Step 10 of this method takes the Net Cash Flow Before Debt Service and refines it a little more by deducting the Future Additions to Working Capital for each year. This money comes out of the company's net cash flow, and it's used to increase the cash reserve, inventory, receivables, or pre-paid expenses - which are all components of working capital. Another way to increase working capital is to pay off some of the current liabilities, since working capital is defined as Current Assets Minus Current Liabilities.

Here's a quick way to figure out whether the working capital should be increased. There is a financial ratio called the "Current Ratio" which is used as an indicator of financial solvency. It tells you whether you have enough working capital. It is defined as Current Assets divided by Current Liabilities, and different types of businesses have different minimum ratios that they try to maintain. You should do some research to find out the *average* current ratio for profitable companies in your particular industry classification. You can get that information from your accountant, or you find it yourself in the reference section of your library. Ask for books on "key financial ratios for private companies", particularly those published by Robert Morris Associates and Prentice Hall.

In this case, let's assume that the average current ratio for private companies in Hammerhead's industry classification is 1.7. Hammerhead's current ratio is 1.87, so we know there is enough working capital for the current level of sales. We suspect that the actual amount of working capital will rise naturally as annual net sales increase, and at about the same rate. Since we assume Hammerhead's net sales will rise 4.5% per year, we will increase working capital by the same amount.

You may notice that Hammerhead has an unusually low ratio of current assets to total assets (43% vs. about 70% as the industry average). However, we assume that this is the result of some healthy circumstances:
- Its real estate has appreciated greatly, and this is reflected on the adjusted balance sheet as a fixed-asset.
- The company has a practice of giving preferential treatment to pre-paid orders, thus keeping trade receivables low (a current asset).
- The company's products are in such great demand that it always has a backlog of orders, so inventory (a current asset) doesn't have a chance to sit around long before it's out the door.

Low current assets are a mixed blessing. On one hand, they indicate that the company is converting its financial assets to income very efficiently. On the other hand, there is less money available on short notice for unexpected problems. It's important to have enough liquidity to cover your current liabilities, along with a healthy margin for safety. You might be called upon to pay those off without notice.

Deduct those additions to working capital from the cash flow. Then subtract the total amount of annual loan payments (debt service). In this case, that includes:

- The line of credit - starting at $2.5MM and increasing by 4.5% each year (@ 9.5% interest) for an average interest cost of $295,968 per year.

- Amortization of the non-current liabilities at $39,794 per year.
- The equipment loan, at $122,508 per year.
- The real estate mortgage, at $135,852 per year.

Total debt service for these = $594,122

Average annual interest for these
= $419,238

In addition, we have to include the payments on an acquisition loan. To do that, you must predict the loan amount. We will use 80% of the value calculated in the Ability To Pay Method (above): ($12,459,753 X .80 = $9,9677,000). (Note: If the result of this method is a value that's different from the amount we predicted here, we can go back and interpolate until they are about the same. If you are working with a computer spreadsheet, that process is very simple.) Anyway, here is what we will use for acquisition debt service:

A $9.967 million acquisition loan at 10.5% for 10 years with 25 year amortization. It will have payments of $1,129,279 per year, and an annual interest expense averaging $971,238.

Please note that we have taken some shortcuts here in order to keep this example simple:
- We have used an annual average for depreciation, instead of calculating the actual depreciation for each year. In reality, depreciation will be different in each year, so you should do a detailed depreciation schedule that includes each group of assets, including adjustments for new asset purchases.
- To determine whether working capital should be increased, we have compared the "current ratio" of this company with the average for its industry as a whole. Concluding that it is sufficient to start

out with, we have increased it only to the same extent that net sales increase each year. (That's not necessarily a reliable way to do it.)
- We guessed at average capital expenditures ($200,000 per year). You really should investigate those needs carefully and project them as accurately as possible.

Short-cuts can really throw your figures off, so in a real valuation, you should do a spreadsheet that calculates these for each year separately. Nonetheless, here is how we got our figures below:
- For each year, we used the Net Sales figure from the Ability To Pay example, multiplied by the Operating Profit Percentage from our adjusted statement (7%).

- Then we adjusted the interest expense and the depreciation expense in accordance with the instructions for Steps 3 and 4.

- We deducted taxes (Step 5), but not an investment tax credit, since that tax benefit is currently repealed.

- Then we add back the predicted amount of interest and depreciation (Steps 7 and 8), and deduct $200,000 per year as our guess at annual capital expenditures (Step 9). That gives us the "cash flow" figure in the first column.

- From that we deduct our short-cut estimate for annual additions to working capital (Step 10) and we also deduct the total annual Debt Service (Step 11).

- The result is the "cash flow safety cushion", which keeps you out of trouble and represents the return on the Buyer's cash investment.

Here are the results in summary form:

Year	Cash Flow	Step 10: Deduct New Working Cap.	Step 11: Deduct Debt Service	Safety Cushion
1	$2,414,559	- 135,076	- 1,664,933 =	$ 614,550
2	$2,460,600	- 141,154	- 1,675,620 =	$ 643,826
3	$2,508,712	- 147,506	- 1,686,789 =	$ 674,417
4	$2,558,990	- 154,144	- 1,698,460 =	$ 706,386
5	$2,611,433	- 161,080	- 1,710,656 =	$ 739,697
6	$2,666,433	- 168,329	- 1,723,401 =	$ 774,703
7	$2,719,272	- 175,904	- 1,736,720 =	$ 806,648
8	$2,783,764	- 183,820	- 1,750,638 =	$ 849,306
9	$2,846,419	- 192,092	- 1,765,182 =	$ 889,145
10	$2,911,893	- 141,119	- 1,780,380 =	$ 990,394

Next (Step 13) you calculate the present value of each year's Cash Flow Safety Cushion. At a 12.5% discount rate, that translates to the following amounts:

year 1	$ 614,550	
year 2	$ 572,289	
year 3	$ 523,873	
year 4	$ 496,118	
year 5	$ 461,789	
year 6	$ 429,905	
year 7	$ 397,895	
year 8	$ 372,389	
year 9	$ 346,539	
year 10	$ 343,111	$4,558,458

Then (Step 14), you add the present value of the assets you believe will be present at the end of this 10-year holding period. In this example, we just used the asset values from the Economic Value of Assets Method (above), projecting them into the future for ten years, and then bringing them back to present value at a 12.5% discount rate. As you can imagine, there's a lot of guesswork involved in projecting those values - which is one reason this method is sometimes criticized.

Asset	Value Now	Future Value	Present Value
Real Estate	$1,800,000	$3,223,520	$1,116,756
Realty Sale	$4,200,000	---	$4,200,000
Inventory	$4,006,948	$5,954,325	$2,062,813
Cash Reserve	$1,256,524	$1,867,314	$ 646,911
Receivables	$2,246,428	$3,338,192	$1,156,481
Equipment	$1,537,500	$2,284,725	$ 791,519
Intangibles	$1,507,249	$2,239,772	$ 775,945
Notes	$ 330,400	---	$ 330,400
		Total =	$11,080,825

Next we add the result from Step 13 to this figure, giving us a total of $15,639,283.

Finally (Step 15), we subtract any liabilities we expect to remain at the end of the holding period. We used "present value" in the previous calculations, so we should also probably use present value for the liabilities. That will make those numbers smaller. In other words, I would rather owe someone $1000 ten years from now than owe them $1000 today, because in the meantime I can make a significant investment return on the money. In fact, I can take a much smaller amount of money and invest it at a certain rate, and in ten years it will become $1000. Using our 12.5% discount rate, I would need only $346 in today's dollars to make that happen. So, here's how we value the liabilities:

Liability	Projected Balance	Present Value
Acquisition Loan	8,386,660	2,905,469
Line of Credit	3,593,707	1,245,001
Payables	1,184,553	410,375
Mortgage	0	0
Equipment Loan	0	0
Other Non-Current Liability	0	0
Misc. Current & Non-Current	900,000	311,795
Total Liabilities =		4,872,640

End Result: To get the value of the company, we subtract this amount from $15,639,283 to get $10,766,643. We have assumed that the Buyer would pay off the Seller's loan ($1,048,333) up front at acquisition time. (That's why our calculations did not include any interest payments or amortization on that loan.) With that loan added to our figure, the total price becomes $11,814,976.

Note: Another way to finish this method is to take the result of Step 12 (the sum of the present values of the cash flow safety cushions), and then add the present value of what you think the company will be worth at the end of the ten-year projection period. Here, we've just done that a different way, since "netting out" the future liabilities against the future asset value amounts to a safe estimate of the future value of the company. Either way, there's plenty of room for dispute due to all of the subjective judgment and downright guesswork involved. All you can really do is use your best judgement and record all of your assumptions so that others have the chance to examine them.

Example of Capitalization of Income Stream Method

First, find the Net Income Before Tax. On Hammerhead's adjusted statement, the Net Income is $1,421,000. Remember: in this method we use Net Operating Income *before* depreciation and interest expenses are deducted. That means we add those two amounts back to the figure on the statement:

$1,421,000 Net Income Before Tax
533,617 Current Annual Interest Expense
+ 748,081 Current Annual Depreciation Expense

$2,702,698 Total

Next, divide this by the Capitalization Rate (12.5%) we selected for Hammerhead. That gives you $21,621,584.

Then deduct all present liabilities (i.e., all of the liabilities helped produce the interest expense that we just added back.)

Current Liabilities:
Line of credit	3,500,000
Trade Payables	1,797,142
Taxes Payable	148,000

Long-Term Liabilities:
Equipment Loan	898,571
Mortgage Loan	876,000
Loan from Owner	1,048,333
Deferred Taxes	118,184
Other Non-Current Liability	300,000

Total liabilities 8,686,290

$21,621,584 - $8,686,290 = $12,935,294

Note that if the Buyer doesn't assume these liabilities, the seller will have to pay them off at settlement. The seller's *net* proceeds will be the same either way.

Some versions of this method do not add interest and depreciation back to net operating income, but in that case you can't deduct the liabilities at the end. If we took that approach in this example, we would have capitalized the net income of $1,421,000 at 12.5%, giving a value of $11,368,000. This is about 9% less than the value we calculated the other way. On one hand, it's still in the ballpark. On the other hand, $1.6 million is a lot of money.

Our preference is to adjust the depreciation on the fixed assets. Realistically, a buyer should consider the real economic depreciation of those assets, because those assets are wearing out a little bit each year. Yet this Capitalization of Earnings Method assumes that those assets will continue to produce that amount of income indefinitely. That won't happen if they are worn out, so you really should deduct something to reflect the average annual cost of replacing them, or at least keeping them in good working order. We don't want to use the actual depreciation figure from the financial statement, because it doesn't necessarily correspond to the real decline in value. It just represents the deduction allowed by the tax laws. You should try to figure out the real annual cost to maintain the quality of those assets, but the figure should not reflect the cost to make them better than they are now.

In our case this means the seller probably won't get $12,935,294. In this case, a reasonable estimate of the real economic depreciation on the fixed assets might be $225,000 per year. One part of that is for plant and warehouse repair costs of $75,000 per year. Also, since the market value of the machinery and equipment is $1,537,500, and we those items will last about 10 years (on average), that means their average replacement cost will be about $150,000 per year. The two figures combine to give a cost of $225,000 per year.

Recall that Net Operating Income before interest and depreciation was $2,702,698. From that we subtract $225,000 per year for economic depreciation of the real estate, equipment, and machinery. That gives $2,477,698, which we capitalize at our rate of 12.5%. The result is $19,821,584. Then we deduct the liabilities of $8,686,290 since our figures reflect no interest expense deduction, giving a final value of $11,135,294.

Example of Excess Earnings Method

In this method, the value is defined as:
The capitalized value of any "excess earnings" (the amount of earnings over-and-above the basic return you'd expect from an investment in this company's tangible assets and working capital)
+ PLUS +
The net value of those fixed assets and working capital.

The adjusted balance sheet lists the following tangible assets, which would be transferred to a new owner if the company is sold:

	Book Value	Adjusted Value
Real estate	1,425,397	6,000,000
Equipment	1,330,200	1,537,500
Leasehold Imps.	335,810	335,810
Total:		$ 11,880,258

The next step is to figure out how much working capital is needed to run the business. Recall that when we did the Discounted Cash Flow method, we determined that Hammerhead's working capital is adequate for its present level of sales. On the other hand, if Hammerhead's "current ratio", compared to the industry average, had told us that the working capital was too thin, we would add enough additional working capital to bring the ratio up to the industry average, but we would need to see a return on that additional

money as well. In this case we don't need to do that.

Here's how we calculate the amount of net working capital:

	Book Value	Adjusted Value
Current Assets:		
Inventory	4,006,948	4,006,948
Cash	1,256,524	1,256,524
Receivables	2,246,428	2,224,000
Note Payable	413,000	330,400
Prepaids	149,761	149,761
Total:		7,967,633

Current liabilities:	
Line of credit	$ 3,500,000
Trade Payables	$ 1,797,142
Taxes Payable	$ 148,000
Total:	$ 5,445,142

Net Working Capital: $ 2,522,491

Next, we add the value of the tangible fixed operating assets to the net working capital:

$11,880,258 + $2,522,491 = $14,402,749

Next we multiply that total by the rate of return that would probably be expected by someone investing in those assets. To find that rate, use the same rationale you use for selecting a capitalization rate. Recall that we selected a cap rate for Hammerhead of 12.5%. Therefore, if you decide to use the same rate for this, you would multiply $14,402,749 by 12.5%. The result is $1,800,343. That's your estimate of how much basic investment return an investor would expect. Now look to see if the company is producing a greater return than that - excess earnings. To find that, look on the adjusted income statement for the net operating income before tax ($1,421,000), then add back the interest expense and depreciation expense from that adjusted statement:

$1,421,000 Net Income Before Tax

+   533,617 Current Annual Interest
              Expense
+   748,081 Current Annual
              Depreciation Expense

= $2,702,698 Total

Next, subtract the average amount by which the company's fixed assets really do depreciate in value each year. (Recall that in the last method we figured that to be $225,000 per year.) The result is $2,477,698.

Next, subtract the basic return the investor will expect on the fixed assets and working capital ($1,800,343). The result is $677,355. This figure represents the "excess earnings".

Divide the excess earnings by the capitalization rate of 16.5%. The result ($5,418,840) is the dollar value of that future stream of excess earnings.

Next, add the total value of the tangible fixed operating assets to be acquired ($15,840,943). Then subtract the amount of any liabilities to be assumed by the buyer ($8,686,290 - as listed in the last example).

The result is $12,573,493. This would be the value of the company according to this method.

Summary of results:

All of the following values include the value the owner's loan to the company:

Asset Value Method: $10,046,045

Discounted Cash
    Flow Method: $11,814,976

Capitalization of
    Income Method: $11,135,294

Excess Earnings
    Method: $12,573,493

Ability To Pay Method: $12,459,753

Remember that we do not average these values to obtain a final result. We think in terms of a range of possible values, and we zero-in on a particular number only when the method that produced it is most theoretically-appropriate for the situation we are dealing with.

In this case, asset value is the least appropriate method because the company is very profitable. It obviously has earnings value over and above the value of the assets. Since asset value is the lowest number we can discard it. The Ability to Pay Method seems to justify a price of up to $12,459,753 for the company, which is probably the upper limit for this firm.

The Capitalization of Income Method and Excess Earnings Method both apply extremely well to Hammerhead, but the Discounted Cash Flow Method may be even better, due to the cyclical popularity of most recreational sports. In addition, there is no assurance that any company in this field can retain its competitive edge for an extended period of time. Therefore, it may be wise to assume a short holding period for this kind of company. Therefore, our range of possible values is $11,135,294 to $12,573,493 - and we have reason to believe that a value of about $11,815,000 may be most appropriate. Recall that the seller is asking $10,600,000 plus repayment of her $1,048,33 loan to the company, for a total of $11,648,333. Rarely will your valuation results be that close to what the other side wants.

There may be numerous mistakes in these calculations. Certainly, there are plenty of assumptions with which one could argue. And many of the shortcuts that were taken here would be inadvisable under ordinary circumstances. But the example demonstrates how one person might apply these methods to a particular situation.

26 CFR 1.1001-1: Computation of gain   Rev. Rul. 65-192
or loss.

The general approach, methods and factors outlined in Revenue Ruling 59-60, C.B. 1959-1, 237, for use in valuing closely-held corporate stocks for estate and gift tax purposes are equally applicable to valuations thereof for income tax purposes and also in determinations of the fair market values of business interests of any type and of intangible assets for all tax purposes.

The formula approach set forth in A.R.M. 34, C.B. 2, 31 (1920), and A.R.M. 68, C.B. 3, 43 (1920), has no valid application in determinations of the fair market values of corporate stocks or of business interests, unless it is necessary to value the intangible assets of the corporation or the intangible assets included in the business interest. The formula approach may be used in determining the fair market values of intangible assets only if there is no better basis therefor available. In applying the formula, the average earnings period and the capitalization rates are dependent upon the facts and circumstances pertinent thereto in such case.

SECTION 1. PURPOSE.

The purpose of this Revenue Ruling is to furnish information and guidance as to the usage to be made of suggested methods for determining the value as of March 1, 1913, or of any other date, of intangible assets and to identify those areas where a valuation formula set forth in A.R.M. 34, C.B. 2, 31 (1920), as modified by A.R.M. 68, C.B. 3, 43 (1920), both quoted in full below should and should not be applied. Since it appears that such formula has been applied to many valuation issues for which it was never intended, the Internal Revenue Service reindicates its limited application.

SEC. 2. BACKGROUND.

A.R.M. 34 was issued in 1920 for the purpose of providing suggested formulas for determining the amount of March 1, 1913, intangible asset value lost by breweries and other businesses connected with the distilling industry, as a result of the passage of the 18th Amendment to the Constitution of the United States. A.R.M. 68 was issued later in the same year and contained a minor revision of the original ruling so that its third formula would be applied in accordance with its purpose and intent.

SEC. 3. STATEMENT OF POSITION.

.01 Although the formulas and approach contained in A.R.M. 34, were specifically aimed at the valuation of intangible assets of distilling and related companies as of March 1, 1913, the last two paragraphs of the ruling seemingly broaden it to make its third formula applicable to almost any kind of enterprise. The final sentences, however, limit the purpose of such formula by stating that "In * * * all of the cases the effort should be to determine what net earnings a purchaser of a business on March 1, 1913, might reasonably have expected to receive from it, * * *," "and by providing certain checks and alternatives. Also, both A.R.M. 34 and A.R.M. 68 expressly stated that such formula

was merely a rule for guidance and not controlling in the presence of "better evidence" in determining the value of intangible assets. Furthermore, T.B.R. 57, C.B. 1, 40 (1919), relating to the meaning of "fair market value" of property received in exchange for other property, which was published before A.R.M. 34 and A.R.M. 68 and has not been revoked, set forth general principles of valuation that are consistent with Revenue Ruling 59-60, C.B. 1959-1, 237. Moreover, in S.M. 1609, C.B. III-1, 48 (1924) it was stated that "The method suggested in A.R.M. 34 for determining the value of intangibles is * * * controlling only in the absence of better evidence." As said in *North American Service Co., Inc. v. Commissioner*, 33 T.C. 677, 694' (1960) acquiescence, C.B. 1960-2, 6, "an A.R.M. 34 computation would not be conclusive of the existence and value of good will if better evidence were available * * *."

.02 Revenue Ruling 59-60 sets forth the proper approach to use in the valuation of closely-held corporate stocks for estate and gift tax purposes. That ruling contains the statement that no formula can be devised that will be generally applicable to the multitude of different valuation issues. It also contains a discussion of intangible value in closely-held corporations and some of the elements which may support such value in a given business.

SEC. 4. DELINEATION OF AREAS IN WHICH SUGGESTED METHODS WILL BE EFFECTIVE.

.01 The general approach, methods, and factors outlined in Revenue Ruling 59-60 are equally applicable to valuations of corporate stocks for income and other tax purposes as well as for estate and gift tax purposes. They apply also to problems involving the determination of the fair market value of business interests of any type, including partnerships, proprietorships, etc., and of intangible assets for all tax purposes.

.02 Valuation, especially where earning power is an important factor, is in essence a process requiring the exercise of informed judgment and common sense. Thus, the suggested formula approach set forth in A.R.M. 34, has no valid application in determinations of the fair market value of corporate stocks or of business interests unless it is necessary to value the intangible assets of the corporation or the intangible assets included in the business interest. The formula approach may be used in determining the fair market values of intangible assets only if there is no better basis therefor available. In applying the formula, the average earnings period and the capitalization rates are dependent upon the facts and circumstances pertinent thereto in each case. See *John Q. Shunk et al. v. Commissioner*, 10 T.C. 293, 304-5 (1948), acquiescence, C.B. 1948-1, 3, affirmed 173 Fed. (2d) 747 (1949); *Ushco Manufacturing Co., Inc. v. Commissioner*, Tax Court Memorandum Opinion entered March 10, 1945, affirmed 175 Fed. (2d) 821 (1945); and *White & Wells Co. v. Commissioner*, 19 B.T.A. 416, nonacquiescence C.B. IX-2, 87 (1930), reversed and remanded 50 Fed. (2d) 120 (1931).

For convenience, A.R.M. 34 reads as follows:

The Committee has considered the question of providing some practical formula for determining value as of March 1, 1913, or of any other date, which might be considered as applying to intangible assets, but finds itself unable to lay down any specific rule of guidance for determining the value of intangibles which would be applicable in all cases and under all circumstances. Where there is no established market to serve as a guide the question of value, even of tangible assets, is one largely of judgment and opinion, and the same thing is even more true of intangible assets such as good will, trade-marks, trade brands, etc. However, there are several methods of reaching a conclusion as to the value of intangibles which the Committee suggests may be utilized broadly in passing upon questions of valuation, not to be regarded as controlling, however, if better evidence is presented in any specific case.

Where deduction is claimed for obsolescence or loss of good will or trade-marks, the burden of proof is primarily upon the taxpayer to show the value of such good will or trade-marks on March 1, 1913. Of course, if good will or trade-marks have been acquired for cash or other valuable considerations subsequent to March 1, 1913, the measure of loss will be determined by the amount of cash or value of other considerations paid therefor, and no deduction will be allowed for the value of good will or trade-marks built up by the taxpayer since March 1, 1913. The following suggestions are made, therefore, merely as suggestions for checks upon the soundness and validity of the taxpayers' claims. No obsolescence or loss with respect to good will should be allowed except in cases of actual disposition of the asset or abandonment of the business.

In the first place, it is recognized that in numerous instances it has been the practice of distillers and wholesale liquor dealers to put out under well-known and popular brands only so much goods as could be marketed without affecting the established market price therefor and to sell other goods of the same identical manufacture, age, and character under other brands, or under no brand at all, in such cases the difference between the price at which whisky was sold under a given brand name and also under another brand name, or under no brand, multiplied by the number of units sold during a given year gives an accurate determination of the amount of profit attributable to that brand during that year, and where this practice is continued for a long enough period to show that this amount was fairly constant and regular and might be expected to yield annually that average profit, by capitalizing this earning at the rate, say, of 20 per cent, the value of the brand is fairly well established.

Another method is to compare the volume of business done under the trade-mark or brand under consideration and profits made, or by the business whose good will is under consideration, with the similar volume of business and profit made in other cases where good will or trade-marks have been actually sold for cash, recognizing as the value of the good will or the first the same proportion of the selling price of the second, as the profits of the first attributable to brands or good will is of the similar profits of the second.

The third method end possibly the one which will most frequently have to be applied as a check in the absence of data necessary for the application of the preceding ones, is to allow out of average earnings over a period of years prior to March 1, 1913, preferably not less than five years, a return of 10 per cent upon the average tangible assets for the period. The surplus earnings will then be the average amount available for return upon the value of the intangible assets,

and it is the opinion of the Committee that this return should be capitalized upon the basis of not more than five years' purchase—that is to say, five times the amount available as return from intangibles should be the value of the intangibles.

In view of the hazards of the business, the changes in popular tastes, and the difficulties in preventing imitation or counterfeiting of popular brands affecting the sales of the genuine goods, the Committee is of the opinion that the figure given of 20 per cent return on intangibles is not unreasonable, and it recommends that no higher figure than that be attached in any case to intangibles without a very clear and adequate showing that the value of the intangibles was in fact greater than would be reached by applying this formula.

The foregoing is intended to apply particularly to businesses put out of existence by the prohibition law, but will be equally applicable so far as the third formula is concerned, to other businesses of a more or less hazardous nature. In the case, however, of valuation of good will of a business which consists of the manufacture or sale of standard articles of every-day necessity not subject to violent fluctuations and where the hazard is not so great, the Committee is of the opinion that the figure for determination of the return on tangible assets might be reduced from 10 to 8 or 9 per cent, and that the percentage for capitalization of the return upon intangibles might be reduced from 20 to 15 per cent.

In any or all of the cases the effort should be to determine what net earnings a purchaser of a business on March 1, 1913, might reasonably have expected to receive from it, and therefore a representative period should be used for ever-aging actual earnings, eliminating any year in which there were extraordinary factors affecting earnings either way. Also, in the case of the sale of good will of a going business the percentage rate of capitalization of earnings applicable to good will shown by the amount actually paid for the business should be used as a check against the determination of good will value as of March 1, 1913, and if the good will is sold upon the basis of capitalization of earnings less than the figures above indicated as the ones ordinarily to be adopted, the same percentage should be used in figuring value as of March 1, 1913.

SEC. 6. QUOTATION OF A.R.M. 68.

Also for convenience, A.R.M. 68 reads as follows:

The Committee is in receipt of a request for advice as to whether under A.R.M. 34 the 10 per cent upon tangible assets is to be applied only to the net tangible assets or to all tangible assets on the books of the corporation, regardless of any outstanding obligations.

The Committee, in the memorandum in question, undertook to lay down a rule for guidance in the absence of better evidence in determining the value as of March 1, 1913, of good will, and held that in determining such value, income over an average period in excess of an amount sufficient to return 10 per cent upon tangible assets should be capitalized at 20 per cent. Manifestly, since the effort is to determine the value of the good will, and therefore the true net worth of the taxpayer as of March 1, 1913, the 10 per cent should be applied only to the tangible assets entering into net worth, including accounts and bills receivable in excess of accounts and bills payable.

In other words, the purpose and intent are to provide for a return to the taxpayer of 10 per cent upon so much of his investment as is represented by tangible assets and to capitalize the excess of earnings over the amount necessary to provide such return, at 20 per cent.

SEC. 7. EFFECT ON OTHER DOCUMENTS.

Although the limited application of A.R.M. 34 and A.R.M. 68 is reindicated in this Revenue Ruling, the principles enunciated in those rulings are not thereby affected.

Valuation of intangible assets of a business where separate appraisal of tangible and intangible assets may not be possible. See Rev. Rul. 65-193, page 370.

26 CFR 20.2031-2: Valuation of stocks and bonds.

(Also Section 2512.)

(Also Part II, Sections 811 (k), 1005, Regulations 105, Section 81.10.)

Rev. Rul. 59-60

In valuing the stock of closely held corporations, or the stock of corporations where market quotations are not available, all other available financial data, as well as all relevant factors affecting the fair market value must be considered for estate tax and gift tax purposes. No general formula may be given that is applicable to the many different valuation situations arising in the valuation of such stock. However, the general approach, methods, and factors which must be considered in valuing such securities are outlined. Revenue Ruling 54-77, C.B. 1954-1, 187, superseded.

SECTION 1. PURPOSE.

The purpose of this Revenue Ruling is to outline and review in general the approach, methods and factors to be considered in valuing shares of the capital stock of closely held corporations for estate tax and gift tax purposes. The methods discussed herein will apply likewise to the valuation of corporate stocks on which market quotations are either unavailable or are of such scarcity that they do not reflect the fair market value.

SEC. 2. BACKGROUND AND DEFINITIONS.

.01 All valuations must be made in accordance with the applicable provisions of the Internal Revenue Code of 1954 and the Federal Estate Tax and Gift Tax Regulations. Sections 2031(a), 2032 and 2512(a) of the 1954 Code (sections 811 and 1005 of the 1939 Code) require that the property to be included in the gross estate, or made the subject of a gift, shall be taxed on the basis of the value of the property at the time of death of the decedent, the alternate date if so elected, or the date of gift.

.02 Section 20.2031-1(b) of the Estate Tax Regulations (section 81.10 of the Estate Tax Regulations 105) and section 25.2512-1 of the Gift Tax Regulations (section 86.19 of Gift Tax Regulations 108) define fair market value, in effect, as the price at which the property would change hands between a willing buyer and a willing seller when the former is not under any compulsion to buy and the latter is not under any compulsion to sell, both parties having reasonable knowledge of relevant facts. Court decisions frequently state in addition that the hypothetical buyer and seller are assumed to be able, as well as willing, to trade and to be well informed about the property and concerning the market for such property.

.03 Closely held corporations are those corporations the shares of which are owned by a relatively limited number of stockholders. Often the entire stock issue is held by one family. The result of this situation is that little, if any, trading in the shares takes place. There is, therefore, no established market for the stock and such sales as occur at irregular intervals seldom reflect all of the elements of a representative transaction as defined by the term "fair market value."

SEC. 3. APPROACH TO VALUATION.

.01 A determination of fair market value, being a question of fact, will depend upon the circumstances in each case. No formula can be devised that will be generally applicable to the multitude of different valuation issues arising in estate and gift tax cases. Often, an appraiser will find wide differences of opinion as to the fair market value of a particular stock. In resolving such differences, he should maintain a reasonable attitude in recognition of the fact that valuation is not an exact science. A sound valuation will be based upon all the relevant facts, but the elements of common sense, informed judgment and reasonableness must enter into the process of weighing those facts and determining their aggregate significance.

.02 The fair market value of specific shares of stock will vary as general economic conditions change from "normal" to "boom"[3] or "depression," that is, according to the degree of optimism or pessimism with which the investing public regards the future at the required date of appraisal. Uncertainty as to the stability or continuity of the future income from a property decreases its value by increasing the risk of loss of earnings and value in the future. The value of shares of stock of a company with very uncertain future prospects is highly speculative. The appraiser must exercise his judgment as to the degree of risk attaching to the business of the corporation which issued the stock, but that judgment must be related to all of the other factors affecting value.

.03 Valuation of securities is, in essence, a prophecy as to the future and must be based on facts available at the required date of appraisal. As a generalization, the prices of stocks which are traded in volume in a free and active market by informed persons best reflect the consensus of the investing public as to what the future holds for the corporations and industries represented. When a stock is closely held, is traded infrequently, or is traded in an erratic market, some other measure of value must be used. In many instances, the next best measure may be found in the prices at which the stocks of companies engaged in the same or a similar line of business are selling in a free and open market.

SEC. 4. FACTORS TO CONSIDER.

.01 It is advisable to emphasize that in the valuation of the stock of closely held corporations or the stock of corporations where market quotations are either lacking or too scarce to be recognized, all available financial data, as well as all relevant factors affecting the fair market value, should be considered. The following factors, although not all-inclusive are fundamental and require careful analysis in each case:

(a) The nature of the business and the history of the enterprise from its inception.

(b) The economic outlook in general and the condition and outlook of the specific industry in particular.

(c) The book value of the stock and the financial condition of the business.

(d) The earning capacity of the company.

(e) The dividend-paying capacity.

(f) Whether or not the enterprise has goodwill or other intangible value.

(g) Sales of the stock and the size of the block of stock to be valued.

(h) The market price of stocks of corporations engaged in the same or a similar line of business having their stocks actively traded in a free and open market, either on an exchange or over-the-counter.

.02 The following is a brief discussion of each of the foregoing factors:

(a) The history of a corporate enterprise will show its past stability or instability, its growth or lack of growth, the diversity or lack of diversity of its operations, and other facts needed to form an opinion of the degree of risk involved in the business. For an enterprise which changed its form of organization but carried on the same or closely similar operations of its predecessor, the history of the former enterprise should be considered. The detail to be considered should increase with approach to the required date of appraisal, since recent events are of greatest help in predicting the future; but a study of gross and net income, and of dividends covering a long prior period, is highly desirable. The history to be studied should include, but need not be limited to, the nature of the business, its products or services, its operating and investment assets, capital structure, plant facilities, sales records and management, all of which should be considered as of the date of the appraisal, with due regard for recent significant changes. Events of the past that are unlikely to recur in the future should be discounted, since value has a close relation to future expectancy.

(b) A sound appraisal of a closely held stock must consider current and prospective economic conditions as of the date of appraisal, both in the national economy and in the industry or industries with which the corporation is allied. It is important to know that the company is more or less successful than its competitors in the same industry, or that it is maintaining a stable position with respect to competitors. Equal or even greater significance may attach to the ability of the industry with which the company is allied to compete with other industries. Prospective competition which has not been a factor in prior years should be given careful attention. For example, high profits due to the novelty of its product and the lack of competition often lead to increasing competition. The public's appraisal of the future prospects of competitive industries or of competitors within an industry may be indicated by price trends in the markets for commodities and for securities. The loss of the manager of a so-called "one-man" business may have a depressing effect upon the value of the stock of such business, particularly if there is a lack of trained personnel capable of succeeding to the management of the enterprise. In valuing the stock of this type of business, therefore, the effect of the loss of the manager on the future expectancy of the business, and the absence of management-succession potentialities are pertinent factors to be taken into consideration. On the other hand, there may be factors which offset, in whole or in part, the loss of the manager's services. For instance, the nature of the business and of its assets may be such that they will not be impaired by the loss of the manager. Furthermore, the loss may be adequately covered by life insurance, or competent management might be employed on the basis of the consideration paid for the former manager's services. These, or other offsetting factors, if found to exist, should be carefully weighed against the loss of the manager's services in valuing the stock of the enterprise.

(c) Balance sheets should be obtained, preferably in the form of comparative annual statements for two or more years immediately preceding the date of appraisal, together with a balance sheet at the end of the month preceding that date, if corporate accounting will permit. Any balance sheet descriptions that are not self-explanatory, and balance sheet items comprehending diverse assets or liabilities, should be clarified in essential detail by supporting supplemental schedules. These statements usually will disclose to the appraiser (1) liquid position (ratio of current assets to current liabilities); (2) gross and net book value of principal classes of fixed assets; (3) working capital; (4) long-term indebtedness; (5) capital structure; and (6) net worth. Consideration also should be given to any assets not essential to the operation of the business, such as investments in securities, real estate, etc. In general, such nonoperating assets will command a lower rate of return than do the operating assets, although in exceptional cases the reverse may be true. In computing the book value per share of stock, assets of the investment type should be revalued on the basis of their market price and the book value adjusted accordingly. Comparison of the company's balance sheets over several years may reveal, among other facts, such developments as the acquisition of additional production facilities or subsidiary companies, improvement in financial position, and details as to recapitalizations and other changes in the capital structure of the corporation. If the corporation has more than one class of stock outstanding, the charter or certificate of incorporation should be examined to ascertain the explicit rights and privileges of the various stock issues including: (1) voting powers, (2) preference as to dividends, and (3) preference as to assets in the event of liquidation.

(d) Detailed profit-and-loss statements should be obtained and considered for a representative period immediately prior to the required date of appraisal, preferably five or more years. Such statements should show (1) gross income by principal items; (2) principal deductions from gross income including major prior items of operating expenses, interest and other expense on each item of long-term debt, depreciation and depletion if such deductions are made, officers' salaries, in total if they appear to be reasonable or in detail if they seem to be excessive, contributions (whether or not deductible for tax purposes) that the nature of its business and its community position require the corporation to make, and taxes by principal items, including income and excess profits taxes; (3) net income available for dividends; (4) rates and amounts of dividends paid on each class of stock; (5) remaining amount carried to surplus; and (6) adjustments to, and reconciliation with, surplus as stated on the balance sheet. With profit and loss statements of this character available, the appraiser should be able to separate recurrent from nonrecurrent items of income and expense, to distinguish between operating income and investment income, and to ascertain whether or not any line of business in which the company is engaged is operated consistently at a loss and might be abandoned with benefit to the company. The percentage of earnings retained for business expansion should be noted when dividend-paying capacity is considered. Potential future income is a major factor in many valuations of closely-held stocks, and all information concerning past income which will be helpful in predicting the future should be secured. Prior earnings records usually are the most reliable guide as to the future expectancy, but resort to arbitrary five-or-ten-year averages without regard to current trends or future prospects will not produce a realistic valuation. If, for instance, a record of progressively increasing or decreasing net income is found, then greater weight may be accorded the most recent years' profits in estimating earning power. It will be helpful, in judging risk and the extent to which a business is a marginal operator, to consider deductions from income and net income in terms of percentage of sales. Major categories of cost and expense to be so analyzed include the consumption of raw materials and supplies in the case of manufacturers, processors and fabricators; the cost of purchased merchandise in the case of merchants; utility services; insurance; taxes; depletion or depreciation; and interest.

(e) Primary consideration should be given to the dividend-paying capacity of the company rather than to dividends actually paid in the past. Recognition must be given to the necessity of retaining a reasonable portion of profits in a company to meet competition. Dividend-paying capacity is a factor that must be considered in an appraisal, but dividends actually paid in the past may not have any relation to dividend-paying capacity. Specifically, the dividends paid by a closely held family company may be measured by the income needs of the stockholders or by their desire to avoid taxes on dividend receipts, instead of by the ability of the company to pay dividends. Where an actual or effective controlling interest in a corporation is to be valued, the dividend factor is not a material element, since the payment of such dividends is discretionary with the controlling stockholders. The individual or group in control can substitute salaries and bonuses for dividends, thus reducing net income and understating the dividend-paying capacity of the company. It follows, therefore, that dividends are less reliable criteria of fair market value than other applicable factors.

(f) In the final analysis, goodwill is based upon earning capacity. The presence of goodwill and its value, therefore, rests upon the excess of net earnings over and above a fair return on the net tangible assets. While the element of goodwill may be based primarily on earnings, such factors as the prestige and renown of the business, the ownership of a trade or brand name, and a record of successful operation over a prolonged period in a particular locality, also may furnish support for the inclusion of intangible value. In some instances it may not be possible to make a separate appraisal of the tangible and intangible assets of the business. The enterprise has a value as an entity. Whatever intangible value there is, which is supportable by the facts, may be measured by the amount by which the appraised value of the tangible assets exceeds the net book value of such assets.

(g) Sales of stock of a closely held corporation should be carefully investigated to determine whether they represent transactions at arm's length. Forced or distress sales do not ordinarily reflect fair market value nor do isolated sales in small amounts necessarily control as the measure of value. This is especially true in the case of closely held stocks, no prevailing market prices are available, there is no basis for making an adjustment for blockage. It follows, therefore, that such stocks should be valued upon a consideration of all the evidence affecting the fair market value. The size of the block of stock itself is a relevant factor to be considered. Although it is true that a minority interest in an unlisted corporation's stock is more difficult to sell than a similar block of listed stock, it is equally true that control of a corporation, either actual or in effect, representing as it does an added element of value, may justify a higher value for a specific block of stock.

(h) Section 2031(b) of the Code states, in effect, that in valuing unlisted securities the value of stock or securities of corporations engaged in the same or a similar line of business which are listed on an exchange should be taken into consideration along with all other factors. An important consideration is that the corporations to be used for comparisons have capital stocks which are actively traded by the public. In accordance with section 2031(b) of the Code, stocks listed on an exchange are to be considered first. However, if sufficient comparable companies whose stocks are listed on an exchange cannot be found, other comparable companies which have stocks actively traded in on the over-the-counter market also may be used. The essential factor is that whether the stocks are sold on an exchange or over-the-counter there is evidence of an active, free public market for the stock as of the valuation date. In selecting corporations for comparative purposes, care should be taken to apparent by a cursory check of the rates of return and dividend yields in terms of the selling prices of corporate shares listed on the major exchanges of the country. Wide variations will be found even for companies in the same industry. Moreover, the ratio will fluctuate from year to year depending upon economic conditions. Thus, no standard tables of capitalization rates applicable to closely held corporations can be formulated. Among the more important factors to be taken into consideration in deciding upon a capitalization rate in a particular case are: (1) the nature of the business; (2) the risk involved; and (3) the stability or irregularity of earnings.

Sec. 7. Average of Factors.

Because valuations cannot be made on the basis of a prescribed formula, there is no means whereby the various applicable factors in a particular case can be assigned mathematical weights in deriving the fair market value. For this reason, no useful purpose is served by taking an average of several factors (for example, book value, capitalized earnings and capitalized dividends) and basing the valuation on the result. Such a process excludes active consideration of other pertinent factors, and the end result cannot be supported by a realistic application of the significant facts in the case except by mere chance.

Sec. 8. Restrictive Agreements.

Frequently, in the valuation of closely held stock for estate and gift tax purposes, it will be found that the stock is subject to an agreement restricting its sale or transfer. Where shares of stock were acquired by a decedent subject to an option reserved by the issuing corporation to repurchase at a certain price, the option price is usually accepted as the fair market value for estate tax purposes. See Rev. Rul. 54–76, C.B. 1954–1, 194. However, in such case the option price is not determinative of fair market value for gift tax purposes. Where the option, or buy and sell agreement, is the result of voluntary action by the stockholders and is binding during the life as well as at the death of the stockholders, such agreement may or may not, depending upon the circumstances of each case, fix the value for estate tax purposes. However, such agreement is a factor to be considered, with other relevant factors, in determining fair market value. Where the stockholder is free to dispose of his shares during life and the option is to become effective only upon his death, the fair market value is not limited to the option price. It is always necessary to consider the relationship of the parties, the relative number of shares held by the decedent, and other material facts, to determine whether the agreement represents a bonafide business arrangement or is a device to pass the decedent's shares to the natural objects of his bounty for less than an adequate and full consideration in money or money's worth. In this connection see Rev. Rul. 157 C.B. 1953–2, 255, and Rev. Rul. 189, C.B. 1953–2, 294.

Sec. 9. Effect on Other Documents.

Revenue Ruling 54–77, C.B. 1954–1, 187, is hereby superseded.

use only comparable companies. Although the only restrictive requirement as to comparable corporations specified in the statute is that their lines of business be the same or similar, yet it is obvious that consideration must be given to other relevant factors in order that the most valid comparison possible will be obtained. For illustration, a corporation having one or more issues of preferred stock, bonds or debentures in addition to its common stock should not be considered to be directly comparable to one having only common stock outstanding. In like manner, a company with a declining business and decreasing markets is not comparable to one with a record of current progress and market expansion.

Sec. 5. Weight To Be Accorded Various Factors.

The valuation of closely held corporate stock entails the consideration of all relevant factors as stated in section 4. Depending upon the circumstances in each case, certain factors may carry more weight than others because of the nature of the company's business. To illustrate:

(a) Earnings may be the most important criterion of value in some cases whereas asset value will receive primary consideration in others. In general, the appraiser will accord primary consideration to earnings when valuing stocks of companies which sell products or services to the public; conversely, in the investment or holding type of company, the appraiser may accord the greatest weight to the assets underlying the security to be valued.

(b) The value of the stock of a closely held investment or real estate holding company, whether or not family owned, is closely related to the value of the assets underlying the stock. For companies of this type the appraiser should determine the fair market values of the assets of the company. Operating expenses of such a company and the cost of liquidating it, if any, merit consideration when appraising the relative values of the stock and the underlying assets. The market value of the underlying assets give due weight to potential earnings and dividends of the particular items of property, underlying the stock, capitalized at rates deemed proper by the investing public at the date of appraisal. A current appraisal by the retrospective opinion of an individual. For these reasons, adjusted net worth should be accorded greater weight in valuing the stock of a closely held investment or real estate holding company, whether or not family owned, than any of the other customary yardsticks of appraisal, such as earnings and dividend paying capacity.

Sec. 6. Capitalization Rates.

In the application of certain fundamental valuation factors, such as earnings and dividends, it is necessary to capitalize the average of the current results at some appropriate rate. A determination of the proper capitalization rate presents one of the most difficult problems in valuation. That there is no ready or simple solution will become

A procedure to be used as a guideline by all persons making appraisals of donated property for Federal income tax purposes.

SECTION 1. PURPOSE.

The purpose of this procedure is to provide information and guidelines for taxpayers, individual appraisers, and valuation groups relative to appraisals of contributed property for Federal income tax purposes. The procedures outlined are applicable to all types of noncash property for which an appraisal is required such as real property, tangible or intangible personal property, and securities. These procedures are also appropriate for unique properties such as art objects, literary manuscripts, antiques, etc., with respect to which the determination of value often is more difficult.

SEC. 2. LAW AND REGULATIONS.

.01 Numerous sections of the Internal Revenue Code of 1954, as amended, give rise to a determination of value for Federal tax purposes; however, the significant section for purposes of this Revenue Procedure is section 170, Charitable, Etc., Contributions and Gifts.

.02 Value is defined in section 1.170-1(c) of the Income Tax Regulations as follows:

* * * The fair market value is the price at which the property would change hands between a willing buyer and a willing seller, neither being under any compulsion to buy or sell and both having reasonable knowledge of relevant facts. * * *

.03 This section further provides that:

* * * If the contribution is made in property of a type which the taxpayer sells in the course of his business, the fair market value is the price which the taxpayer would have received if he had sold the contributed property in the lowest usual market in which he customarily sells, at the time and place of contribution (and in the case of a contribution of goods in quantity, in the quantity contributed). * * *

.04 As to the measure of proof in determining the fair market value, all factors bearing on value are relevant including, where pertinent, the cost, or selling price of the item, sales of comparable properties, cost of reproduction, opinion evidence and appraisals. Fair market value depends upon value in the market and not on intrinsic worth.

.05 The cost or actual selling price of an item within a reasonable time before or after the valuation date may be the best evidence of its fair market value. Before such information is taken into account, it must be ascertained that the transaction was at arm's length and that the parties were fully informed as to all relevant facts. Absent such evidence, even the sales price of the item in question will not be persuasive.

.06 Sales of similar properties are often given probative weight by the courts in establishing fair market value. The weight to be given such evidence will be affected by the degree of similarity to the property under appraisal and the proximity of the date of sale to the valuation date.

.07 With respect to reproductive cost as a measure of fair market value, it must be shown that there is a probative correlation between the cost of reproduction and fair market value. Frequently, reproductive cost will be in excess of the fair market value.

.08 Generally, the weight to be given to opinion evidence depends on its origin and the thoroughness with which it is supported by experience and facts. It is only where expert opinion is supported by facts having strong probative value, that the opinion testimony will in itself be given appropriate weight. The underlying facts must corroborate the opinion; otherwise such opinion will be discounted or disregarded.

.09 The weight to be accorded any appraisal made either at or after the valuation date will depend largely upon the competence and knowledge of the appraiser with respect to the property and the market for such property.

SEC. 3. APPRAISAL FORMAT.

.01 When it becomes necessary to secure an appraisal in order to determine the values of items for Federal income tax purposes, such appraisals should be obtained from qualified and reputable sources, and the appraisal report should accompany the return when it is filed. The more complete the information filed with a tax return the more unlikely it will be that the Internal Revenue Service will find it necessary to question items on it. Thus, when reporting a deduction for charitable contributions on an income tax return, it will facilitate the review and the acceptance of the returned values if any appraisals which have been secured are furnished. The above-mentioned regulations prescribe that support of values claimed should be submitted and a properly prepared appraisal by a person qualified to make such an appraisal may well constitute the necessary substantiation. In this respect, it is not intended that all value determinations be supported by formal written appraisals as outlined in detail below. This is particularly applicable to minor items of property or where the value of the property is easily ascertainable by methods other than appraisal.

.02 In general, an appraisal report should contain at least the following:

(1) A summary of the appraiser's qualifications.
(2) A statement of the value and the appraiser's definition of

donated property, the Service may either accept the value claimed based on information or appraisals submitted with the return or make its own determination as to the fair market value. In either instance, the Service may find it necessary to:

(1) contact the taxpayer and ask for additional information, or

(2) refer the valuation problem to a Service appraiser or valuation specialist,

(3) recommend that an independent appraiser be employed by the Service to appraise the asset in question. (This latter course is frequently used by the Service when objects requiring appraisers of highly specialized experience and knowledge are involved.)

The "formula" approach may be used in determining the fair market value of intangible assets of a business only if there is no better basis available for making the determination; A.R.M. 34, A.R.M. 68, O.D. 937, and Revenue Ruling 65–192 superseded.

SECTION 1001.—DETERMINATION OF AMOUNT OF AND RECOGNITION OF GAIN OR LOSS

26 CFR 1.1001–1: Computation of gain or loss. (Also Section 167; 1.167(a)–3.)   Rev. Rul. 68–609 [1]

The purpose of this Revenue Ruling is to update and restate, under the current statute and regulations, the currently outstanding portions of A.R.M. 34, C.B. 2, 31 (1920), A.R.M. 68, C.B. 3, 43 (1920), and O.D. 937, C.B. 4, 43 (1921).

The question presented is whether the "formula" approach, the capitalization of earnings in excess of a fair rate of return on net tangible assets, may be used to determine the fair market value of the intangible assets of a business

The "formula" approach may be stated as follows:

A percentage return on the average annual value of the tangible assets used in a business is determined, using a period of years (preferably not less than five) immediately prior to the valuation date. The amount of the percentage return on tangible assets, thus determined, is deducted from the average earnings of the business for such period and the remainder, if any, is considered to be the amount of the average annual earnings from the intangible assets of the business for the period. This amount (considered as the average annual earnings from intangibles), capitalized at a percentage of, say, 15 to 20 percent, is the value of the intangible assets of the business determined under the "formula" approach

[1] Prepared pursuant to Rev. Proc. 67–6, C.B. 1967–1, 576.

---

the value he has obtained.

(3) The bases upon which the appraisal was made, including any restrictions, understandings, or covenants limiting the use or disposition of the property.

(4) The date as of which the property was valued.

(5) The signature of the appraiser and the date the appraisal was made.

.03 An example of the kind of data which should be contained in a typical appraisal is included below. This relates to the valuation of art objects, but a similar detailed breakdown can be outlined for any type of property. Appraisals of art objects, paintings in particular, should include:

(1) A complete description of the object, indicating the size, the subject matter, the medium, the name of the artist, approximate date created, the interest transferred, etc.

(2) The cost, date, and manner of acquisition.

(3) A history of the item including proof of authenticity such as a certificate of authentication if such exists.

(4) A photograph of a size and quality fully identifying the subject matter, preferably a 10'' x 12'' or larger print.

(5) A statement of the factors upon which the appraisal was based, such as:

(a) Sales of other works by the same artist particularly on or around the valuation date.

(b) Quoted prices in dealers' catalogs of the artist's works or of other artists of comparable stature.

(c) The economic state of the art market at or around the time of valuation, particularly with respect to the specific property.

(d) A record of any exhibitions at which the particular art object had been displayed.

(e) A statement as to the standing of the artist in his profession and in the particular school or time period.

.04 Although an appraisal report meets these requirements, the Internal Revenue Service is not relieved of the responsibility of reviewing appraisals to the extent deemed necessary.

SEC. 4. REVIEW OF VALUATION APPRAISALS.

.01 While the Service is responsible for reviewing appraisals, it is not responsible for making appraisals; the burden of supporting the fair market value listed on a return is the taxpayer's. The Internal Revenue Service cannot accord recognition to any appraiser or group of appraisers from the standpoint of unquestioned acceptance of their appraisals. Furthermore, the Service cannot approve valuations or appraisals prior to the actual filing of the tax return to which the appraisal pertains and cannot issue advance rulings approving or disapproving such appraisals.

.02 In determining the acceptability of the claimed value of the

The percentage of return on the average annual value of the tangible assets used should be the percentage prevailing in the industry involved at the date of valuation, or (when the industry percentage is not available) a percentage of 8 to 10 percent may be used.

The 8 percent rate of return and the 15 percent rate of capitalization are applied to tangibles and intangibles, respectively, of businesses with a small risk factor and stable and regular earnings; the 10 percent rate of return and 20 percent rate of capitalization are applied to businesses in which the hazards of business are relatively high.

The above rates are used as examples and are not appropriate in all cases. In applying the "formula" approach, the average earnings period and the capitalization rates are dependent upon the facts pertinent thereto in each case.

The past earnings to which the formula is applied should fairly reflect the probable future earnings. Ordinarily, the period should not be less than five years, and abnormal years, whether above or below the average, should be eliminated. If the business is a sole proprietorship or partnership, there should be deducted from the earnings of the business a reasonable amount for services performed by the owner or partners engaged in the business. See *Lloyd B. Sanderson Estate v. Commissioner*, 42 F. 2d 160 (1930). Further, only the tangible assets entering into net worth, including accounts and bills receivable in excess of accounts and bills payable, are used for determining earnings on the tangible assets. Factors that influence the capitalization rate include (1) the nature of the business, (2) the risk involved, and (3) the stability or irregularity of earnings.

The "formula" approach should not be used if there is better evidence available from which the value of intangibles can be determined. If the assets of a going business are sold upon the basis of a rate of capitalization that can be substantiated as being realistic, though it is not within the range of figures indicated here as the ones ordinarily to be adopted, the same rate of capitalization should be used in determining the value of intangibles.

Accordingly, the "formula" approach may be used for determining the fair market value of intangible assets of a business only if there is no better basis therefor available.

See also Revenue Ruling 59–60, C.B. 1959–1, 237, as modified by Revenue Ruling 65–193, C.B. 1965–2, 370, which sets forth the proper approach to use in the valuation of closely-held corporate stocks for estate and gift tax purposes. The general approach, methods, and factors, outlined in Revenue Ruling 59–60, as modified, are equally applicable to valuations of corporate stocks for income and other tax purposes as well as for estate and gift tax purposes. They apply also to problems involving the determination of the fair market value of business interests of any type, including partnerships and proprietorships, and of intangible assets for all tax purposes.

A.R.M. 34, A.R.M. 68, and O.D. 937 are superseded, since the positions set forth therein are restated to the extent applicable under current law in this Revenue Ruling. Revenue Ruling 65–192, C.B. 1965–2, 259, which contained restatements of A.R.M. 34 and A.R.M. 68, is also superseded.

26 CFR 1.1001–1: Computation of gain or loss.

Loan charges incurred by a seller to assist the purchaser of his house in obtaining a mortgage loan. See Rev. Rul. 68–650, page 78.

Rev. Proc. 77-12

Section 1. Purpose.

The purpose of this Revenue Procedure is to set forth guidelines for use by taxpayers and Service personnel in making fair market value determinations in situations where a corporation purchases the assets of a business containing inventory items for a lump sum or where a corporation acquires assets including inventory items by the liquidation of a subsidiary pursuant to the provisions of section 332 of the Internal Revenue Code of 1954 and the basis of the inventory received in liquidation is determined under section 334(b)(2). These guidelines are designed to assist taxpayers and Service personnel in assigning a fair market value to such assets.

Sec. 2. Background.

If the assets of a business are purchased for a lump sum, or if the stock of a corporation is purchased and that corporation is liquidated under section 332 of the Code and the basis is determined under section 334(b)(2), the purchase price must be allocated among the assets acquired to determine the basis of each of such assets.

In making such determinations, it is necessary to determine the fair market value of any inventory items involved. This Revenue Procedure describes methods that may be used to determine the fair market value of inventory items.

In determining the fair market value of inventory under the situations set forth in this Revenue Procedure, the amount of inventory generally would be different from the amounts usually purchased. In addition, the goods in process and finished goods on hand must be considered in light of what a willing purchaser would pay and a willing seller would accept for the inventory at the various stages of completion, when the former is not under any compulsion to buy and the latter is not under any compulsion to sell, both parties having reasonable knowledge of relevant facts.

SEC. 3. PROCEDURES FOR DETERMINATION OF FAIR MARKET VALUE.

Three basic methods an appraiser may use to determine the fair market value of inventory are the cost of reproduction method, the comparative sales method, and the income method. All methods of valuation are based on one or a combination of these three methods.

.01 The cost of reproduction method generally provides a good indication of fair market value if inventory is readily replaceable in a wholesale or retail business, but generally should not be used in establishing the fair market value of the finished goods of a manufacturing concern. In valuing a particular inventory under this method, however, other factors may be relevant. For example, a well balanced inventory available to fill customers' orders in the ordinary course of business may have a fair market value in excess of its cost of reproduction because it provides a continuity of business, whereas an inventory containing obsolete merchandise unsuitable for customers might have a fair market value of less than the cost of reproduction.

.02 The comparative sales method utilizes the actual or expected selling prices of finished goods to customers as a basis of determining fair market values of those finished goods. When the expected selling price is used as a basis for valuing finished goods inventory, consideration should be given to the time that would be required to dispose of this inventory, the expenses that would be expected to be incurred in such disposition, for example, all costs of disposition, applicable discounts (including those for quantity), sales commissions, and freight and shipping charges, and a profit commensurate with the amount of investment and degree of risk. It should also be recognized that the inventory to be valued may represent a larger quantity than the normal trading volume and the expected selling price can be a valid starting point only if customers' orders are filled in the ordinary course of business.

.03 The income method, when applied to fair market value determinations for finished goods, recognizes that finished goods must generally be valued in a profit motivated business. Since the amount of inventory may be large in relation to normal trading volume in relation to normal trading volume and best use of the inventory will be to provide for a continuity of the marketing operation of the going business. Additionally, the finished goods inventory will usually provide the only source of revenue of an acquired business during the period it is being used to fill customers' orders. The historical financial data of an acquired company can be used to determine the amount that could be attributed to finished goods in order to pay all costs of disposition and provide a return on the investment during the period of disposition.

.04 The fair market value of work in process should be based on the same factors used to determine the fair market value of finished goods reduced by the expected costs of completion, including a reasonable profit allowance for the completion and selling effort of the acquiring corporation. In determining the fair market value of raw materials, the current costs of replacing the inventory in the quantities to be valued generally provides the most reliable standard.

SEC. 4. CONCLUSION.

Because valuing inventory is an inherently factual determination, no rigid formulas can be applied. Consequently, the methods outlined above can only serve as guidelines for determining the fair market value of inventories.

Present Value/Future Value Tables

Present Value of $1

$$P = F_n(1 + r)^{-n}$$

r = discount rate; n = number of periods until payment; $F_n = \$1$

Periods = n	¼%	½%	¾%	1%	1½%	2%	3%	4%	5%	6%	7%	8%	10%	12%	15%	20%
1	.99751	.99502	.99256	.99010	.98522	.98039	.97087	.96154	.95238	.94340	.93458	.92593	.90909	.89286	.86957	.83333
2	.99502	.99007	.98517	.98030	.97066	.96117	.94260	.92456	.90703	.89000	.87344	.85734	.82645	.79719	.75614	.69444
3	.99254	.98515	.97783	.97059	.95632	.94232	.91514	.88900	.86384	.83962	.81630	.79383	.75131	.71178	.65752	.57870
4	.99006	.98025	.97055	.96098	.94218	.92385	.88849	.85480	.82270	.79209	.76290	.73503	.68301	.63552	.57175	.48225
5	.98759	.97537	.96333	.95147	.92826	.90573	.86261	.82193	.78353	.74726	.71299	.68058	.62092	.56743	.49718	.40188
6	.98513	.97052	.95616	.94205	.91454	.88797	.83748	.79031	.74622	.70496	.66634	.63017	.56447	.50663	.43233	.33490
7	.98267	.96569	.94904	.93272	.90103	.87056	.81309	.75992	.71068	.66506	.62275	.58349	.51316	.45235	.37594	.27908
8	.98022	.96089	.94198	.92348	.88771	.85349	.78941	.73069	.67684	.62741	.58201	.54027	.46651	.40388	.32690	.23257
9	.97778	.95610	.93496	.91434	.87459	.83676	.76642	.70259	.64461	.59190	.54393	.50025	.42410	.36061	.28426	.19381
10	.97534	.95135	.92800	.90529	.86167	.82035	.74409	.67556	.61391	.55839	.50835	.46319	.38554	.32197	.24718	.16151
11	.97291	.94661	.92109	.89632	.84893	.80426	.72242	.64958	.58468	.52679	.47509	.42888	.35049	.28748	.21494	.13459
12	.97048	.94191	.91424	.88745	.83639	.78849	.70138	.62460	.55684	.49697	.44401	.39711	.31863	.25668	.18691	.11216
13	.96806	.93722	.90743	.87866	.82403	.77303	.68095	.60057	.53032	.46884	.41496	.36770	.28966	.22917	.16253	.09346
14	.96565	.93256	.90068	.86996	.81185	.75788	.66112	.57748	.50507	.44230	.38782	.34046	.26333	.20462	.14133	.07789
15	.96324	.92792	.89397	.86135	.79985	.74301	.64186	.55526	.48102	.41727	.36245	.31524	.23939	.18270	.12289	.06491
16	.96084	.92330	.88732	.85282	.78803	.72845	.62317	.53391	.45811	.39365	.33873	.29189	.21763	.16312	.10686	.05409
17	.95844	.91871	.88071	.84438	.77639	.71416	.60502	.51337	.43630	.37136	.31657	.27027	.19784	.14564	.09293	.04507
18	.95605	.91414	.87416	.83602	.76491	.70016	.58739	.49363	.41552	.35034	.29586	.25025	.17986	.13004	.08081	.03756
19	.95367	.90959	.86765	.82774	.75361	.68643	.57029	.47464	.39573	.33051	.27651	.23171	.16351	.11611	.07027	.03130
20	.95129	.90506	.86119	.81954	.74247	.67297	.55368	.45639	.37689	.31180	.25842	.21455	.14864	.10367	.06110	.02608
22	.94655	.89608	.84842	.80340	.72069	.64684	.52189	.42196	.34185	.27751	.22571	.18394	.12285	.08264	.04620	.01811
24	.94184	.88719	.83583	.78757	.69954	.62172	.49193	.39012	.31007	.24698	.19715	.15770	.10153	.06588	.03493	.01258
26	.93714	.87838	.82343	.77205	.67902	.59758	.46369	.36069	.28124	.21981	.17220	.13520	.08391	.05252	.02642	.00874
28	.93248	.86996	.81122	.75684	.65910	.57437	.43708	.33348	.25509	.19563	.15040	.11591	.06934	.04187	.01997	.00607
30	.92783	.86103	.79919	.74192	.63976	.55207	.41199	.30832	.23138	.17411	.13137	.09938	.05731	.03338	.01510	.00421
32	.92321	.85248	.78733	.72730	.62099	.53063	.38834	.28506	.20987	.15496	.11474	.08520	.04736	.02661	.01142	.00293
34	.91861	.84402	.77565	.71297	.60277	.51003	.36604	.26355	.19035	.13791	.10022	.07305	.03914	.02121	.00864	.00203
36	.91403	.83564	.76415	.69892	.58509	.49022	.34503	.24367	.17266	.12274	.08754	.06262	.03235	.01691	.00653	.00141
38	.90948	.82735	.75281	.68515	.56792	.47119	.32523	.22529	.15661	.10924	.07646	.05369	.02673	.01348	.00494	.00098
40	.90495	.81914	.74165	.67165	.55126	.45289	.30656	.20829	.14205	.09722	.06678	.04603	.02209	.01075	.00373	.00068
45	.89372	.79896	.71445	.63905	.51171	.41020	.26444	.17120	.11130	.07265	.04761	.03133	.01372	.00610	.00186	.00027
50	.88263	.77929	.68825	.60804	.47500	.37153	.22811	.14071	.08720	.05429	.03395	.02132	.00852	.00346	.00092	.00011
100	.77904	.60729	.47369	.36971	.22563	.13803	.05203	.01980	.00760	.00295	.00115	.00045	.00007	.00001	.00000	.00000

Index

Please see Glossary and Table of Contents as well

accountant 1, 3, 4, 6, 16, 26, 30, 66, 84, 89, 101, 106, 113
. . . . 168, 172-, 180, 198-, 218, 221-, 240-
accounting firm 40, 131, 199, 219
accounts payable 19, 90, 103, 225, 229
accounts receivable 18, 32, 62, 79, 86, 90, 100, 160, 225-
acquisition agreement 1, 10, 123, 200, 226
adjusted income statement 59, 73, 75, 79, 84, 90, 95, 102, 155
adjustments 8, 26, 36, 75, 83, 102, 108, 122, 128, 170, 195, 208
amortization 88, 114, 191, 226-
asking price 109, 159, 165, 190
asset appraisal 62, 100
asset value 35, 59-62, 69-71, 159, 170, 176, 200
attorney 6, 106, 130, 168-, 180, 185-, 221-
auction 8, 9, 27, 33, 51, 119, 159, 162, 235
bad debt 18, 231, 237
book value 18, 34, 37, 61, 69-71, 84, 100, 105, 107, 125,
. . . . 160, 207, 222, 225-
brand name 64
cap rate 41-58, 59, 76, 78, 155, 175-, 195-
capitalization 17, 20, 30, 37, 41-44, 52, 58, 65, 73-79, 81, 93, 99,
. . . . 102, 155, 106-108, 129, 169-, 222, 228-
cash flow safety cushion 88, 92, 96, 114, 119
common stock 206, 209, 229, 237-
competition 1, 2, 5, 19, 46, 52, 63, 179, 196-, 216, 232
consulting contract 178, 192
copyright 64, 180, 227
covenant not to compete 66, 179
current assets 38, 78, 101, 199, 208, 217, 227-, 241-242
debt service 38, 82, 89, 92-96, 114, 229
depreciation 11, 17, 24, 29, 38, 58, 61, 69, 73, 77, 81, 83, 89, 95, 100,
. . . . 105, 112, 125, 128, 162, 172-, 218, 224, 226-, 233-, 240
discount rate 35, 41, 44, 54, 64-68, 93, 156, 228-, 238
divorce 6, 8, 9,167
doubtful accounts 33, 157
employees . . . . 6, 14, 19 ,23 ,31, 48, 105, 155, 168, 178-, 187, 198
. . . . 214, 216, 234
employment contracts 20, 67, 178, 204
entertainment expense 28, 233
ESOP 8, 105, 213, 223
estate tax 105-108

excess earnings 30, 38, 63, 92, 96, 99, 102, 107, 114, 236
feasibility 81, 94, 111, 117
financial ratios 47, 52, 58, 91, 101, 125, 179, 200, 232
fixed assets 5, 38, 46, 53, 99, 157, 162, 168, 217, 227-
future depreciation 83, 116
future value 93
gift tax 38, 105
golf course 40
hardball 186, 196
income statement 22, 25-35, 38, 43, 59, 65, 73, 77, 81-91, 102, 112,
. . . . 118, 123, 155, 167, 176-, 228-
income taxes 20, 73, 81, 88, 95, 113, 155, 166, 233
industry average 51, 56, 83, 101
insurance . . . . 5, 18, 22 ,28, 31, 36, 39, 87, 100, 121-, 156, 227-
. . . . 162, 218
intangible assets 35, 38, 60-68, 70, 75, 93, 99-102, 107,
. . . . 121, 156, 161, 224, 227-
interest expense 30, 73, 86, 89, 95, 116-
intermediary 15, 182, 194
inventory 18, 47, 59, 62, 78, 86, 90, 100-104, 112, 128, 157, 160, 168-
. . . . 196-, 217, 226-, 231-, 242
investment tax credit 29, 33, 89, 95, 113,
lease 21, 29, 34, 100, 112, 163, 204, 211, 227, 234
leasehold improvements 34, 75, 99, 227, 234
leveraged buyout 70, 234
liabilities 11, 16, 29, 31, 35, 38, 47, 53, 58, 62, 69-71, 76-79,
. . . . 90-96, 99-104, 107, 155, 168-, 193-, 218, 228-, 235-, 241-
line of credit 86, 114, 175
liquidation value 34, 37, 61, 70, 86, 93, 100, 157, 159-
. . . . 168-, 235
loan interest 56, 86, 112, 175, 236
loan structure 112
machinery and equipment 47, 75, 85, 161
managers 20, 23, 26, 85, 175, 178, 187, 210, 216
market value 2, 4, 6, 29, 33, 38, 43, 60, 71, 73, 78, 86, 94, 99-105
. . . . 110, 121-, 159-, 167-, 196, 226-, 235-
medical practice 40, 130
negotiation 2, 4, 10, 39, 105, 166, 170-, 182, 185, 192-197, 236
net operating income 24, 30, 38, 45, 56, 73, 77, 83-95, 104, 112,
. . . . 121-, 155, 175, 231-
net operating loss 173
obsolescence 47, 175, 230
offer 3, 12, 15, 45, 49, 51, 69, 85, 118, 166-, 186-,
. . . . 211, 216, 239
operating expenses 24, 35, 38, 81, 111, 122-, 155, 216, 231
opinion of value 3
P/E ratio 123, 125-, 189
perks 111, 217, 237
post-acquisition changes 117, 188
preferred stock 58, 87, 96, 112, 206, 210, 229, 237

present value 35, 38, 41, 44, 54, 64-68, 81, 93, 96, 114, 156,
. . . . 222, 228-, 238-
pre-paid expenses 34, 79, 100, 227, 238
pro forma 23, 75, 83, 102, 118, 240
product development 17, 180
production capacity 21, 110
project an increase in sales 111
projections 17, 53, 82, 90, 117, 156, 198, 215-, 221
purchase of assets 11, 30, 61, 74, 79, 89, 113, 172, 224
purchase of stock 11, 30, 58, 70, 79, 84, 103, 172
range of values 37
real estate 6, 17, 31, 34, 38, 47, 50, 59-62, 71, 74, 77, 85-90, 99, 114,
. . . . 122, 130, 160-, 170-, 189, 219, 228, 234
replacement cost 5, 33, 62, 100, 121
replacement value 34, 39, 121, 162
retail 7, 17, 38, 55, 64, 79, 124, 129
risk 1, 2, 8, 12, 17, 32, 38, 41-58, 64, 73, 81, 87, 93, 101, 107-,
. . . . 117, 131, 155, 160, 167-, 190-, 217, 230-
risk free rate 56
rule-of-thumb 30, 93, 128, 198, 236
sale proceeds 11, 74, 166, 174, 207, 224
seller financing 162, 207
service business 47, 59, 155-
shareholders 21, 35, 128, 169, 176, 205, 210-, 223, 228, 239-
spouse 167, 205
synergy 110, 180
tax laws 4, 26, 34, 85, 88, 105, 167-, 213, 218, 224
taxes 2, 8, 20, 24, 26, 28, 38, 73, 77, 81, 88, 95, 105,
. . . . 113-, 121-, 166-, 205, 218, 221, 226-, 232-235
timing the sale 190, 215
travel and entertainment 3, 28, 233, 237
useful life 34, 64-67, 69, 84, 102, 224, 227, 230
vehicles 17, 78, 85, 100, 104, 227
weighted average 31, 38, 55, 57, 66, 75, 78, 82, 111, 128, 155, 235, 241
working capital 38, 53, 78, 89-92, 101, 104, 112, 119, 200-,
. . . . 160, 241-242

Order Additional Copies at your *Special Reorder Price*

Charter Oak Press
Attn: Orders
6 Brook Circle
Ephrata, PA   17522

Please send me _____ copies of *Unlocking the Value of Your Business.*

Enclosed is $24.95 plus $4 ground shipping per book. ($27.95)

Sales tax: Pennsylvanians, please add 6% sales tax ($1.50)

Name: _____

Address: _____

City: _____

State: _____   Zip: _____

Order Additional Copies at your *Special Reorder Price*

Charter Oak Press
Attn: Orders
6 Brook Circle
Ephrata, PA   17522

Please send me _____ copies of *Unlocking the Value of Your Business.*

Enclosed is $24.95 plus $4 ground shipping per book. ($27.95)

Sales tax: Pennsylvanians, please add 6% sales tax ($1.50)

Name: _____

Address: _____

City: _____

State: _____   Zip: _____